The BlaQ Market

ESSAYS & PLAYS from Afrikan Centered Theatre

A Sakhu Publication

The BlaQ Market

ESSAYS & PLAYS from Afrikan Centered Theatre

Edited By Shepsu Aakhu
With A Forward By Chuck Smith

A Sakhu Publication

The BlaQ Market
ESSAYS & PLAYS from Afrikan Centered Theatre

© 2006 Sakhu Publications a Division of MPAACT Inc.

1st printing

ISBN #: 0-9714033-1-7

Dedication

*For those who have created and performed
upon the sacred boards
and now have passed on*

*for
Charles Michael Moore
Alger Bozwell*

and so many more

*We feel your spirit
and continue to be moved*

Contents

Foreward

Dancing In the Dark - Black Theater in Chicago 2006
By Chuck Smith

I was introduced to Shepsu Aakhu in the early 1990's at a large regional arts conference held in a Chicago hotel. He was serving notice to anyone who would listen that he was going to join the Chicago theater community with a new kind of Black theater company. Later his company, MPAACT set up shop in my neighborhood at the South Shore Cultural Center, a beautiful location sitting on the edge of the lake but a space new to theater. The company is committed to the difficult task of producing original works. Mounting world premieres is a noble task for any theater and especially true for a Black company. This is because the Black theater community still doesn't have the varied *published* body of work needed for growth and training.

I first worked with MPAACT there at the center at an event celebrating the life of Paul Robeson and was immediately impressed with their technical skills. A year or so later at the center they fell prey to what I call, "The Curse of the News - a new theatre company, in a new space, doing new plays." They relocated to the well established Victory Gardens Theater and while still doing all original works have been gaining attention and respect ever since. I worked with them again in 2000, directing **Chris T** filling a long time desire to direct a play by Nambi E. Kelley one of their resident playwrights. It was a challenging experience mainly because I felt that the Victory Gardens' studio space was much too small. However during tech, the expertise of this technically savvy ensemble showed me the error of my ways and the result proved to be one of my most proud productions to date**.** Experiencing an MPAACT performance is like watching a classic black and white, fine arts movie. It doesn't try to be anything other than what it is, a thought provoking informative story fused with live music. Anyone doubting my words should revisit their 2003 production of **SOST** to help explain some of the confusion and issues in today's 2006 immigration headlines.

Recently I attended a MPAACT performance of **SOFTLY BLUE** and during intermission Shepsu commented that one of the major critics had refused to attend the production because of the subject matter. The play dealt with depression among African Americans. A few months earlier at an African American Arts Alliance of Chicago board meeting another artistic director had made a similar comment. While I can't imagine a critic refusing to attend a show *for any reason* at one of Chicago's major theaters it does clearly illustrate that the Chicago theater community is indeed huge, and the few seasoned theater critics are stretched past their limit. The inability to cover all gives them the legitimate ability to pick and choose.

Included in this huge Chicago theater community are six Black companies hiring professional actors, and producing full seasons. In no particular order they are MPAACT, Chocolate Chips (a theater for the young), ETA, Chicago Theater Company, Congo

Square, and Black Ensemble, which recently joined ETA as a property owner. Year round, a visitor coming to Chicago seeking Black theater can always be accommodated with a wide range of work. Yet with all of this activity a certain missing element keeps most of these theater companies at a continued disconnect with the Black community at large. With all due respect to Earl Calloway of the Chicago Defender the time has come for another respected media voice to take on the very serious responsibility of critiquing the art of Black theater, and the Black theater artist in Chicago.

Given that each of Chicago's theater companies, regardless of race, all rely on word of mouth to generate a healthy return at the box office, and while a great review in any Chicago newspaper doesn't assure the box office phone to ring, it certainly doesn't hurt. All things considered in order to move forward *the Black theater community of Chicago needs an arts savvy Black champion ("X") of the press, radio, and television* to relate to the public at large who is doing what and where plus their own expert opinion of the work. This is no small task given the number of Black theater companies, Black shows at non-Black companies, and Black artist in non-Black shows.

During previews of a recent show I directed, the production's young Black female playwright disclosed to me that her work had never been performed in front of an all, or predominantly Black theater audience. This wasn't the first time I was told this but being theatrically raised here in Chicago's Black theater community I am still taken aback when I come in contact with a Black artist who has never experienced their work with the Black community at large. I always remind my actors of the difference in performing for the Black and the white theater audience and for the first two previews they were nearly all Black. The response they gave the show literally shocked the young playwright. They caught and reacted to every line, every nuance, plus laughed so much at unexpected times that the playwright wondered if she had actually written a comedy by mistake. The third and final preview was sold out to a group of college students, all white, and while their attention was riveted to the stage there was little to no response. The young, now converted, playwright found the silence so deafening she had to leave the theater. Fortunately, since critics were there, it didn't throw the actors. However, one did mention that following the response of the two previous nights it seemed they were dancing in the dark.

Of course every audience, regardless of color, gets the same show, but we Chicago Black theater artist are continuously asking, "What did Mr. A at the Sun-Times, or Ms. B at the Tribune write about our show?" - If they wrote anything at all. In the best of all possible worlds we should first be asking, "What did "X" say?" – Knowing, that "X" has the keys to the kingdom.

Chuck Smith
Resident Director
Goodman Theatre

About MPAACT

The Ma'at Production Association of Afrikan Centered Theatre

MPAACT is a multi-disciplinary theatre arts organization dedicated to producing original works. Based in Chicago since 1992, MPAACT has built a reputation for innovation and excellence by solely producing "world premiere" productions which utilize language, music, and movement in a manner that captivates both the critical and commercial audience. This style of production has been labeled *Afrikan Centered Theatre.*

MPAACT has grown from a campus movement at the University of Illinois in the late 1980's and early 1990's into a strong cultural institution which helps fortify Chicago's vibrant arts community. MPAACT continues to provide services to Chicago and the nation through their many Art-in-Education programs, Literary Development programs, the Institute of Afrikan Centered Theatre, and a variety of touring productions.

The Meaning of Ma'at

Ma'at (Ma'aut) represents the fourth sphere of the tree of life in the spiritual system of the ancient east Afrikan civilization of Kamit. Ma'at corresponds to the energy of the planet Jupiter, and rules truth, love, balance, and law. Ma'at is symbolized by a single feather. In the Kamitic spiritual system this feather is weighed against the heart of an individual on the day of judgment. If the heart balances with the feather, it is recorded in the sacred scroll that this person has lived their life according to divine law-living truth, being just in her/his actions while giving selflessly and seeking nothing in return for their upright behavior. We have chosen Ma'at to represent a goal which we will continually strive to meet; giving of ourselves, living truth, achieving harmony and balance, thus making our heart as light as a feather.

Essays on Afrikan Centered Theatre

When you go into any culture, I don't care what the culture is, you have to go with some humility. You have to understand the language, and by that I do not mean what we speak, you've got to understand **the language,** *the interior language of the people. You've got to enter their philosophy, their world view. You've got to speak both the spoken language and the metalanguage of the people.*
--Wole Soyinka

[ACT] lives and breathes in both "*word*" and "*ritual*". Objective viewpoints are not the goal, *...the exercise is concerned with reaching beyond objective reality, to touch the spirit and awaken the soul -- a necessary condition for the affirmation of existence. ...Ritual is the affectual technique common to most theatrical exercises in the black world. Within these exercises, the word is not simply a mechanism of discourse. It is rather, a creative elixir--nommo force--that activates the dramatic mode ...Embedded in this mode are references to common experience, myths, and significations that define a collective moral universe.*
--Totem Voices, Paul Carter Harrison

I Ars Ergo Sum
By William S. Carroll

I first became aware of just how wide an analytical divide exists between theatre artists and theatre scholars when I was a graduate student at the University of Illinois. In my time there, I only had two classes where the acting students and MA/PhD students commingled. When this did happen, we approached each other the way supporters of rival political parties often do: with a certain grudging respect and the assurance that you are following the illuminated path.

In the time since then, I have had the opportunity to instruct actors in academic and private settings with charges ranging in ages preteen to retiree. I have seen a practiced intellectual laziness, not from every student, but from far too many. Perhaps I am describing this poorly. There seemed to be an attitude and fear among a number of them that if they analyzed the creative process too thoroughly and understood it too well, they would destroy the MAGIC.

Let us then extend the metaphor of MAGIC to represent the creative process. Magic is shrouded in mystery and beyond the understanding of the audience, but for the magician, there is no mystery. All the good magicians study not only what tricks work and why, where, how and before whom, but they also study the history of prestidigitation. Some, like Ricky Jay, are virtual museums of their craft. Even in such non-intellectual pursuits as athletics, the only way to succeed is to stay current, to know what training methods, rules and opposing strategies you may face and devise and practice responses for them.

Why do you suppose theatre artists are often expected to be highly functioning idiot savants, *mentally handicapped, but demonstrates proficiency in a specific area.* rather than scholars of their chosen profession? I understand surprise when Mike Tyson waxes rhapsodically regarding the work of Rousseau, but shouldn't a person whose job description is equal parts psychologist, detective, shaman, clown, mimic and empath also be fairly bright?

The training of any artist is a tricky proposition in both theory and practice. The very concept makes some skittish. How do you make someone more sensitive, aware, perceptive or talented? If not, what is the purpose of the many MF programs? To make smooth and regular the way artists practice their craft? Is the purpose to prepare artists for the marketplace, or for acceptance, and if so, accepted by whom? If we train artists in order to produce better artists then we must figure out what that means. What makes an artist better, to be more honest, curious, passionate, playful or real, if these things are not to be found in the classroom, then where can they be found? Is Broadway or Hollywood the guide? If not, what about major regional repertory theatre? Should we look abroad?

Making art is not a way to avoid intellectual pursuits. Instead, it is a synthesis of intellect, intuition, training and talent. If there is a type of job a person can be too smart to do well, the job of a theatre artist is not that job. If you don't like thinking, you won't like acting, writing, dancing, directing, designing etc

Philosophy defines humanity on the concept: "I Cogito Ergo Sum"- "I think therefore I am".   Try defining the artist on this concept: "I Cogito Ergos Ars" – I think therefore I Art.

Reflections on Afrikan Centered Theatre
by Shepsu Aakhu

Who are we and why do we do what we do?

In our attempt to discuss what Theatre is, we often get caught up in the notion of Western theatre, and thus our discussion gets sidetracked into a form of theatre which serves a fundamentally different purpose for Europeans and their Diaspora as opposed to Afrikans and our Diaspora. In order to get any real understanding of theatre (e.g. ritual and performance) in an Afrikan context, we have to take a good look at the indigenous spiritual systems of Afrika, the enslavement of Afrikans through the triangular slave trade, and contemporary American society. Quite a mouthful at first glance, but quite necessary if we want to have any clarity on whom, and why we are, what we are in a contemporary context. Join together the dynamic nature of Afrikan spiritual traditions and their longevity, and you are looking not at an archaic system, but rather a system which has had 50,000 years with which to refine itself -- 50,000 years to get rid of that which does not serve the community. It has evolved into a supremely practical system which has as its mandate to serve the needs of the community, no matter how the community changes over the millennia. Contrast this to most of the founder based religions [Buddhism, Judaism, Christianity, and Islam] and you will find that they are in their developmental infancy. Add to that they are text based, which by it's very nature makes them more resistant to change, to evolving with the community they are designed to serve. It is important to note that this is not a discussion of the value of any religious system, but rather the dynamics of spiritual systems, community needs, and their co-evolution.

Indigenous Afrikan spiritual systems

The Afrikan continent contains several hundreds, if not thousands, of ethnic groups. Each has their own language, cultural, and spiritual traditions. Despite this diversity, there are some common threads which unite most of the indigenous traditions:

1. **Indigenous Afrikan Spiritual systems do not have founders**. They are an evolved communal understanding of the relationship between community, spirit, and divinity. As such, they rarely have a sacred text. There is no need to write down the system because it exists as an everyday tangible part of life.

2. **Equally important is the concept of adaptability**. Indigenous traditions are mandated to continue to evolve, refine themselves, and incorporate change into their very fabric. If there is a golden role for Indigenous Afrikan spiritual systems it would be: "If it doesn't work, get rid of it".

3.   **Indigenous Afrikan spiritual systems typically place community at the center of the relationship between humanity and Divinity/God.** The community and its laws are one with the divine. The community acts as an extension of God. For many cultures there is no distinction, whether in language or thought, between the community and God. This of course is a radical difference from most Western concepts of God as an external force to both the person and the community.

So where does this leave us? At the core of the Afrikanized mind, there is no life/spirit without community, because community and divinity are inseparable Simply put, "we are part of the living god. Whatever my needs, God will address them through community." This concept was reinforced through 50,000 years of collective experience.

Ritual and Performance as an Expression of Community.

Theatre in a traditional Afrikan context is about ritual. It is about community coming together and through its "pageants and practices" collectively saying: "This is who we are! This is where we came from! This is our relationship to Divinity/God! This is our relationship to each other, and we will always be here for each other!"   In the traditional sense, there is hardly a concept of Afrikan theatre that is not grounded in these ideas.

The Failure of Community as an Agent of God.

The transatlantic slave trade ripped apart to fabric of the Afrikanized mind. Slavery was not just an assault upon the physical person, but it was a spiritual assault as well. In addition to the roughly four hundred years of forced physical servitude, chattel slavery redefined the relationship between the individual and community, thus the individual and God. The act of being enslaved meant separation from spiritual elders (e.g. loss of collective wisdom), separation from a shared language (e.g. loss of the ability to self express) and most critically the loss of community (i.e., loss of self/God/collective identity). Even in this damaged state, the Afrikanized mind holds to the central tenants of the faith. The golden rule is still in effect: "If it doesn't work, get rid of it. Community has failed, because it has not prevented my enslavement. Community cannot be the sacred institution." So what then are the forces at work in this new place, this place that is devoid of my community, thus devoid of my concept of god? If the enslaved person, being infinitely practical, looks for (or is forced to adopt) clues as to the new order of things, they will quickly find the Europeans (i.e. those with white skin privilege) at the top of this society. With the application of the Golden rule, the Afrikanized mind begins to adopt their way of thinking and thus incorporate it into a new understanding of the world.

I imagine the reasoning was such... "If they control everything, they must have a system that works. I'll take a little of this and a little of that and come up with something that works better than the stuff that landed me in chains." It is in this moment that the African-American mind (the hybrid mind) was born. This mind learned to place personal survival above community survival. This mind came to accept that community was transient, unreliable, and perhaps even undesirable. This mind came to believe in a European centered world view, where everything in the society was geared to providing comfort for the enslavers. This mind came to want to *be* just like the Europeans, to have what they had, do what they did, and believe what they believed. This is not to say that there was not resistance, but overt resistance was a self modifying behavior. That is to say that 'being murdered' has a way of extinguishing a behavior.

Ritual and Performance as an Expression of Community.

Scattered by slavery, with the loss of cultural wisdom, ethnic identity, language and other cultural practices, ritual expression took on a new purpose. The 'pageants and practices' of theatre in an African-American context were less concerned with saying: "This is who we are!" but rather "Who the hell are we?" Not, "This is where we came from!" But rather, "How did I get here?" Not, "This is our relationship to Divinity/God!" But rather, "is there a God anymore?" Not even, "This is our relationship to each other, and we will always be here for each other!" The new question was "who are you and why should I trust you/ invest in you?" WE became hyper concerned with the question of distinguishing self from other. In all fairness, this was due to the fact that others made a concerted effort to exclude us from a place of social value in this new world.   In the contemporary sense there is hardly a concept of Afrikan theatre that is not grounded in these ideas.

Contemporary Afrikan Centered Theatre

Afrikan Centered Theatre is living in two worlds. There is the element that concerns itself with the traditional purposes of ritual in Afrikan society. "This is our relationship to Divinity/God! This is our relationship to each other".   Then there is the element that is concerned with the Diaspora's experience in the Americas: "How did I get here? Who is God to me in this world? Why didn't you have my back when all the ugly shit went down?" Then there are the meta-issues, the issues that truly encapsulate the agenda of Afrikan Centered Theatre, namely: "We are community. Together we are at the center of the relationship between humanity and Divinity/God. The community is an extension of God. There is no distinction, whether in language or thought, between the community and God. No matter what has happened before, I am you, you are me and we are Divinity/ God." All forms of Afrikan Centered expression, whether theatre, film, music, or dance, are concerned with this meta-issue: How do we get back to the "you and me" of God and community; how can we be whole again?

This is why we are not driven by marketing and commercialism, why our material is often challenging, even difficult to work through. Why in fact you can't shake a show for weeks or months or ever. We are not trying to entertain you. We are trying to reconnect with you. As artists, we have no other objective. This is a far cry from the notion that our generation is only concerned with money, status, and notoriety, because these things seldom accompany our chosen path.

Environmentalism and Black Expression
by Shepsu Aakhu

The environmental movement has taken a firm grip on the music, film, and theatre industries. If Americans recycled newspapers and aluminum cans the way the industry recycles samples, beats, remakes, sequels, and revivals, the world's energy problems would cease to exist. What drives this phenomenon? The quest for marketability, but I suspect you already knew that. What is the cost of this phenomenon? That is a far more interesting question.

American Music Industry

Let's start with music. Hip Hop/R & B will serve as able examples largely because their transgressions are so egregious. Tune your radio to any Black/Urban contemporary/ Rap/Dusty/ Top Forty/R&B station. I know this may seem like a diverse sample, but it is essentially the same music. Listen to the station of your choice for ten minutes. How many songs contain a sample from a hit song that was recorded 5 to 25 years ago? How many of them recycle the lyrics, in whole or in part, from someone else's hit song? How many of them ARE someone else's hit, with rap lyrics laid on top? How many contain no original elements (music, lyrics or arrangement) except the name of the recording artist (and I use the term "artist" extremely loosely)? How many sing nowhere near the key in which the song was written? The last question does not so much pertain to my argument here as much as it just annoys the f**k out of me: what is the effect of this practice?

The industry is selling you material that you previously purchased. Usually, you don't even like the remake. But that doesn't stop you from bobbin' your head to the song because you love the P-Funk sample, not because you like JaRule, Jay-Z, J-Lo (insert insipid music mogul here). We are conditioned to buy an inferior knock off. This is akin to buying a Gucci handbag for $600 only to discover that it is a Kmart special with a designer label. And yet the damage seems minimal. Who is it hurting, right? We know that the music is recycled, don't we? We can still shake our ass at the club, can't we? It's party music not revolution. Like a revolution, let's see what's gonna come back around and bite us in the ass. Where is the creativity? The originality? The expression that is unique to this generation? Where are our novel ideas in this soup of environmental mediocrity?

There is a generation plus that is in danger of having no music that reflects its perspectives, its ideas, concerns, passions (that is unless getting paid can be considered a passion). But the damage is even more significant. Remember that off the cuff comment that I made about singing on key? Can a lay person even tell the difference anymore? Has our collective ear been deadened to the point that we can't discern good singing from the mediocre? Then there are those who have no idea that a song has a key. *Why is JaRule allowed to sing at all?* Other than the guerilla artists, those who work the circuit for next to nothing in the name of ideas and expression, who is nurturing us?

American Film Industry

The prime directives of American film:
1. If it's a hit, make it again, and again, and again. If it was a cartoon, sell it to them again as live action.
2.   If it was hit T.V. show, bring it back as a feature film (can you say "The Dukes of fu***ng Hazzard" and "Welcome Back Kotter"?).
3. If the first film made a dime, make three sequels.
4. If someone else's film was profitable, let's make one just like it.
5. [and my personal favorite] We've run out of sequels so lets do three prequels.

Does Hollywood even deserve to be thought of as a vehicle for artistic expression when it refers to its own product as a franchise? Spinning out bland, uninspired, assembly line, drivel like McDonalds and Taco f**king Bell? I won't even bother to go deeper into such an obvious force of creative destruction.

American Theatre

Does American theatre recycle? Without a doubt. In the profit sector (read Broadway and Broadway tours) the result mirrors the film industry. Many production companies in theatre have the film company as their parent company. This is why we get *The Lion King* followed by *The Lion King the Musical*. The same can be said for music/theatre, recycling the music of Billy Joel, Elton John, Andrew Lloyd Webber, and Tim Rice. Elton is unique. He gets to triple dip with the soundtrack for the film, the musical, and the musical featuring only his compositions. Then of course there is Mel Brooks and *The Producers*. He has the dubious distinction of having a film (The Producers) made into a Broadway musical, and then made yet again into a film musical. The agony!

Does non-profit theatre behave any differently than the profit houses? Tough question, brutal answer: not often enough for my taste. Non-profit has a tendency to hedge, that is to say to try and have it both ways. We want to be expressive, but we also want butts in seats. Our solution? Recycle! After all, it's easier to sell a known commodity like *A Soldiers Play*, *A Raisin in the Sun*, *The Colored Museum*, *Fences*, *For Colored Girls*, etc. And that's why these plays are done dozens and dozens of times per year across the country.   The thinking goes something like this: IF we produce three *Colored Museums*, we can do one *Nobody Ever Heard of This*. Many companies don't even bother with the one *Nobody Ever Heard of This* figuring that it's better to produce four or five *Colored Museums* and stay fiscally solvent. Thus theatre's environmental movement is also in full swing.

Now things get really interesting. Most younger theatre companies (under twenty years old) begin to only produce older material in hopes of garnering their share of the ticket buying public. All of a sudden theatre looks a lot like music. I'm getting Jay-Z in my P-Funk. How can this be a good thing? It is important to note that I do believe there is a place on Black stages for Black plays, regardless of when they were originally produced. But when we almost exclusively recycle, what are we losing? Where are the voices of contemporary Black America? Who is chronicling the voices and perspectives of this generation in this time and place? Have we like popular music abandoned that in pursuit of marketability?

To make matters worse, white theaters have discovered the New Black play as a marketing tool. At first glance, this may appear to be useful. It implies that these otherwise neglected works will find increased stage time and therefore acceptability in a broader context. So what's wrong with that? Let's look a little deeper. White theatre companies are seeking to diversify their audiences in the face of dwindling gate receipts from their ageing traditional audience. Foundations are enlisted to aid in this new initiative that will prolong the life of these white institutions. Again, no real damage, right?

White theaters which develop Black works or Black expression typically leave an indelible imprint upon the work. It all boils down to this: a white theatre typically serves a mostly white middle to upper-class audience, the white company says to the Black writer, I need you to make this change and that change to accommodate our audience. During the process of development, the changes to the new play mount. The writer often feels compelled to accommodate the theatre requests, believing (often rightfully so) that such changes are necessary to secure a production. In the end, your Blackness has been sifted through a white filter. An original work of Black expression has been skewed to serve an external viewpoint. We are now in the business of explaining and decoding our Blackness for white America. We as artists have engaged in the ultimate mind fuck, namely: we have put the white experience at the center of our creative process. How can this be a good thing?

All of that to say this: We must MAKE own art! We must OWN our ideas! We must CREATE new and original work. We must develop and produce ART that serves our needs both as artists and as a community. In an ecological context, environmentalism is a productive force in conservation. With artistic expression, particularly *Black* artistic expression, environmentalism erodes our sense of self, our creativity, and our ability to be expressive. If we do not endeavor to create a vibrant and relevant voice for this generation, grounded in the here and now, we surrender our collective expression to the commercial marketplace, and perhaps even more destructive, we free it to serve the agenda of others.

Directing for Afrikan Centered Theatre

by Mignon McPherson Nance

The primary job of a director is to work with other artists to create a production that communicates the essence of the playwright's story to the audience. A director must provide a safe space where artists will give freely of themselves knowing the gift is appreciated. They must encourage in each member of the production the understanding that their contribution to the work is valued and instrumental in the production's success.

How is this accomplished? First, a director must do their homework. They must study the text seeking to understand the playwright's vision. When working on new scripts the director must communicate with the playwright in an honest and creative manner. Rather than telling the playwright what they should do with their script, the director needs to listen and ask questions. You are not trying to mold the script in to your vision, but helping the playwright clarify their own. A clear grasp on the script and the playwright's intent is key, and this is not possible when working on new scripts without trust and dialogue between you and the playwright.

The director must then determine what kind of rehearsal process best suites the particular play. In western theatre it is often assumed that there is a standard rehearsal structure that can be applied to all plays of a genre. In our work, we cannot make this assumption. Each play is a different story, includes unique theatrical elements, presents different challenges for the actors, and has specific mode of storytelling. A director needs to examine all that makes a play unique and create a rehearsal journey that will lead to a production that expresses that particular work.

Whatever structure you determine is required for the production at hand, there are elements that are key to any rehearsal process. The rehearsal process should be one of exploration for all artists involved. The director knows the play that is their job. They then create the environment where the actors and other artists can play unhampered. Instincts are the stuff of art, yet so many artists shut themselves off. They are stifled by insecure directors and at some point no longer trust their own gut. I work with many actors who I have to coax in to following their own impulses on stage. This can be a difficult process, but it is necessary to creating honest storytelling. Theatre is about being in the moment. It is about trusting that impulse when it comes, not second-guessing. If a director wants to truly create moments of beauty on stage, they must let go and create an environment where this kind of openness is possible. When a director creates this kind of rehearsal environment, a synergy emerges among the artists in the production where every one focuses on communicating the story as the playwright intended.

Just as the performers must trust the moment, a director must strive to do the same. You do the preparation and then you have to release. Directing is not about placing your stamp on the play. It is not about forcing a preconceived structure on the work. It is about entering in to the ritual space of rehearsals and trusting the story to guide you. It is about asking questions, listening and watching the work of the performers as they investigate the script and embody their characters. Your job is then to process this input and that of your designers and shape it in a way that it clearly communicates the story to the audience. A director has to be open and let their intuition and understanding guide their choices. When you do this, you can feel those moments when you, the other artists and the work click. When you then add the final element, the audience, to the mix and you feel them respond to the work; it is golden.

Associative Storytelling: defining the non-linear plot
By Shepsu Aakhu

How much useful information can be provided by telling you what something is NOT? Imagine someone describing their mother and all they can say about her is "she's *not* Adolph Hitler". Not much help? Closer to a detriment, perhaps? Likewise the same mother may spend an enormous amount of energy describing how wonderful her son is by telling you what *he* is not. "He's *not* on drugs", "He doesn't have any children", "He's not in a gang". In the end, do we have a clear picture of her son?

We have a similar problem describing storytelling in theater and film. Chronology is king in western theater. So much so that the lexicon essentially permits only two definitions for story structure: linear and non-linear. The definition for linear storytelling is simple: when told, the story's sequence of events (plot) can be best represented by a line. That is to say, all of the events happen in chronological order from first to last, or in some instances last to first. Non-linear, then, is any story structure which "cannot" best be represented by a straight line.

So we know what non-linear is NOT, but what IS it? In order to answer this question, we must first ask ourselves, "What is the organizing force at work in our story?" In a linear story, it's obvious that the organizing force is time. More precisely, it is the relentless march forward of time. If you doubt it, watch any western play/film and take note of how often the relentless march forward of time is diverted. Any diversion from linear chronology is a rare occurrence, except of course with Quentin Tarantino's *Pulp Fiction*. But can you name another film? For those of you who said *Memento*, I regret to inform you that telling a story backwards is still linear storytelling. The only tangible example in Western/American theatre/film of diverting the relentless march of time is the "flashback" (and its evil step sister the "flash forward"), which basically gives license to the storyteller to incorporate a non-linear element briefly (usually less than five minutes) before once again kneeling at the altar of time.
I do not have a problem with western/American theater and film being a slave to chronology. The fact is that linear thought and chronology are deeply imbedded in the psyche of the westernized mind. They can hardly imagine a world without it. But we can both imagine such a place, and reflect it in our art.

All of this talk and still we have not defined what has been vaguely identified as non-linear storytelling. So we come back to the question of the organizing force. What if we organized a story around a deeper connection or relationships between events? What if the most important force in our story centered around the interdependence and connection between events, not their chronological relationship to each other? Suddenly a new world is possible. Now we can bounce forward and backward in time and watch the effect of actions as they relate to each other, as opposed to waiting for all of those years to transpire in our story, or simply trying to create an ellipse of time?

Perhaps an example would better illustrate the point. Let's say we have a story where our primary character (Olivia) lives in 2006. She's a mother and is having trouble raising her daughter. Her mother (Maggy) also had similar troubles raising Olivia in 1976. Maggy's mother (Sandra) also encountered similar trouble with her in 1956. In a traditional linear format, we would tell each of these stories one after the other and watch the events of their lives slowly unfold over three generations. When the story concludes, we would then be able to make the connections regarding the impact of individual life choices on our characters. We would see how the present "results" from all of the events that lead up to today.

Here's another way to tell this story. If we organize the story around associated elements, that is to say we clump events together based on their mutual relevance/impact, and ignore chronology, we end up with a story that moves based upon the interconnected nature of these three generations. Effectively we eliminate the "present" as the result of everything that has come before it, and instead make it interdependent/interconnected with past and future. "When" something happens is of less significance. The emphasis now lays on the fact "that" it happened at all. Furthermore, the impact of the action and its effect on other events/characters/eras is underscored by placing such events proximal to each other in the plot. Essentially I can now see the interconnected interdependent nature of life, because the illusion of time has been removed. In essence this is the traditional Afrikan view of life. According to many Afrikan spiritual traditions, our existence is not linear, all events have associations, and these associations are relatively independent of the concept of time. In simple terms: the past, present, and future coexist in ONE reality. Therefore they each have the power to impact one another. Everything else (e.g. time, death, isolation) is illusion.

To mix things up a little bit more, associative storytelling does not have to end with the ordering of events (plot). Characters also can speak and convey ideas in complex associations. At first glance this may appear to be a series of random tangents, but upon closer inspection you will discover that these characters have a range of expression and connection that is profound. These associations of language and speech emphasize the connections between ideas and interactions. The linear characteristics of language are modified and/or abandoned to reveal a more compelling sense of relationships between ideas, motives, perspectives and beliefs.

Looking for some tangible examples of "associative storytelling"? Four plays by Shepsu Aakhu offer varying degrees of the association as an organizing force: *SOST, Kiwi Black, Fascia*, and *The Abesha Conspiracy*. Also the work of Nambi E. Kelley is an excellent example of associative language in storytelling. Selections from her catalogue include *MiLK, Hoochie Mama, Chris T, and Bus Boyz*.

What do we gain, and what do we sacrifice by telling stories in this manner? The trade off is that you can get vibrant and provocative connections in the moment that they are presented, but you may not understand their chronological relationship until the end of the work you are experiencing. This has proven most difficult for those who cannot suppress the western desire to know the "when" before they know the "what" and the "why". In such instances it is your concept of time that hinders your enjoyment of the associative story.

I recognize that associative storytelling asks a lot of the audience. It requires that you stop "actively" working to reconstruct a linear/chronological context for the work. It is not as if associative storytelling is absent of chronological clues, but the chronology is not emphasized. If one gives one's full attention to reconstructing a viable time line, frustration will likely result. Additionally, the power of the associations, the very reason a story is being told, may be lost.

Music Outside The Margins
By Shepsu Aakhu

Music sits so central in the lives of Afrikan people and it has burrowed so deeply into our professional theater. This partnership between music and theater is a delicate art. It appears so natural and effortless when well executed, when the music exists in service to the storytelling. It is often little understood, and approached with fear and trepidation by the classically trained professional. In order to function at its highest level, however, this partnership demands a radical rethinking of how and why music functions in Afrikan Centered Theatre (ACT). A conflict between the Western (American/European) and Afrikan aesthetics is at the heart of the matter.

 The vast majority of American professional theater artists, directors in particular, have been trained in American colleges and conservatories. These institutions are heavily invested in the Western (American /European) canon and suffice it to say, they are self affirmed by the practice. Afrikan and African-American theatre artists must become proficient in the aesthetics of Western theater in order to survive and excel in these institutions. Unfortunately, this very Western-centered proficiency, and the relative lack of proficiency in Afrikan-centered works, can and often does lead to conflict. Central to such conflict is the notion of "creative control."

In the contemporary sense, Western drama is about language (i.e., the power of sufficiently motivated spoken language; text). Anything that may detract from that language is viewed as negative, the exception being the uniquely American animal called "The Musical" (which I will address later in this essay). Music is pushed out of the drama proper and exists only in the margins. It rarely occupies the same space and time as dialogue/monologue, largely because there is a notion that music is superfluous, incidental, and distracting, and thus a potentially undermining force. As a result, music largely exists as either an expository element telling us the where and when of a scene/ event, or as purely transitional and affective in nature. It carries us from the end of one scene to the beginning of another and may carry some aspect of mood/ambiance for the scene to change. Whether serving its expository function and/or its transitional one, this music is most often recorded. It is fixed and unchanging throughout the life of the particular mounting of the production. Essentially, the Western perspective on music in theatre is: live music is a dangerously distracting, unwieldy beast. It must be tamed, or better yet house broken. In order to do that, we are willing to sacrifice the most elegant and evocative aspects of the form. We will relegate it to a supportive but non-essential function. Everything else we will leave to "The Musical".

As if operating in an all or none principal, the American musical takes the notion of "music in the margins" and flips it. The result is a highly stylized and fairly rigid form of theater where much of the dialogue/monologue is sung to a preexisting score. Unlike American drama and comedy, in "The Musical," the music is center stage. In fact, the entire genre has been named after the music. Nonetheless, the perspective of music as an unwieldy beast has not changed. In American musicals, we recognize the power and evocative nature of music, but we must tame it first. It must be made docile and submissive. Toward that end, we must regiment the music by fixing it in a pre-written score. This score is often played live but EXACTLY the same night after night. To insure this precision of accompaniment, the score is typically written well in advance and is often sight-read by the musicians during the performance. The music has been domesticated, thus "control" rests solely with the director and/or conductor.

The director's job is to guide the artistic process and shape the production. All too often this is simply reduced to controlling the process, fixing the elements (set, lights, costume, props, music, sound, etc.), and shaping the performances. The result is that everything is *supposed* to be fixed and unchanging except for the actor's performances which, in the best circumstances, will continue to develop and nuance for the life of the production. The notion presented here is not that the traditional western use of music in theatre is somehow wrong, but rather there are more vibrant and viable alternatives. In all fairness to western theatre, the manner in which music has been traditionally used has served it well. Many compelling works have been created with music as little more than an accoutrement, (often a meticulously composed, highly specialized, deftly utilized, recorded accoutrement, but an accoutrement none the less). Afrikan centered theatre (ACT) presents a vastly different take on the power and viability of live music (soundscape).

If western drama is about language, Afrikan centered theatre is about resonance (e.g. the power of sufficiently motivated expression). Music in ACT does not live in the margins. It is central to the storytelling. The music co-exists with language and action without being confined to purely expository or transitional roles. Unlike "The Musical", music in ACT is improvisational in nature and a versatile blend of sophisticated accompaniment which grows and changes with each performance. This approach to "music/sound" liberates the medium from its more traditional role of pre-recorded songs, and effects, thereby allowing the soundscape to exist as both character and thematic carrier.

Great language, but what does it mean? Simply put, the music (soundscape) is not fixed, it's adaptive. Additionally, its relevance is dictated by the feeling/emotion it evokes and supports within the performer and the viewer. Much like an actor is free to explore pace, tone, and intent within the confines of the text and blocking, so then is the music. This is where conflict typically arises between director and musician. The director, highly trained in western theater and highly skilled in their craft, often wants to "fix" the music. The director wants to know exactly what they are getting so that the actors can rely upon it as a constant. Additionally, the director wants to fix the music to insure that the show/scenes' intent is not undermined. In ACT, the music and actor interact and affect each other in the interest of the play. Asking for the music to be fixed and unchanged is akin to asking an actor's performance to be fixed and unchanged. Nothing good can come from this.

Who then is in control? The ideal of "control" is misleading. It is the director's job to help shape the interpretation of a work. Understanding the give and take necessary to get the most from an actor is a well honed skill employed by the contemporary theatre director. The same can be said of the relationship between director and musician/music director. Directors have to know both the potential and the process of scoring music for African centered theatre. The most important element in this relationship is accountability. Often the director and musician are trying to be accountable to two different "texts". A musician playing what they want, when they want, flies in the face of a director's sensibilities. Directors want control; it is part of the job description. In western theatre, who can stomach musicians acting in the role that is reserved for the director? Grumbling is sure to follow, and sound something like this: Musicians are not trained directors, they often cannot see the fragility, or intensity of the entire show. They play too loud and detract from the "language" of the play. They are attention seeking, etc., the list continues. The difference is the ACT musician is trained to translate the *affective* nature of a scene WHILE the scene is being performed. The result is that the improvised music is dictated by the performers. This interplay between the musician and performer creates a unique form of expression which is drastically different from pre-recorded and pre-scored live music that accompanies the western drama/comedy or the American musical. Unfortunately, the western trained director all too often interprets this as a loss of control. The reasoning tends to follow this path: I have not approved that music. If the music can change without notice, then it must follow that the music is sometimes "wrong" for the scene. "Wrong" is unacceptable. Make it "right" by staying with the choice that I approved, regardless of how the actors change their performances, or the production changes its tone. This is akin to a jazz musician being told to read sheet music during a performance. It may be pretty to hear once, but it is not interactive with the other musicians, the audience, or the eccentricities of the particular performance. In the interest of honesty, I will acknowledge that these concerns are not entirely without merit. But we are not talking about musicians in a generic sense. We are talking about specialists. The same arguments listed above are often levied against untrained and undisciplined actors. That does not mean that the highly trained, highly disciplined actor should be dismissed as undesirable.

In order to understand and hopefully embrace this concept, we have to expand the notion of text to mean that article (written or not) from which the artist is to base their primary interpretations. I am now calling something text (i.e. words on a page) that is clearly simply an actor's interpretation. For the director, this is the script (traditional text), and likewise for the actors and most designers. They are equally concerned with the writer's intent as well as what the writer actually wrote on the page. For the musician in ACT this is neither practical nor practicable. If one is to play music for a scene, the soundscape must be as nuanced and evocative as the performance. One of the joys of live theatre is that actors can change the depth and resonance of a production as they nuance their performances. Over the course of a production, actors often collectively transform a play into something entirely different in tone and temperament than what hit the stage on opening night. In ACT we recognize that it is not in the service of the storytelling to have musicians playing music for an interpretation of a production which no longer exists on stage. Scoring is about intent, action, tension, motivation, mood, and silence. These "variables" are just that --"variable". The actors collectively define and redefine the interplay of these factors from scene to scene and from performance to performance. If the text from which a musician is to make his/her interpretations is dynamic in nature, and frequently dramatically so, it is counterproductive to assume that the music be static, fixed or unchanging. A musician's instinct is to demand that the text dictate what is appropriate to a scene. Since the actor's performance is the "text" for the musician, the improvised music must flow from the actor's interpretation. Sometimes this means that the music will vary very little from show to show, and cues which are set by the musicians for entrances and the like cannot be altered without undermining a performance. But in some instances, particularly with new works, the music HAS to evolve rapidly and dramatically to keep pace with the actors evolving portrayals.

American filmmaking offers perhaps the best example to illustrate my point. In American film a score is often utilized in a manner where it co-exists with dialogue and action. We easily grasp its power and importance. Rarely do we engage in a discussion of how the "sound/music" is distracting or unimportant. We readily recognize that music greatly enhances the power of the medium. A reoccurring musical theme may create vital connections between events and characters. A depth of emotion and connection is evoked between actors and the audience which otherwise might not be evidenced. In film, however, the score is most often created by a composer after (s)he has seen the film. The score is sometimes created while viewing the film. This is the practice of ACT. The music is created as the musicians view, feel, and experience the performance. There is an interaction, a depth of sharing that occurs in that moment which is greater than the sum of its parts.   To make the music fixed and unchanged is to sever this partnership and lessen the experience for all involved.

To further extend the comparison, the soundscape for ACT is akin to scoring different "takes" of the same scene live during filming. Occasionally, a "take" has a wildly different interpretation. Other times, it may be subtle. The musicians must intuit the nature of the "take" (interpretation) and improvise appropriate music on the spot. We know what the director has requested, we see what the actors are creating, and we contribute something dynamic and evocative based on our understanding of the two. Every night that the curtain goes up is like scoring the same film over and over again, but the actors are making new "takes" every night. This sometimes requires completely different music, other times not. Such is the challenge and the art. In the end, we have to be as free as the actors or we cease to be able to support them and the stories we tell. A large amount of trust is required. Trust which quite frankly is not required in traditional western theatre.

Are you still concerned about who's in control? The answer hasn't changed: the story is in charge.

The Creation: The Internal vs. The External
by Carla Stillwell

I recently assisted a friend, who is a director, with helping one of her actors get physically connected to a character he's playing in her show. In my workshop session with the actor, I made the statement, "I don't believe that one can get connected to a character until they understand how the character physically relates to the world." My friend and I disagreed, but since we were there to help this actor and not have a full-scale debate about the craft, I let it go and did the workshop. That moment stuck with me for weeks and I thought this might be the perfect forum to make my point.

In the 20 years that I have been on stage, I have always been cast against "type". As an overweight child/teen/young adult/grown ass woman, I have always been cast well outside of my age group. As a child and young adult, that meant playing the grandmother or the aunt. In the professional arena, it meant that since I am not physically "suitable" to be the wife or the love interest, I am cast in roles that require an actress to undergo an extreme physical metamorphose: to be the 'Transformer' or 'Thunder Cat' of the Chicago stage. I have been asked to be anywhere from 5 to 60 years old. I have played men, animals, and the occasional gimp. I've been Jamaican, many different varieties of generic African, and one or two white women. It is my opinion that the 'internal' approach of creating a character is counter productive in the beginning of the rehearsal process, especially when you are being asked to create a character that is physically and socially removed from your personal experience, which most African American actors are asked to do on a daily basis.

Now some of you are saying to yourself, "What the hell is she talking about!? You have to internalize your character! She has lost her mind!" I'm not disputing anything that we were taught in the infinite number of acting classes that most of us sat in for way more years than we care to remember. It is important to understand technique, all the different methods, how to write an effective character bio, and actually sit down and write the damn bio. It is important to know how go through your script and dissect each scene, each moment, beat by beat. As an artist, you have to understand the rules before you can break them. You will get no argument from me on that point. However, there are a certain set of rules that should be taught to African American actors first, and one of them is the act of 'externally' creating a character.

Let's face it; you can count the Negro leading men and women in Hollywood on one hand. The rest of them are character actors. In this society, there can only be one Hallie at a time. The rest of us have to scrap for the "sassy black neighbor" or "Kizzy" roles. Most of us must tap into our inner slave to decipher how Kizzy lived. You have to decide how one walks with a welt tree on their back, what an average young slave mother wore to the fields to put in 15 hours worth of free labor with her child strapped to her body, how quickly you can move with 30 lbs. of cotton and a child hanging from your person, barefoot in 95-100 degree weather. These are all physical choices that the actress needs to make so that you believe that she is an American Negro slave in Mississippi circa 1789. It won't matter how many books the actress has read on acting theory and technique. It won't matter how many bios she's written about which one of her children was sold at auction and on what day. It won't matter how many times the actress decided that Massa crept into her quarters, if that same well-fed, over-educated, middle class (by middle class, I speak in the Negro since of the word…she was raised by somebody that had a job and she never had to wear the clothes and shoes of anyone other than her siblings and not too distant cousins) Negro woman does not spend at least one day fasting to figure out what it feels like to be hungry, you won't believe that she's Kizzy because she will be lacking any physical connection to that way of life. She simply has no point of reference.

So, the girl they cast to play "Carla" in the movie of my life might not have to be 5' 2", but she will sure as hell have to spend several days walking in nothing lower than a 3" heel. To create the "Carla" persona, you have to be able to walk like "Carla". To walk like "Carla" you need 3-4 inch heels. The girl can go all Psych 101 and write the 5-page bio about how the character always felt she was being looked down on because she was so short, so she wears the high ass shoes. But if you have never been 3 sheets to the wind wearing a pair of 4 inch stacks, you know nothing of my life. That's all physical.

Acting is as much observation, imitation, and channeling as it is theory and method.

A Safe Black Universe
Shepsu Aakhu

My voice has its own metronome. It comes from an amalgam of my personal experiences, as well as a deep commitment to introspection. I essentially write a world that is populated by the people I have known, and the many facets of my own spirit. I do not write to sell. I write to explore, discover, and reveal.

In this practiced art of mining my own soul, I have found freedom in style and subject. I have since discovered it to be largely unappreciated, unheralded, and unrewarded on the American stage, especially as it relates to the diversity of Black stories.

I define a Black story as a story where Black characters are central to the narrative.   That is in contrast to the common practice of placing Black characters in the periphery of the narrative. In such stories, the Black characters exist only to support others (typically the white characters). These characters rarely have a rich internal life and are rarely motivated beyond simple ethnic stereotypes. They certainly are not reflective of the Black people that I have known, feared, loved, or admired.   Essentially, they are only tools to tell the story of someone else and not people in their own right.

There is a book entitled: ***Toms, Coons, Mulattoes, Mammies, & Bucks*** by Donald Bogle**.** The book has a simple yet effective premise. Black stereotypes (i.e., Toms, Coons, etc.) were the only characters we were permitted and encouraged to create or portray. Unfortunately, over twenty years later audiences are still being fed a steady diet of *Toms, Coons, Mulattoes, Mammies, & Bucks***.** The cultural landscape has not changed significantly enough to erase those pervasive archetypes, but enough to create an equally detrimental alternative. I call it the *Safe Black Play*, full of safe Black characters inhabiting a safe Black Universe. Ironically, however, that safe Black universe provides little actual safety for the Black audience as to not offend White sensibilities.

To better understand this point we need look no further than the American "*Race Play*". What does the topic of race look like in the *Safe Black Play*? First, it must not make the White audience, or the affluent Black audience for that matter, uncomfortable. Removing the story from a contemporary setting is the easiest way to accomplish this goal. A period piece, set anytime in American history before 1975, will typically get the job done. We can draw bold characters steeped in overt racial opposition without the fear of offending the great masses. I call it the "Thirty-Year Barrier". The thirty-year barrier represents old America - confused, obstructionist, unenlightened America. When the audience sees this America on stage, they see it as a politically or historically *Dark Age* and not an extension or commentary of themselves. This *Dark Age* was an unfortunate time, but it is not at all reflective of our present enlightened society.

The thirty year barrier facilitates the notion that the evil has passed, which may be unintentional on the writer's part. The work may have higher aspirations, but inevitably exists as a work that does not directly force its audience to examine themselves within a contemporary context. The audience is given an out and allowed to cloak themselves in a well worn deception. *"Those people back then had it bad. Boy, aren't things better now?"* This disconnection allows the audience to empathize without taking any responsibility for the issue being explored, thus the *"Safe Black Play."*

For the Black community, it is anything but safe – it takes racism out of its usual institutional context and personified it instead. It is embodied in a flesh and blood character that exists as the antagonist. Any writing teacher will tell you that this is a good idea because, in theory, it gives the audience a clear villain and creates clear motivations for the protagonist. Functionally, however, this device undermines the Black community's sense of reality. The obstructions of racism are rarely limited to one individual. We effectively tell the Black audience that what you know to be true will not be seen on this stage. For the white audience we go in the other direction; what you WISH to be true will be validated on this stage - white society has allegiance and responsibility, only the white individual.

In this scenario, the white audience is safe while the Black audience is not. The race play requires a certain truth telling. We have to see race in a contemporary context, with all of its complexity, and with an acceptance/understanding that we will be made uncomfortable from time to time.

In American theater we are allowed to be angry, violent, impoverished, anti-social and generally self-destructive. We are allowed to be comical. Our comedy, no matter how subversive the creator's intent, is largely consumed as a docile or passive diversion. From this comes the concept of the coon. We are allowed to be objects of lust and exoticism. Can it be healthy to think of oneself as exotic? This is by definition an outsider's viewpoint. Forming one's self-image from an external viewpoint has to be considered a destructive practice.

None of this imagery challenges audiences to view us with any depth. As BLACK artists we have to OWN and utilize these images. I am not of the school of thought that purports all representations of Black culture have to be positive and uplifting, but we have to be more complex than this. We have to be more than what makes others comfortable when they interact with us. We have to be the conflicted, contradictory, profoundly heroic, and deeply flawed people that we all know and share our lives with. We must be and represent our true selves.

Do we exist in American theater outside the boundaries of the race play? The answer is yes. Are these stories widely produced? Not really. Why? Because once the race play is put aside, Black characters exist in a world with conflicts that are not bound by our relationships to white America. The white audience does not see itself in the story. Their interest in a Black story typically declines sharply when their experiences, culture, and sense of superiority, are not referenced textually, or within the greater subtext. Simply put – if the story is not clearly about them, they tend to divest. If you doubt it, ask yourself this question: how many reviews of Black stories do you see with the following line buried in the body of the critique: *"It is a universal story about...".* Decoded, this simply means that white America doesn't need to worry, because they will see themselves (their culture and values) in the story.

When was the last time you saw those words in reference to *Hamlet, Death of a Salesmen, The Producers, Blueman Group*, or *UrineTown*? We are not *allowed* to be ourselves yet. We are not allowed to tell our stories for their value to us. In the Black Market, we exist largely to entertain and amuse white America. This is a problem, one we help to create and reinforce.

We have to value our own stories. We must come to view our art as a reflection of ourselves. We must view our work as more than an opportunity for escapism. When you give your time and your hard earned money, you deserve more than just a laugh. You deserve a good cry whether in joy or pain. You deserve the tingle of self recognition when characters that look like you and share your experiences move across the stage. You deserve to be challenged instead of pandered to by the production. You deserve to be welcomed by a sense that your stories are valued in this space, upon this stage, by these performers. The Black universe should portray a world that is populated by the people you have known, and the many facets of your own spirit.

You've been getting short changed. Frankly, the industry doesn't think that we have been paying attention. And quiet honestly, far too many of us have not. This is the only safe Black universe that matters - one where we are secure enough to be our selves.

The Plays

MiLK
by Nambi E. Kelley

Fascia
by Shepsu Aakhu

She Calls Up The Sun
by Addae Moon

The Divine Order of Becoming
by Carla Stillwell

MiLK
By NAMBI E. KELLEY
World Premiere 1995

MiLK
Director's Notes

The years 1994 to 1995 were a pivotal time in my life. I had just lost my father and was becoming a bit demoralized by the status of my acting career. Three years of playing "ensemble member #3" and the "non-traditional" part of several shows was taking a toll on my artistic soul. I was simultaneously offered several directing projects which led me to MPAACT and Nambi E. Kelley's MiLK. MiLK gave me hope at a time when I was not feeling good about the opportunities I had as a Black theater artist.

When asked to direct MiLK, I read the script and immediately accepted the challenge. The language and the style drew me to the play. Nambi's use of language in MiLK is an intricate blend of stream of conscious flow and dialogue straight from the projects (the play's setting). This unique use of language adds to the vibrancy of her storytelling. Nambi is a playwright with a keen awareness that the ridiculous and the tragic can coexist. This creates a style that extends the reality of her characters and takes her audience on a thrilling journey. Here was a play focused on the life of a young woman growing up in Chicago's public housing (Chicago Housing Authority) -- not your typical theater fare. It was invigorating to meet this young black woman telling her story in a way that was honest and unrestrained, and reminded me of former female schoolmates. MiLK is funny and disturbing, and I felt very fortunate to direct such an important play.

I was naïve when we began working on the world premiere production of MiLK. I was unaware of the tremendous amount of faith being given to me by this production company, and unphased by the complexity of this script. This was probably for the best. My "greenness" was an advantage because it allowed me to just do the work, unencumbered by anxiety or fear. I was not daunted or intimidated by the work or the risks. I connected with this story. I knew these people and I felt that I could successfully bring Nambi's story to the stage. My challenge was to let the production match the ingenuity of the script. Just as the playwright juxtaposed humor and tragedy, urban reality and ritualism in her storytelling, I tried to bring these elements into balance in the staging, design elements and performances of the production. In the end, the story guided the production, and I like to think that it was successful. As I look back on it now, the lasting impression was recognition from the audience as they watched the lives of these black folks from the Ida B. Wells housing projects play out in all its complexity on stage, and my pride at being a part of it all.

MiLK
Playwright's Statement

This work speaks about the "milk" of our life experiences which we swallow and hold in our soul. In that sense it is a journey that everyone goes through from childbirth, passing through the birth canal, to life outside the womb. Entering into this world is a physical and spiritual transformation, a transformation which no person can elude.

MiLK

Original Cast

Magaly Colimon	WOMACLOWN
Tijuana Gray	BABY
Dushon Monique Brown	SHADOW
Nicole Bush	BROWN
James Meridith	LEE
Renardo Bell	FIVE –OHH
Kenneth Johnson	MR. CONN

Staff

Director	Mignon McPherson
Assistant Director	Kerri Richardson
Production Stage Manager	Mark Franklin
Musical Director	Georges Blaise
Technical Director	Sean R. Neron
Set Design	Dirk DeLaCour
Lighting Design	Sean R. Neron
Choreographer	Lisa Biggs
Sound Design	William S. Carroll
Costume Design	Tiffany Trent
Properties	Shepsu Aakhu
Producer	Reginald Lawrence

CHARACTERS:

WOMACLOWN: Womaclown is BABY's soul; or her as a child-self. She is constantly in the same physical space as BABY, and reacting as BABY's truest self. Her reactions are entirely physical and movement-based. She is invisible. No one ever sees her, but BABY, and even sometimes not BABY.

BROWN: 20-25 African-American female to play 13-18; street-smart and wise with a love for making pencil marijuana, BABY's friend; ALSO DOUBLES AS COMPANY MEMBER.

SHADOW: 20-25 African-American female to play 13-18; somewhat androgynous, BABY's best friend; ALSO DOUBLES AS COMPANY MEMBER.

BABY: 20-25 African-American female to play 13-18; beautiful and innocent, tries to act tougher than she is.

LEE: 20-25 African-American male to play 15-20; BABY's boyfriend; in need of a father figure.

FIVE-OHH: 40-60; African-American male; BABY's eccentric but loveable and deeply spiritual uncle.

MR. CONN: 25-40; any race; the neighborhood homeless man who later poses as an exterminator and school teacher.

SETTING:

Chicago, mid 1990s in the housing projects on the southside.

ACT I

[*Lights fade up slowly as a figure dressed all in black carries a purple glass of milk from the house towards the stage. WOMACLOWN sets the full glass down and begins to feel the parameters of a womb which she is inside of. Lights are now dim and we can see her face. She is very dark complexioned. Her features are very pronounced, African, full. She has a full natural afro which stands tall & wide. She is beautiful. She struggles and struggles within the womb. Freezes. Stares at the audience. She looks largely, examining every face in the audience with her large black eyes. She cowers, then speaks.*]

WOMACLOWN:

Inside.
Inside it is warm.
I feel liquid
Thru finger tips
and her air
Air!
She is safe,
warm
and all around
are her walls which
hold
me tighly
and her Tube
which feeds me
French fries, peanut butter,
milk
and soul.

Inside.

I don't want to leave
Don't want to go
Don't want to know
Woman's journey
          thru
kids teasing me
'bout my raggedy
tragedies
nah nah nah nah nah!
t.v. with face
brady-bunch paste
menstruatin'
people hatin'
graduatin'
free!

sex with men
whose penises offend
thru shit,
muck
senseless fucks

I smack
gum
I can't
cum
Don't want to know
Just don't!
But
I am the wisher
the watcher
the dreamer
I hold warm warm soul.
I taste sweet milk.
NO!
I don't want to go

Don't want to leave
her womb
to the dying tomb
But it's time
to be born.

[WOMACLOWN breaks free of womb, sips the milk, and skips upstage and watches *BABY. Enter BABY, SHADOW,* and *BROWN* skipping across aisles to stage. *WOMACLOWN* tosses a rope. The girls don't ever see *WOMACLOWN* because she is *BABY'S* soul and therefore invisible.*]*

SHADOW [*grabs rope*]: First!

BROWN: Second!

SHADOW: Pull that end, Brown. I'll pull the other-

BROWN: O.k. One--two--three!

SHADOW: Let's play "Take a peach."

BROWN: You can turn, can't you?

BABY: Yeah, girl! Just bring on that rope and I'll show you what I can do!

BROWN: You sure you not double-handed?

BABY: If I was double handed you'd see another little hand sticking from out and between my thumbs wouldn't you?

BROWN: Just like Five-Ohh, right?

BABY: Don't you be talkin' 'bout my blood.

BROWN: Why else he been baggin' at the A&P for 30 years?

SHADOW: Come on, let's just play. I'm first.

BABY: I never get to go first.

SHADOW: That's cause it my rope, little puddin' head girl.

BABY: I never get to go first!

SHADOW: I'm the one who cut the ends offa my Mamma's extention cord to make this rope. When YOU cut off YO' Mamma's extention cord-

BROWN: That's some suicide right there.

BABY: OOH! I know y'all heard 'bout that real smart girl with the long braids in the seventh grade?

BROWN: The one they call "Computer?"

BABY: Yeah. Tyronda Wilson.

BROWN: They said she was gon' get to graduate early wit us next month.

SHADOW: Yeah. I heard. Just jumped right off the top o'that project buildin'.

BROWN: Did you see it, Baby?

BABY: Umm hmm. I saw it all!

BROWN: You did, girl?!

BABY: Umm hmm-

BROWN: You see blood and everything?

BABY: Yup.

WOMACLOWN: Unn!

SHADOW [*steps on the rope*]: Two turns each. No overs!

BABY: I never get to go first!

BROWN: Yeah, whatever, Baby.

BABY [*seeing* WOMACLOWN]: Maybe that girl over there wanna play. HEY GIRL!

BROWN: Ain't nobody there, Baby. Let's just play.

BABY: Yes there is. She sittin' right over there. HEY GIRL, YOU WANNA PLAY-?!

[BABY *looks up, doesn't see* WOMACLOWN *anymore.*]

I could just swear-

BROWN: Tol' you wudn't nobody there, Baby. Now just shut up and turn!

SHADOW: Brown, sing that song, now!

BROWN: Alright hit it!
[*singing*]
Take a peach
Take a plumb
Take a pocketful of gum
Don't like it
Don't take it
Shake it up
Shake it down
Shake it all the way around-

[SHADOW'S *feet get caught in the rope.*]

SHADOW: Shoot! Brown, why don't you guide her so she can turn right?

BABY: Why don't you go on and pick up yo' big feet so I can turn?

BROWN: You want that over?

SHADOW: I said no overs! Keep singin'!

BROWN: Baby, turn!

BABY: I AM turning!

SHADOW: Sing!

BROWN [*singing*]: Shake it all the way around
Hot dog baby
Chicken in the gravy
Here come da lady wit da bald headed baby
So one all around
Two all around
Three all around-

[SHADOW *gets caught in the rope.*]

BABY: See? There go Shadow's big feet gettin' caught ALL up in the rope again!

SHADOW: I ain't got no big feet!

BROWN: Oh yes you do, girl!

SHADOW: Ya'll betta get on these ends and give me my last turn!

BROWN: Naw! It's my turn now!

BABY: My mamma want me home fo' the street lights come up. Why come you in such a hurry?

BROWN: 'Cause my Mamma gon' press my hair tonight!

SHADOW: Yo' Mamma need to do somethin' wit that Diana Ross FRO, girl!

BROWN: Don't you be talkin' 'bout my fro Miss Two hundred and twenty one tons-o-fun! You said "two turns each, no overs!" It's my turn!

BABY: Both ya'll need to quit cause I'm the only one here who even know how to jump. It's my turn!

SHADOW: What you mean, girl? It's still my turn!

BROWN: No it ain't either!

BABY: What 'bout me?

BROWN: Yo' mama!

BABY: Don't you be talkin' bout my Mamma now or we gon' have to fight!

SHADOW: Tell her "Yo' whole generation!"

BABY: Don't be tellin' me what to say. I know what to say!

SHADOW: Then go on and say it to her! Tell her this- Yo' mama, and yo' grandpappy's mamma, and yo' great great great grandpappy's mamma's whole generation!

BABY: You don't need to tell me. I'm gon' cuss Brown out when I'm good and ready!

SHADOW: You ain't gon' do nothin'.

BABY: You need to quit, Shadow. You cain't even jump let alone cuss nobody out!

SHADOW: Alright then. You gon' be all like that when I'm tryin' to help you out? I'm gon' trip on you too!

BROWN: Shadow! Baby's mama so ugly when she was born the doctor thought she was E.T!

SHADOW: Naw, I got one, watch this! Baby's mama so black, doctor thought she was a piece of charcoal!

BROWN: Wait a minute girl, get this! Baby mama so ugly, her first name is DAMN!

BABY: OOOO! Look at you up there cussin' like yo'mama in the grave!

BROWN: Shet up! And she may as well be anyway!

SHADOW: Hold up! Baby mamma so ugly, she walk by the bathroom and the toilet flush!

BROWN [*gestures to breast, pelvis, and rear*]: OOOH! Listen! Baby mama ho on the corner sellin' her fruit-cock-tail!

BABY: Yo' mama, yo' mama...yo' mama stink like Magic Johnson's dookey!

BROWN [*laughing*]: Girl, that's tired like Michael Jackson's care-free curl!

SHADOW [*laughing*]: Chill now! Baby tryin' to EDUCATE us-!

BROWN [*laughing*]: 'Bout her Mama's dookey stains!

SHADOW [*laughing*]: Brown, shut up!

BABY: You both double-handed anyway!!!

BROWN: We got her! C'mon and slap me some five, Shadow!

SHADOW: Hold up that hand up high!

BROWN: SLAM IT--! YES!

[BROWN *and* SHADOW *slap high-five.*]

BABY: Alright. Y'all wanna go and trip on me, that's cool. I'm just gon' go home then. And y'all cain't play no rope without me. So see ya!

BROWN [*laughing*]: Come here, Baby!

SHADOW: Don't leave, girl. We just trippin'. I'll let you jump next?

BABY: You forreal?

SHADOW: Yeah, girl. Come on.

BROWN: What 'bout me?

BABY: Yo' Mamma!

BROWN: Aw, Baby gettin' hard!

BABY: That's right! Now turn that rope!

SHADOW: Alright, hit it!

[*Enter* MR. CONN *with sprayer. He watches* BABY. BROWN *notices him watching* BABY. WOMACLOWN *peers at him strangely.*]

BROWN: Unn! What he lookin' at?!

SHADOW: Just sing! "My Mamma!"

BROWN [*singing*]: My Mamma sent me to the store
She told me not to stay out late
I fell in love with the grocery boy
Who took my heart away way way!

Who's the mamma?

BABY: Baby!

BROWN: How's the baby?

BABY: Just fine!

BROWN: What you gon' feed it?

BABY: Baby food!

BROWN: What you gon' feed it wit?

BABY: A spoon!

BROWN: Who's the father?

BABY: None o' yo' business-!

BROWN: So J-I Gypsy
Yo' Mamma can see
Tell me who on earth
Could yo husband be?
He a lover
Unda cover
Gettin' down
Wit yo' mother so
Spell yo name on one feet!

BABY: Capital B-A-B-and-Y!

[BABY *gets caught in rope, but is exhuberant.* BABY *sees and smiles at the* WOMACLOWN.]

SHADOW: OOOH! BABY was tearin' it up in that rope!

BROWN: Who you smilin' at?!

BABY: That girl! She loved my jumpin'!

BROWN: You don't need to gloat!

[*Beat.* BABY *turns around to see* WOMACLOWN. WOMACLOWN'S *gone, and* MR. CONN *has replaced her. He smiles and exits slowly.*]

[*Beat.*]

BABY: Wait?

BROWN: Jumpin' so long she lost the brains in the rope. And so what that ol' fool in the Orkin hat is smilin' at you! He don't know I could jump betta!

SHADOW: OOOH! Baby! She was gettin' down!

BROWN: Yeah, whatever.

SHADOW: She was! OOH! Baby know she can jump!

BROWN: Umm hmm. Yeah. Sure.

[BROWN *whacks* BABY *with rope*.]

You it, Baby!

BABY: Ow! Why you hit me in the head!

BROWN: Cuz you it!

SHADOW: My Mamma always tell me Jealousy-February.   And Brown got it.

BROWN: It ain't even February! And I ain't jealous. I just wanna play somethin' else. YOU IT, Baby!

SHADOW: Umm Hmm. Alright!

[*Beat*.]

You it, Baby!

BABY: I don't wanna be it! I'm goin' home! Y'all play too much! Why come she gotta come up and hit me in my head like I'm a can o' spam?

SHADOW: Aw right. Then I'm it! One-two-three-get off my Mamma's apple tree!

BROWN: Run!

BABY: Alright. Y'all wanna play. I'ma play. You can't catch me!

SHADOW: Ahh! I almost got you!

BROWN: We're runnin', We're runnin'-

BABY: As fast as we can-

BROWN: You cain't catch me-

BABY: I'm the Gingerbread man!

SHADOW: Ahh! I got you-Ahh!

BROWN: Girl, you betta leggo my arm for I come knock you up side the head wit my Mr. T. fist!

SHADOW: You it!

BROWN: Alright! Since you refuse to buckle down to the Force of the A-team! Here I come!

SHADOW: Quit talkin' 'bout Mr. T. and run!

BROWN: Shut up, girl! T. the boy!

SHADOW: And yo' Mamma look like him, so come on! You started the game.

BABY: Are we playin' or what?

BROWN: Mr. T. aka B.A. Barracus and the Force of the A-Team go to war to save lost p.o.w.'s. "I pity the fool who mess wit me!"

BABY: The street lights gon' be out soon-

BROWN: We dig deep in the trenches for lost American men!

[BROWN *digs in trenches behind ladder, starts giggling.*]

SHADOW: What you laughin' at?

BABY: What you got there?

SHADOW: Girl, I wanna see! I wanna see?

BABY: OOOH! Brown found somethin' in the trenches!

SHADOW: Girl! Ain't no trenches in no project playground!

BABY: Well look like she got somethin' in that little plastic bag. I bet some whino left it there.

SHADOW: Brown! Quit jumpin' around and show us what you found!

BROWN [in teasing song]: I got somethin' you don't got!
I'm gon' keep it till I drop!
I'm gon' keep it till I choke!
Got myself some stash to smoke!

BABY: What you got?

BROWN: Shavin's!

SHADOW: OHHH! Baby, come here!

BABY: What?

BROWN: Shavin's. Shavin's. Shavin's!

SHADOW: Toss me that bag!

BROWN: Catch!

SHADOW: Got it!

BROWN: Let's do the shavin's dance!

SHADOW: Brown know every song and dance in the projects!

BABY: But she can't jump like I can!

BROWN: Anyway, Baby. La-tee-dah-tee-!

SHADOW: We like ta party!
BROWN: La-tee-dah-tee!

SHADOW: We's like ta party!

SHADOW/BROWN: Heyyyyy!

BROWN: What do you ever imagine we could possibly do wit a bag full o' shavin's from the whino?

SHADOW [*laughing*]: OOh girl, I don't know. We could...throw it away.

BROWN: OOOH! But my Mamma told me never throw away a gift from god!

SHADOW: We could...eat it!

BROWN: My mamma tol' me never eat anything up off the ground less you wanna get club foot and diarrhea!

SHADOW: OOOH! Then what you think we should do?

SHADOW/BROWN [*to* BABY]: HMMM!

BROWN: What YOU think we should do, Baby?

BABY: The street lights just 'bout out. My mamma 'pect me home. I'm gon' go.

BROWN: OOH NOOOO! You cain't go yet. Yo' Mamma may be ugly, but she know you got to have a lil' fun sometimes.

SHADOW: That's right, Baby.

BROWN: And this is gon' be somethin' serious, Baby.

[*Beat.*]

Come to think of it, I bet you Baby can't even do this.

SHADOW: YUP.

BROWN: Only thing Baby can do is jump.

BABY: That ain't true. I can smoke yo' ol' pencil reefer if I want to. That's IF I wanted to. Just cause you a fool don't mean I got to be a fool wit you.

BROWN: You cain't do it, that's why! Baby scared.

BABY: I'm not scared. I could do anything you could do better.

BROWN: Shadow, she lyin'.

SHADOW: I s'pose we gon' find out.

BROWN: We ain't 'bout to find out nothin' 'cept that Baby weak!

BABY: Alright. You gon' be like that. Show me how we's gon' have some fun wit a bag o' whino shavin's that we don't know what to do wit?

BROWN: I'll show you. You got a notebook?

BABY: Yeah.

BROWN: Where is it?

BABY: Under the swing.

BROWN: Bring it to me.

BABY: What for?

BROWN: Just bring it already!

[BABY *goes to grab notebook.* WOMACLOWN *tries to block her unsuccessfully.*]

BABY: Here.

BROWN: Thank you.

SHADOW: Girl! Why you rippin' pages out-

BROWN: Cause I was watchin' reruns o' Kojak, me and this boy-

SHADOW: Raymond!

BABY: Raymond?

SHADOW: Raymond the first boy Brown ever-

BROWN: KISSED! The first boy I ever kissed, so shet up, Shadow!

SHADOW: Did I say you didn't just kiss?

BROWN: Shet up about him, alright? Or else I'ma have to talk 'bout yo' daddy.

BABY: What 'bout yo' daddy Shadow?

BROWN: Nothin'. 'Cept he-

SHADOW: I said I wouldn't say nothin' bout Raymond, Brown!

[*Beat.*]

BROWN: Baby, find some matches.

BABY: This ain't "What's happenin'? Roj, DeWayne, and Re-run wouldn't be doin' this-

SHADOW: That's cause they'd be runnin' up and dancin' on the Gong Show wit Mamma Mabel and Dee-

BROWN: Dee got some pretty hair.

SHADOW: It kinda look like Baby's hair don't it rown?

BROWN: Yeah, um hm.

SHADOW: Yup. Jealous.

BROWN: Quit, Shadow! I thought you wasn't scared, Baby?

BABY: I'm not. You just bring it on. And I'll show you I ain't scared. You still ain't shown me how to do it yet!

BROWN: Be cool. Just watch.

SHADOW: Aw right, girl, do it.

BROWN: See first you rip it into little squares-

BABY: Um hmm.

BROWN: Then you take the shavin's and put equal amounts in each square.

SHADOW: And then-

BROWN: And then you roll it...like this-

BABY: Girl, where you say you learn that?
BROWN: On Kojak--

SHADOW: OOH! I saw that one too!

BROWN: SLAM IT--! YES!

[BROWN *and* SHADOW *slap high-five.*]

BROWN: Baby! What I say about gettin' some matches? I saw some up unda the swing.

BABY: All right. I'm gettin' 'em.

BROWN: Hurry up!

BABY: I cain't find 'em!

BROWN: Girl! Look up unda ova there!

BABY: Oh. Here.

BROWN: Watch this.

SHADOW: Look at her light that baby!

BABY: Ohh, Brown! You betta put that out fo' the po-lice come!

SHADOW: Girl! How many times I gotta tell you? Ain't no po-lice in no project playground either!

BROWN: "I'M NOT SCARED! I'M NOT SCARED!" Cry baby. It ain't nothin' but pencil shavin's. Here, Shadow.

SHADOW: Yeah.

BROWN: Baby!

BABY: Give it here!

BROWN: Ohh, Baby gettin' a little hard!

BABY: Give it to me!

SHADOW: Alright, girl. Brown? Relight this?

BROWN: Sure thing, girl. Here, Baby.

BABY: Now I'm gonna see how bad this is. [*Pause.*] Alright. Here I go. [*Pause.*] Y'all gon' stop me?

BROWN: Naw, girl. Hurry on up.

BABY: Alright. I'm finna do it.

BROWN: Go on, girl. Smoke it. Now!

[BABY *smokes, coughs.* WOMACLOWN *pats* BABY'S *back.*]

BABY: Woo! Wee! I feel it too.

SHADOW: No you don't girl.

BROWN: That's why you coughin', right?

BABY: Woo! Wee! I feel it!

SHADOW: No you don't girl. You just wanna be like us.

BROWN: You lyin', girl!

BABY: I ain't lying. Woo! Wee!

BROWN: Then come over here and take another puff.

SHADOW: Yeah, girl.

BABY: Naw, I think I had enough. I can't even see my eyeballs.

BROWN: That's cause you coughin' smoke all up in 'em!

SHADOW: Yup!

BROWN: Here, Baby...Take it.

BABY: Alright. Alright!

BROWN: Go, girl.

[BABY *smokes, coughs.* WOMACLOWN *pats* BABY'S *back.*]

BABY: Alright...Woo-

BROWN [*laughing*]: There she go coughin' up smoke like she don't know where she gon' sleep tonight.

BABY: You the one neva know where you gon' sleep!

[*Beat.*]

BABY: It almost dark. I'm gon' home!

BROWN: Go on home then! I'm tired of her!

BABY: And I'm tired o' you.

SHADOW: You the one always smokin' them shavin's!

BROWN: Quit! Otherwise you ain't gettin' no more.

SHADOW: You don't need to be smokin' 'em everytime the teacher tell you to clean out the pencil sharpener!

BROWN: So at least teacher ask me to. Only thing he ask you to do is grade all his papers. Brown noser!

SHADOW: Only thing Brown know how to do is smoke.

BROWN: Only thing Shadow know how to do is kiss teacher boodie!

BABY: Y'all both need to quit. Especially you smokin' all the time.

BROWN: It don't matter. It not like it the real thing.

SHADOW: Always doin' somethin' dumb.

BABY: Umm hmm.

BROWN: Ain't done nothin' dumb. 'Cept sharin' it wit you fools!

BABY: I didn't want none o'it no way. It gettin' dark out. My mamma said she might be home when I get there, so I'm finna go, awright?

SHADOW: Awright, Baby. Come on, Brown. I know you cain't stay mad at me too long or-

BROWN: Or what?

SHADOW: Or I'ma hafta talk 'bout yo' mama like she burnt hair in a greasy hot comb.

[*Beat.*]
Come on, girl. Slam it?

[SHADOW *raises her hand for a high-five.*]

BROWN: Hmpf!

BABY: Go on and slap the girl hand so I can go!

BROWN: Why you gotta wait for that?

BABY: Cause I can't stand to see my two girls fightin' like cats havin' spats-

BROWN: I don't know 'bout all that!

SHADOW: You gon' leave me hangin'? You GON' leave me hangin'!! I won't talk 'bout Raymond no more-

BROWN: Promise?

SHADOW: Cross my heart
Hope to die-

BABY: And gon' stick a needle up in MY eye!

BROWN: Alright. I forgive you. This time-

[*Finishing high-five slam.*]
[*In teasing song*]: I got somethin' you don't got!
I'm gon' keep it till I drop!
I'm gon' keep it till I choke!
Baby don't know how to smoke!

[BROWN *laughs ridiculously.*]

BABY: Yeah. Whatever, Brown. See ya'll later.

[SHADOW *and* BROWN *exit.* BABY *comes upon* FIVE-OHH *and* LEE *pitching quarters.*]

FIVE-OHH: Now watch. This the way you do it.

LEE: I'm watchin' ol'man.

FIVE-OHH: You put the quarter in between yuh fo'finguh, and yuh crow thumb, right?

LEE: My daddy showed me this once. I got it.

FIVE-OHH: You say a prayer to the Blessed God in heaven Jesus Christ the lord-

LEE: To who-?

FIVE-OHH: And then, yuhs pitch it up to the skies. Like this.

[FIVE-OHH *goes thru an involved arm movement, pitches, lands right on the line.*]

FIVE-OHH: SHUCKY DUCKY, now!

LEE: Alright.

FIVE-OHH: Now you go on' and try it Lee.

LEE: I'm finna show you, Old man. I can pitch just like that.

FIVE-OHH: I'm watchin', Lee. Now yuh gotta pose it just like I did-

LEE: Just like this?

FIVE-OHH: Naw. Like this. You gotta shoot yuh arm straight up like it's a Tennessee peacock feather-

LEE: Alright. Alright. Watch-!

[LEE *pitches the quarter. It smacks* BABY'S *feet.* WOMACLOWN *echoes* BABY'S *words with movement through out this encounter.*]

BABY: Hey boy! You betta watch that quarter fo' I knock you out!

LEE: Look girl! I ain't even see yo' ol' funky feet comin'!

BABY: I know. Cause if you'da seen my feet comin' you'd a been hidin' cause you'd knowed I'd a stomped yo' face up in that concrete cement!

FIVE-OHH: Bsby! Ain't no need to be talkin' to the boy like he had it in his mind before he knowed it to hit you wit that coin.

BABY: He did! He did it on purpose, Five-Ohh!

LEE: I ain't even knowed you was comin'. And how you know Five-Ohh?

BABY: Everybody know Five-Ohh bag at A&P unless they stupid like you! Duhh! How you know Five-Ohh when he my uncle?

LEE: Cause I be bringin' home people groceries from A&P. And I ain't stupid! Just cause the only reason you go there is to be stuffin' yo' ol' ugly cross eyed-spam-livered greasy haired crustified Aunt Esther face!

FIVE-OHH: Baby! Lee! Ya'll two kids know you need not to be hollerin' out here in the street like yuh mamma's raised you on Sugar Smacks.

BABY: Mamma ain't raise me on no Sugar Smacks, Five-Ohh, but I know when some little nappy headed boy tryin' to hit me.

LEE: Don't you be callin' me no nappy headed boy, girl. You need to take yo'self on.

FIVE-OHH: Baby, I saw yuh mamma this evenin' in the sto' and she said she left yuh some food so you betta get home and ate it befo' it go cold. And Lee, I think Mr. Jackson on Rhodes 116 waitin' on you to bring him the fresh perch up in that bag. Ya'll get which way my air is shiftin'?

BABY: Yeah, Five-Ohh.

LEE: Cain't pitch no mo' quarters no how.

FIVE-OHH: Especially seein' in how it's dark and all. Now Lee, you goin' the same general die-rection as Baby, I think you betta take huh on up to huh do'.

LEE: Aw, man! I don't wanna be wit this ol' funky girl!

BABY: Don't think I want to even be next to you either. Fool!

LEE: Ugly!

BABY: Stank butt!

LEE: PUS-!

FIVE-OHH: Lee! You gon' walk huh home or yuh ain't gon' be carryin' no mo' groceries fuh the A&P! And Baby! You betta let this boy walk you home fo' I tell yo' mamma you been up in the street talkin' like you ain't never knowed huh name!

BABY: I'm gon'.

FIVE-OHH: Now let me introduce yuh proper. Baby Flemings, this Lee. Lee Walker, this Baby.

LEE: What kinda name is Baby?

BABY: It's my name!

FIVE-OHH: Ya'll go on now. Go on. I'm gon' home to feed Nicholas. Damn cat start hissin' at me I don't feed him before ten in the o'clock.

[FIVE-OHH *exits*. BABY *and* LEE *walk in silence*.]

BABY: Hmm.

LEE: What?

BABY: Nothin'. I ain't say nothin'.

LEE: You did. You said "hmm."

BABY: So?

LEE: So what that mean?

BABY: It don't mean nothin'.

LEE: Girls always be sayin' that.

BABY: That ain't true. And you don't know no girls anyway.

LEE: I do.

BABY: You don't.

LEE: Do!

BABY: Don't!

LEE: Do too!

BABY: Do not!

LEE: Wanna bet?

BABY: Yeah!

LEE: Stick out yo' hand!

BABY: I bet five packs o'rainbow now and laters and ten chico sticks.

LEE: Awright.

[LEE *and* BABY *do elaborate betting handshake.*]

BABY: Awright. I bet you cain't name ten girls in the seventh grade.

LEE: I can. I could name twenty!

BABY: O.k. I'm waitin'.

LEE: I know Lucinda. She that girl wit the long braids-

BABY: Is they real braids or fake braids?

LEE: I don't know! That's for girls! I know Katrina.

BABY: If you know Katrina then who she go wit last year?

LEE: She went wit yo' Mamma!

BABY: Yeah, right. Uhh huh. Go on.

LEE: I know Belinda. Smiley-

BABY: Smiley a boy.

LEE: Laqueisha. Francesca-

BABY: Francesca in the sixth grade-

LEE: I thought you was in the sixth grade the way you talk-

BABY: I'm in the eighth grade! I'm 'bout to graduate.

LEE: Why you know all these li' seventh grade girls if you such a big eighth grader like me-?

BABY: Like you? I ain't neva seen you there before!

LEE: That's cause I'm in the "gifted" class-

BABY: Hmpf! Who else you know?

LEE: I know Carmelita, LeVal, and Tyronda-

BABY: You don't know Tyronda!

LEE: I do!
BABY: You don't. Cause she fell off the top o' that buildin' right there last week! And I saw the whole thing!

LEE: You did not. You lyin-!

BABY: I ain't!

LEE: You is!

BABY: Ain't!

LEE: Is!

BABY: Nope!

LEE: Girl!

BABY: Awright! You don't believe me! I'm gon' tell you what I saw-!

[WOMACLOWN *leads the company members enter in a whip like the ice skating game. The whip cracks and each member lands in their own little spaces.* BROWN *and* SHADOW *enter, becoming* BABY'S *interpretation of people who witnessed the event.*]

BABY: My mama sent me out to the-

WOMACLOWN: Store-

BABY: To buy her some-

WOMACLOWN: Milk.

BABY: So I was walkin' along Rhodes avenue-

SHADOW: Just lookin' up at the Ida B. Wells housing projects-

BROWN: Like I didn't even notice the-

WOMACLOWN: "Eat Pussy" red and black graffiti on the-

BABY: World.

[*Beat.*]

SHADOW: Probably just another gang sign-

BROWN: Probably just another hooker's lipstick smear-

GIRL: When her pimp decided she was gonna lay some woman-

SHADOW: Cause he gonna get more money if his womens do women.

WOMACLOWN: All of the sudden some kids was racin' down the street-

BROWN: Shoutin' and cussin' and-

BABY: Sayin' all the things the elders in the church told us only whino's say-

WOMACLOWN: When all the sudden I heard car sirens and ambulances gettin' slowed down by the potholes in the street-

BABY: So I rushed over to where all the other kids were-

SHADOW: To see what was the matter-

WOMACLOWN: And there I saw it-

COMPANY: And there I saw it-

WOMACLOWN: Little girls's brains is crashed onto the concrete floor! Who is she? I don't know who she is! All I see is her long pigtail with the goody flower barrette hangin' offa her skinny braids. Her brains is oozin' into the gutter. Her yellow dress and red socks is all crashed up in her ribs and in her throat and in her --FACE!

BABY: I see her! Tyronda! She beat SHADOW in the spelling bee last year. She spelled the word "nourish" and got to go to district. I was so jealous of her 'cause she beat SHADOW, cause she knew how to spell and SHADOW didn't. All the kids loved her and SHADOW felt stupid.

WOMACLOWN: What happened to her? Who did this to her?!

BABY: Suicide-

LEE: What you say-

BABY: Suicide-

LEE: How you know?

BABY: Suicide. Little girl is home from school. Her momma is gone. Little girl turns on the T.V. and watches cartoons and videos and ice cream commercials-

WOMACLOWN: Little girl hears a knockin' at the door-

[COMPANY *knocks*.]

BROWN: It's the Tuwell brothers lookin' for her brother-

WOMACLOWN: They say he owes them some money-

BABY: They say they wanna see how she can spell "dookey."

WOMACLOWN: But-

BABY: What they really want is her-

WOMACLOWN: So they comin' after her-

SHADOW: With they stuff-

WOMACLOWN: Uncovered and hard-

BROWN: And they wanna make her bleed-

[WOMACLOWN *becomes* TYRONDA. BABY *reacts questioningly to* TYRONDA *being played by* WOMACLOWN. *The ensemble of men chase her as* BABY *recalls the event.*]

BABY: And she doesn't want her mama to find out. She breaks from the boys. They chase her to the elevator shaft. It smells of-

SHADOW: Piss.

BABY: She stops. The boys holler at her, "Teach us how to spell-

BROWN/SHADOW: "Bitch!"

BABY: She screams! She runs to the dank stairwell which leads to the roof. She stops. The boys split up and come at her. She runs up the stairs, pushes the hatch, and is on the roof. She hears them, screamin' and cussin'. One of them got a knife and say he gonna-

SHADOW: Snatch up that little snatch-

BROWN: And eat it for dinner!

BABY: She rushes. They chase. She reaches the edge. She say a prayer. She jumps... suicide-

LEE: Why?

GIRL: Suicide-

LEE: I don't under-

BABY: Suicide! The Tuwell brothers stopped chasin' her when she got to the roof. They was just playin' a joke on her brother. She ran...cause she was lookin' for a way out. [COMPANY *freezes, then abscond off the stage. Beat.*]

LEE: That what happened to Tyronda?

BABY: Cross my heart. Hope to die. Stick a needle up in my eye.

LEE: I ain't know it went down like that.

BABY: Yup.

[*Beat.*]

LEE: Shoot! I lost the bet.

BABY: Umhm. You owe me five packs ' rainbow now and laters. And ten chico sticks.

LEE: When you wan'em?

BABY: When you gon' give'm to me?

LEE: I'll bring em. Next time.

BABY: What you mean "next time?"

LEE: This yo' house ain't it? This Rhodes avenue. It say Flemings on the bell.

BABY: Oh. We here so soon.

LEE: That's cuz you was talkin' so much ol' bean head girl.

[LEE *pops her gently in the head.*]

BABY: Quit. I ain't no bean head girl just cause you lost the bet-

LEE: I ain't lose yet. I still could name twenty girls in the seventh grade-

BABY: But you cain't cause I at home, so that mean I won the bet!

LEE: Even though you funky, I still keep my word. I'll bring you them chico sticks. But I got cobs!

BABY: Awright, Lee. Awright.

[LEE *moves toward* BABY, *then backs away.* LEE *and* BABY *freeze.* LEE *exits.* BABY *looks for her mama.*]
BABY: MMMM-mmmma-mmaaa-MAMA! Mama?! Mama?! Is you here?

[BABY *searches for Mama.* WOMACLOWN *mirrors. Silence.*]

Mama!

[*Silence.*]

WOMACLOWN: Mama I'm scared-

BABY: Please tell me is you here.

[WOMACLOWN *finds a note and puts it in plain view for* BABY *to find.*]

What's this? [*Pause.*] Oh. BABY. Fix your own dinner. I left a mac and cheese with some fish sticks in the fridge. There's milk too if you thirsty. Watch t.v. I think something good on channel 2. I gotta work late. Your mama. P.S. Bathe yourself. And say your prayers the right way." All right Mama! Let me see what up on the tube.

[BABY *turns on an air T.V.* SHADOW *and* BROWN *enter, but they are not their characters, they are in masks acting out what* BABY *is watching on T.V.* WOMACLOWN *sits beside* BABY, *watching and reacting as* BABY *does.*]

SHADOW: Let's get dangerous! We must save the fair-maiden!

BROWN: Lettttttt's GO and shit!

SHADOW: Get up! Get up! We must save this poor child from the Back Alley Beast!

BROWN: O.k. O.k., SHIT-!

WOMACLOWN: Shi-?

SHADOW: Get up! We've got to get dangerous! See poor Genevieve, behind those bars in the clutches of society's evils?! She'll turn to drugs and prostitution! She'll become a "baby having babies" if we don't do something to stop the Back Alley Beast! Let's go save her!

BABY: Me?

[WOMACLOWN *perks up. The whole scene* WOMACLOWN *tries to protect* BABY *from the caped crusaders.*]

SHADOW: Yes, my darling! I hear you, we are coming to save you!

WOMACLOWN: I ain't none-

BABY: O' yo darlin' nobody!

WOMACLOWN: I ain't shootin' up-

BABY: And I ain't no ho!

BROWN: Yeah Mr. Great Caped Crusadered Suh! I see her, struggling and shit, trying to break free from the clutches of FUCKIN' evil!

WOMACLOWN: Fucki-?

BROWN: LETTTTT'S GO---AW, FUCK ME UP!

SHADOW: Stop tripping! Get up! [*to* BABY] My darling Genevieve! We're coming! We're coming-!

[BROWN *and* SHADOW *move toward* BABY *as cartoon characters*.]

WOMACLOWN: I don't need yo' help!

BABY: Mamma!

SHADOW: Genevieve we hear you screaming for our help! You're a victim of the Back Alley Beast! We'll save you and give you a home out of the slums!

WOMACLOWN: I told you. I ain't none-

BABY: O' yo' gin and weave-

WOMACLOWN: Or-

BABY: Jim in tweed-

WOMACLOWN: Or-

BABY: Nothin'!

WOMACLOWN: Do I look like-

BABY: A cartoon character-

WOMACLOWN: To you?!

SHADOW: Listen to us, Genevieve! We know who you are better than you know yourself!

WOMACLOWN: You ain't none-

BABY: O'my mama!

SHADOW: We know who you are.

BROWN: She's resistin' oh caped one!

[BROWN *trips again*.]

AW FUCK ME UP!

WOMACLOWN: Fuck me-?

BROWN: Damn! Don't she know we gotta save her from the beast and shit? We gotta so she don't end up on welfare like all the rest o' them do. The Back Alley Beast don't give a good GODDAMN-!

WOMACLOWN/BABY: What?

BROWN: You heard me! I said the Back Alley Beast don't give a good GODDAMN-!

SHADOW/BROWN: daMN-dAMN-DAMN-!

WOMACLOWN: Damn-?!

BABY: daMN. dAMN. DAMN!

[BROWN *and* SHADOW *freeze. Exit.* WOMACLOWN *covers her ears.* WOMACLOWN *and* BABY *overlap words and thoughts.*]

WOMACLOWN: UT OH! Oh God! I didn't-I didn't. Ohh! I did-I did! I said it! I said a curse word! OH NO! Mama gonna tear up my-

BABY: Ass-!

WOMACLOWN: OHH! I said another one! Ohh no! Mama gonna take out that green belt and -

BABY: FUCK ME UP-!

WOMACLOWN: Oh God? Are you listen' God? You're there, I know you are. If I sing it'll help-Miss Mary Mack Mack Mack

BABY: All dressed in black black black-

WOMACLOWN: With silver buttons buttons buttons-

BABY: All down her back back back. Aw, I don't know anymore o' that song.

[WOMACLOWN/BABY *continue humming.*]

WOMACLOWN: I know! Mama said say my prayers. [*Rapping*]: Now I lay me-

BABY [*rapping*]: Down to sleep.

WOMACLOWN: I pray the lord-

BABY: My soul to keep.

WOMACLOWN: If I should die-

BABY: Before I wake.

WOMACLOWN: I pray the lord-

BABY: My rump do shake!

[BABY *and* WOMACLOWN *shake rump.*]

WOMACLOWN: There. God, please don't let mama find out I swore. Please don't let her know I was sittin' here swearin'. All the sudden I'm saying all these-

BABY: FUCKIN'-!

WOMACLOWN: OOHHH!! OOHH! OOOOHHHHHH-! Unn.

[WOMACLOWN *looks at back of* BABY'S *dress and notices a red spot.*]

BABY: Ohh. Ohh. Ohhh. What's this?

WOMACLOWN: UNN!

BABY: It wet. It smell too. Like cornstarch. OHH!

WOMACLOWN: Unn! It's red.
BABY: Look like some spaghetti sauce.

[BABY *and* WOMACLOWN *sniff.*]

WOMACLOWN: But it smell like cornstarch.

[*Pause.*]

BABY: It blood! Oh God! Are you still listenin'?

WOMACLOWN: Ohh!

BABY: I gotta call the hospital!

WOMACLOWN: I prob'ly got-

BABY: Cancer o' the liver!

WOMACLOWN: No, I saw this on Oprah. I got-

BABY: Liposuction of the heart!

WOMACLOWN: I know--I got-

BABY: Typhoid Mary sclerosis!

[*Beat.*]

BABY: God, I'm gonna die!

WOMACLOWN: I'm gonna bleed to death from-

BABY: The symphonic plague!

WOMACLOWN: I cain't die yet, lord. I ain't even kissed a boy yet-

BABY: Well...I kissed my arm, but that don't count-

WOMACLOWN: I ain't even got to high school yet-

BABY: I won't smoke no more pencil reefer-

WOMACLOWN: And I won't swear-

BABY: And I won't pray my rump do shake. "To TAKE lord, I'll pray the lord my soul to TAKE!"
[*Pause.*]

WOMACLOWN: Maybe-

BABY: If I wash it'll go away.

BABY/WOMACLOWN: God?

WOMACLOWN: Promise me it'll go away.

BABY: Oh, Rub-a-dub dolly? Get ready cause we finna take a bath!

WOMACLOWN: I'll make it go away.

WOMACLOWN/BABY: Right, Lord?

[*We hear a drumbeat. BABY picks up her dolly and begins to dance and sway. Her dance builds to an explosion of sexual freedom. WOMACLOWN mirrors, and half empties the purple glass of milk on baby's vibrating body. Silence. A doorbell buzzes… violently.*]

WOMACLOWN: I'm comin' Mama!

BABY: I'm almost there!

[*A door opens.*]

MR. CONN: I'm from Orkin. Is this the Fleming residence.

WOMACLOWN: Um-

BABY: Yeah. Yes. It is.

MR. CONN: Is your mama here?

BABY: Um...no-

WOMACLOWN: Yes! She here.

MR. CONN: Good. Then I'll just come right in.

BABY: It's eight o'clock. Why come you here so late?

MR. CONN: We work 'til ten so that we can catch people when they're at home.

[*An awkward pause.*]

MR. CONN (Cont-): That's a cute bathrobe you got there little one.

WOMACLOWN: I think you best get to 'terminatin'-

BABY: I'll get my mama.

MR. CONN: Yes. You do that.

BABY: Mamma! Mamma! [*Pause.*] She comin'.

WOMACLOWN: Youse best get to 'terminatin'.

MR. CONN: You're right, you're absolutely right.

BABY: What you doin'?

MR. CONN: Spraying for pests, little one. Hey. What's this glass doing here? Didn't your mama ever tell you not to leave out dirty dishes?

BABY: That ain't dirty. It ain't even empty!

MR. CONN: Whoa! You've got a sharp tongue there little one. Didn't your mama ever tell you not to disrespect adults?

BABY: My mama-

MR. CONN: She should've told you not to let strange men in the house either.

BABY: Only when she here!

MR. CONN: Well, little person. Where is your mama? [*Pause.*] Huh? [*Pause.*] Where is she then?
[*Silence.*] I really like that pink bathrobe you're wearing.

[WOMACLOWN *tightens* BABY'S *robe.*]

MR. CONN (Cont-): What do you say?

WOMACLOWN [mumbling]: Thank you.

MR. CONN: I can't hear you little one.

BABY: I said THANK YOU!

MR. CONN: Easy, baby!

BABY: How you know my name?

MR. CONN: Your name?

BABY: My name-

MR. CONN: Is Baby. That's a pretty name for a pretty little girl. [*Beat.*] I know your mama isn't here.

BABY: She is too!

MR. CONN: Baby, I know your mama is not here.

BABY: How you know?

MR. CONN: Because little one, I saw her leave for work. I watched you play double-dutch. I saw you come home. I heard you screaming for her. I heard you swearing-

BABY: You didn't!

MR. CONN: I did. I heard you swearing, and I have a right mind to tell your mama on you.

BABY: Mama! Mama!

WOMACLOWN: Are you comin' mama?

[WOMACLOWN *checks house for Mama.*]

BABY: You don't know my mama!

MR. CONN: That's where you're wrong little one. I know your mama. I watch her everyday. [*A pause.*] I watch you, too. I liked that little dance you did in the bathtub with your rub-a-dub dolly.

WOMACLOWN: Liar!

BABY: You didn't see me do nothin'!

MR. CONN: Oh I did. It was very...titillating...I know all about your little dance, Baby. And I'm going to tell your mama-

BABY: I didn't do nothin'!

MR. CONN: Where is the milk that was in this glass?

BABY: I spilt it.

MR. CONN: Looks like you "spilt" it all over your mama's rug....I don't think you want your mama to know that you "spilt" this milk do you?

[WOMACLOWN *misses trying to grab and hold* BABY. MR. CONN *touches* BABY'S *ear.*]

MR. CONN (Cont-): Do you?

[*He picks up the glass, grabs* BABY *around the waist, pours the remaining milk down her forehead and watches it run. He licks the milk as it trickles down her face.* WOMACLOWN *quivers.*]

MR. CONN: I like your Minnie Mouse bathrobe, little one. [*Beat.*] And I love milk.

[*Blackout.*]

WOMACLOWN [*in blackout*]:

I am a box.
Inside me is my soul.
Look.
Inside me.

I am a box.
Inside me is my soul.
Look.

Inside me.

[*Lights fade up slowly; four weeks later*]

WOMACLOWN (Cont-):

I am here
Waiting for the next class to begin
Waiting to learn to win
What am I tasting now?
Where are the rivers
that run in
soul
in spirit
in wholes
I miss giggling
and tripping
and patty caking
with the baker's man
But I am here
Waiting for the next class to begin
Waiting to learn to win
Waiting to taste...
I am a box
Inside me is my soul.
Look.
Inside me.

[*A buzzer sounds. Lights up.*]

FIVE-OHH: Baby! Baby! Open up this do' I lef' muh keys at the job.

WOMACLOWN: What you say?

FIVE-OHH: I say open up this do'.

WOMACLOWN: The do'-

FIVE-OHH: Girl. You don't soun' right. Open up this do'. I got a bag o' groceries yuh mama lef' at the sto'.

BABY: I'm comin'. I'm comin.'

[FIVE-OHH *enters.*]

FIVE-OHH: Baby. Tammy so funny. She lef' this bag right up unda the counter. I guess maybe Lee was out runnin' some bags somewhere else when she lef' the sto'. You cold, baby?

BABY: Yeah. It drafty-

FIVE-OHH: Then shut the do'.

BABY: O.k.-

FIVE-OHH: Let me empty out this bag befo' I go so I can return this plastic. Let's see. Tammy 'bought 'lot today. She say somethin' 'bout makin' some succotash and cobbler some time. Look. Cling peaches-

BABY: Um hm.

FIVE-OHH: Cottage fries-

BABY: Yeah.

FIVE-OHH: OOH this fo' yo' gradu-ation ! Cain't show you that yet!

BABY: Hm.

FIVE-OHH: Baby, you tremblin' like a leaf in the summertime when it knowed that winter comin' sooner than death. Go get a sweater.

[WOMACLOWN *moves to* BABY, *puts her arms around her*.]

BABY: Ooooooo-!

FIVE-OHH: Girl what wrong? What wrong wit chu? My cat befo' Nicholas died a some strange kind of cancer, and that's what he sound like-

WOMACLOWN: AAAAGGHHHH!

FIVE-OHH: BABY! You sound'in like the devil that comed up into muh dreams just befo' that cat died! He had a bunch o' evil spirits runnin' all throughout up in him!

BABY: AAAAAGGGGHHH!

FIVE-OHH: Awright, girl. Let me look at yuh-

BABY: AAAAGGGGHHH!

FIVE-OHH: Yuh betta tell me what happen, girl!

WOMACLOWN: AAAAAGGEEGHHHE!

FIVE-OHH: Stop shakin', baby! Come here to uncle.

[BABY *leaves* WOMACLOWN, *comes to* FIVE-OHH.]

WOMACLOWN: I am-

FIVE-OHH: This devil? Comed up in muh dream. And he tried to put his hands 'round muh neck. And I looked him right up in his red eye balls, and I say, "SCAT!" and the devil ran out thru the stairs at Mamma's house wit his tail behin' 'im.

BABY: I-

FIVE-OHH: Baby, there's good spirits too. But to let 'em in you gotta let the devil out. [*Beat.*] Why you shakin' BABY. Why you shakin'. OOHHH. It's alright. [*Beat.*] Who did this to you, Baby? Yuh been sick fo' weeks. I been comin' up over here every which a day tryin' ta do what my sistuh needs her brother to do. And you just sit here and shake and shake a shake. Who did this to you, Baby?

BABY: I got the flu-

FIVE-OHH: You know you cain't fool me. I'ma ol' man. Been fightin' devils a whole lot of years longer than you knowed what breathin' devils was, and you cain't keep lyin' to me, girl.

WOMACLOWN: I am a box.

FIVE-OHH: What that mean, I am a box?

WOMACLOWN: You can hear me?

FIVE-OHH: Yes, I can hear you, Baby. What is it?

WOMACLOWN: Inside me is my soul.

FIVE-OHH: Huh?

WOMACLOWN: Look. Inside me.

FIVE-OHH: Girl I'm lookin' but I don't see.

WOMACLOWN: I am a box.

FIVE-OHH: It was that Lee boy. Tryin' tuh kiss yuh and went on an' gave yuh the chicken poxies-

WOMACLOWN: Inside me is my soul.

FIVE-OHH: Soul...Inside?

WOMACLOWN: Look. Look inside me.

BABY: Look. Look inside me!

[FIVE-OHH *looks up and locks* WOMACLOWN'S *eyes. He's looking into* BABY'S *soul, but he doesn't actually see* WOMACLOWN.]

FIVE-OHH: Lawd oh Lawd or Blessed Father Jesus Christ our Lord in Heaven!

[WOMACLOWN'S *eyes tell* FIVE-OHH *that* BABY *is pregnant.*]

FIVE-OHH: Baby? Yuh's gon' have a...

WOMACLOWN: Soul.

FIVE-OHH: I been knowin' spirits a whole lot o' years, and there be another spirit up in this room beside me and mine and yuh and yourns. An' right now yo' spirit tellin' me yuh's gon' have a-

WOMACLOWN: Soul.

[*Beat.*]

FIVE-OHH: I'm gon' help you, Baby. Don't be scared. I'm gon' help you. It's gon' be alright. Awright? Come to Uncle.

[BABY *goes to* FIVE-OHH. *He embraces her.*]

It won't hurt. It ain't hurt fo' yo' Mamma. I'll be right back as fast as you can shake yuh leg three times and say Tennessee peacock backwards.

[FIVE-OHH *exits.* WOMACLOWN *races frantically around the room.*]

WOMACLOWN [*to* BABY]:
I am left alone
to be the little girl
who is left to die on the sidewalk
on Rhodes Avenue.
You must hold on to me.
You must.
You can't go on without me in you-

[FIVE-OHH *reenters dressed in a white sheet which acts as African ritualisitic garb.* With him, he brings beads, a dead chicken, gourds, an A&P apron with smeared blood, latex gloves & a hanger.]
FIVE-OHH: Baby, I just be needin' yo to relax. Let me put down dis apron. And we be ready. It won't hurt.

BABY: What you gon' do Uncle?

FIVE-OHH: Yuh say yuh have the flu. I'ma gon' get rid' o it fo' yuh.

BABY: What I gotta do uncle?

FIVE-OHH: Just relax. I'm gon' lay this here apron up under yuh.

[FIVE-OHH *lays* BABY'S *legs up on the bed.* WOMACLOWN *motions between them.* BABY *begins a slow humming.* BABY *begins struggling.*]

FIVE-OHH: Blood of fowl! Beads of hands! Gourds o' earth! Part the way for virgin birth!

 [BABY *and* WOMACLOWN *shiver.*]

The devil comed up in her and I got to make 'em leave!

The devil comed up in her and I got to scoot his sleeve!

[FIVE-OHH *chants an ancient African Purification Rhythm.*]

WOMACLOWN:
Hand come
Fitting fingers
Tightly-

FIVE-OHH [*still in rhythm*]: In latex gloves-

WOMACLOWN:
I hear drills,
in stills,
in stillness.
My illness.
She grows till this-

[BABY *whimpers.*]

WOMACLOWN:
Hands
pry at me,
Me.
She hides.
I feel my baby hide.
Deep inside the blue walls,
milk sac.
Inside my soul.
but
hands come.

FIVE-OHH [*inserting hanger between* BABY's *legs.*]

Metal rods!

BABY:
Suction!
Suction!

WOMACLOWN:
She grows till this-
two minutes
one second-

FIVE-OHH: Right now!

[FIVE-OHH *freezes. Blackout.*]

[*Enter* SHADOW *and* BROWN.]

BROWN [*hittin' SHADOW with rope*]: First!

SHADOW: Second.

BROWN: Alright. This how we gon' do it. I'm gon' get on the end like this, and then jump in from my side. You gon' turn that end.

SHADOW: I don't wanna play without Baby.

BROWN: Why not?

SHADOW: You cain't play double-dutch with only two people, Brown. Use yo' brains.

BROWN: So we could play single.

SHADOW: I don't wanna play no single. Single too easy.

BROWN: We ain't played double-dutch in four weeks. Tomorrow graduation. You know we cain't be playin' no double-dutch when we get to high school!

SHADOW: Why not?

BROWN: You s'posed to be the smart one! Raymond say the big girls ain't gon' wanna play, and they gon' laugh at us.

SHADOW: How he know?

BROWN: He only a senior-

SHADOW: Only thing he know 'bout is shavins.

BROWN: He don't. He gon' have a high school diploma soon.

SHADOW: He gon' have him a G.E.D. soon.

BROWN: Why you always be talkin' bad 'bout him?

SHADOW: Cause he usin' you.

BROWN: He ain't.

SHADOW: He is. He just want you to be his dope runner. That's all. We could've played rope last week. And where was you? Out runnin' up and down Rhodes droppin' off bags fo' him. Any fool with half a brain not up on shavins could tell you he usin' you.

BROWN: If you don't wanna play rope, just say so. I came lookin' fo' you to play rope last week, and yo' fat butt was wit yo' Mama tryin' to get some gov'ment cheese. So don't be sayin' that he usin' me.

SHADOW: He is!
BROWN: He ain't!

SHADOW: He is!

BROWN: He ain't! So shet up and grab that end!

[BROWN *slaps* SHADOW. *Beat.*]

SHADOW: Why don't you quit hittin' me and look at the truth that starin' you straight up in yo'face?

BROWN: Don't let me have to talk 'bout yo' daddy!

SHADOW: Don't even-!

BROWN: Naw, I'ma do it! You still gon' talk 'bout Raymond?!

SHADOW: No!

BROWN: What?!

SHADOW: No! I said No!

BROWN [*in teasing song*]:
Shadow daddy ran away!
Left her momma while she on the way
Shadow born and set up camp
Daddy left her gov'ment stamps!

SHADOW: Why you always tryin' to hurt somebody? My mama tol' me I shouldn't be friends wit you, but I say to her, "Naw, Mama. Brown cool. Naw, Mama. It o.k. She don't really smoke dope. Naw, Mama. I know sometimes Brown be hittin' people. But she be o.k. But you know what? My Mama was right all up in around behind and crossways about you!

[*Beat.*]

BROWN: Grab the end! Only thing you care 'bout is BABY! You in love wit that girl or somethin'?

[*Beat.*]

SHADOW: Shut up! I don't go that way and you know it.

BROWN: Not the way you be lookin' at her I don't know it.

SHADOW: She ain't been to school since the last time we played!

BROWN: So!

SHADOW: So maybe somethin' wrong wit her. And if you wasn't up on them shavin's all the time, you'd think maybe somethin' was wrong wit her too.

BROWN: Ain't nothin' wrong. She probly mad cause I got betta at jumpin'. I been practicin' all on my own. She know I could beat her. That's why she ain't been to school.

SHADOW: She ain't stupid! She ain't gon' stop gettin' smart in school 'cause of you!

BROWN: Just grab the end! Let's play!

SHADOW: You dumb, Brown.

[SHADOW *starts turning rope.*]

BROWN: And you gay! But I see you pickin' up that end.

[BABY *enters.*]

BROWN: See? You all worried and here come ol'girl now. Hey Baby! We missed you so much! You been sick?

[BROWN *grabs* BABY, *pushes* SHADOW *away from* BABY.]

SHADOW: Jesus.

BABY: Naw. I ain't been sick. My mamma was sick and I had to stay home wit her.

SHADOW: Why couldn't Five-Ohh stay wit her?

BABY: He workin' all day.

SHADOW: She alright?

BABY: Yeah. Just the flu or somethin'.

[*Beat.*]

BROWN: Well now that you back, let's play. You wanna go first Baby?

BABY: Um, no.

BROWN: Aw, girl! You go first and then I'll go second.

BABY: I don't really wanna play.

BROWN: Come on, girl. Play. Play!

SHADOW [*steps on rope*]: My rope. One turn each. No overs.

[*Beat.*]

BABY: O.k. Medium.

[*Enter Orkin man with sprayer. He eyes* BABY. BROWN *notices.*]

BROWN: What he want again!?

BABY: Who-?

SHADOW: Shut up, Brown! Just sing! "My mama."

BROWN [*singing*]:
My Mamma sent me to the store
She told me not to stay out late
I fell in love wit the grocery boy
Who took my heart away way way!
Who's the mamma?

BABY: Baby.

BROWN: How's the baby?

BABY: Just fine.

BROWN: What you gon' feed it?

BABY: Baby food.

BROWN: What you gon' feed it wit?

BABY: A spoon.

BROWN: Who's the father-? [*Pause.*] Who's the father-?   [*Pause.*] BABY?! Who's the father!

WOMACLOWN: AAAAAAAGGHHHHHHH!

[*Beat.*]

BABY [*covering ears*]: I hear a little girl-!

BROWN: What you mean, girl?! It's time fo' you to get on the end so I could beat you!

SHADOW: Shut up, Brown!

WOMACLOWN:

Is deaf.
Is dead.
Like lead-
Pickin'
up the pieces
of flesh
intermeshed
in
concrete soil-
Same little girl
singin'
rain rain go away.
Please let me drink from my mama
today
Same little girl cryin'-

BROWN: It's my turn!

SHADOW: SHHHH! Listen!

WOMACLOWN:

Mama, mama I'm scared.
Please tell me is you here?
[*Beat.*]
I'm dyin'!
I'm dead!
Decapitate my head!
I exist in raincloud.
Rain hide.
rain suicide.
Chucklin' down-

BABY: Laughin' at me!

[BABY *collapses. She sees* WOMACLOWN.]

BABY: Who that?

BROWN: Girl? What I tell you? She don't know her behin' from her head. Seein' folk that ain't even there!

SHADOW: I'm tired o' you, Brown! Baby, what are you seein'?

BABY [*to* WOMACLOWN]: Who is you?! Where are you going? Why are you leaving me? Wait. Come back. Come back! I need you!

[*Blackout.*]

[SHADOW, BROWN, BABY *in a circular graduation march*; *a saxophone plays* "*Pomp & Circumstance.*"]

WOMACLOWN: Love me. Me in you. Love me. We are two...

SHADOW: And so parent, teachers, students at George Washington, no not Carver, School. As we step out into this WORLD, I hope we each can-

WOMACLOWN: Love me....

BROWN: Learn from the experiences we had within these walls-

WOMACLOWN: Me in you....

BABY: Including the teacher's we've hated-

WOMACLOWN: Love me....

SHADOW: The loves we had or lost-

WOMACLOWN: We are two...

BROWN: Raymond.

WOMACLOWN: Love me...

SHADOW: Daddy.

WOMACLOWN: Me in you...

BABY: Him.

WOMACLOWN: Love me...

BROWN: He said the stuff would make me feel good-

WOMACLOWN: We are two...

SHADOW: He said he'd take care of me-

WOMACLOWN: Love me!

BABY: He told me he wouldn't tell my mama I swore-

WOMACLOWN: Me in you!

BROWN: Then I tried it-

WOMACLOWN: Love me!

SHADOW: Then he left us with only a book a food stamps.

WOMACLOWN: We are two!

BABY: The he spilt milk down my-

WOMACLOWN: Love me.

SHADOW: Bastard!

BABY: Liar!

BROWN [*adoringly*]: Huuuh!

[SHADOW *and* BABY *stare at* BROWN *in disbelief.* WOMACLOWN *motions toward the circle.*]

WOMACLOWN: Love me. Me in you. Love me. We are two.

SHADOW: And the knowledge we've gained.

BROWN: I'm only fourteen. I feel older, though.

SHADOW: Daddy's just can't be trusted.

BABY: I got a soul. Somewhere in these hands. I think-

SHADOW: Let us look upon this passing from birth-

BROWN: To life-

BABY: And on through school after high school after college school-

SHADOW: Not as the beginning of life-

BROWN: Where I can be.

SHADOW: Where I can be.

BABY: Where I can be.

SHADOW: Let us look upon this passing- Not as the beginning of life-

BABY: But as the end-

SHADOW/BABY/BROWN: Of innocence.

WOMACLOWN: Love me.

[*Procession leads to* WOMACLOWN, *who delivers them diplomas made of burned paper sheets which crumble as they receive them.* BABY, SHADOW, BROWN *freeze in pose as lights fade to black.*]

END OF ACT 1

ACT 2

WOMACLOWN: To graduate-

MR. CONN: Yes-

WOMACLOWN:
That was a prize.
To walk the aisle to pomp and circumstance.
To feel the eyes-

MR. CONN: Watching-

WOMACLOWN:
As I walk
As I talk
As I receive the deed
And now I am here.

MR. CONN: Waiting for class to begin.

WOMACLOWN: Waiting to learn to win.

MR.CONN: To taste...

WOMACLOWN: Love.

MR. CONN: To know...

WOMACLOWN: ME!

WOMACLOWN/MR.CONN:
That is what I
need
from she.

[*Enter* BROWN, BABY, SHADOW. WOMACLOWN & MR. CONN *watch.*
The girls are now high school seniors.]

BROWN [*singing*]: I said a boom chicka boom!

BABY/SHADOW: I said a boom chicka boom!

BROWN: I said a boom chicka boom!

BABY/SHADOW: I said a boom chicka boom!

BROWN: I said a boom chicka rocka chicka rocka chicka boom!

BABY/SHADOW: I said a boom chicka rocka chicka rocka chicka boom!

BROWN: Uhh huh!

BABY/SHADOW: Uhh huh!

BROWN: Oh yeah!

BABY/SHADOW: Oh yeah!

BROWN: One mo' time!

BABY/SHADOW: One mo' time!

BROWN: Like you in love!

BABY/SHADOW: Like we in love!

BROWN [*slow & sexy*]: I said a boom chicka boom.

BABY/SHADOW: I said a boom chicka boom.

BROWN: I said a boom chicka boom.

BABY/SHADOW: I said a boom chicka boom.

BROWN: I said a boom chicka rocka chicka rocka chicka boom.

BABY/SHADOW: I said a boom chicka rocka chicka rocka chicka boom.

BROWN: Uh huh.

BABY/SHADOW: Uh huh.

BROWN: Oh yeah.

BABY/SHADOW: Oh yeah.

BROWN: One mo' time!

BABY/SHADOW: One mo' time-

[*Enter* LEE.]

BROWN: Like oh my good god DAMN-

[*Exit* CONN *quickly.*]

BROWN: Who in the fuck is that?

LEE: I said a boom chicka rocka chicka boom boo boo boom!

[BABY & LEE *do a mating dance.*]

BABY: Chicka rocka chicka rock-

LEE: Chicka boo boo boom!

BABY: hicka rock?

LEE: hicka rock?

BABY: hicka rock.

LEE: hicka rock.

BABY: hicka rocka chicka rocka chicka boom boom boom!

[*Beat.*]

SHADOW: Jesus.

BROWN: What wrong wit you?

SHADOW: Why these dumb boys always gotta be comin' around when we tryin' be girls together?

BROWN: That what happen when you a senior, fool. We be smellin' like women. So the young slims gon' come sniffin' around us. And he fine so what do it matter?

BABY: What you doin' here, Lee!

LEE: I on my way to meet Five-Ohh if it's any o' yo business. What ya'll doin'?

BROWN: We practicin' fo' the step squad. And I'd like to step all up in yo fine-

SHADOW [*putting hand on* BABY's *shoulder*]: It's GIRLS only!

LEE: So why I see you up in there then looking like a mooka mooka-cow from Pigs in Space?

BABY: Quit it out, Lee. We should get back to practicin'any ol' way 'stead o' talkin' to you.

LEE: Funky girl.

BROWN: Let's break. I got somethin' I gotta do-

SHADOW: An' I bet I know what-

BROWN: I gotta drop somethin' off fo' Raymond, that's what.

SHADOW: Yeah. Uh huh. Bet.

LEE: I just passin' thru cause I always keep my word. Baby. Turn around and close yo' eyes, and you gon' get a big ol' surprise.

[WOMACLOWN *closes* BABY'S *eyes & spins her around.*]

Now hol' out yo' hands.

BABY: Like this?

LEE: Yeah. Jus' like that!

[*He throws a bag full of candy in her face.*]

BABY: Boy!

LEE: I say I always keep my word.

BABY: That was four years ago!

SHADOW [*grabbing the candy*]: You so immature!

LEE: Naw, forreal. I got somethin' else fo' you too-

SHADOW: Um hmm. Bet.

LEE: Close yo' eyes and turn around, and you gon' get a big ol' surprise-

BABY: Naw, boy.

SHADOW: Not again.

LEE: C'mon. I forreal this time. C'mon. Please?

BABY: Alright.

[WOMACLOWN *closes* BABY'S *eyes, and turns her around.*]

LEE: Now hol' out yo' hands-

BABY: Like this?

LEE: Yeah.

[LEE *kisses* BABY *on the lips & runs away laughing.* SHADOW & BROWN *run after him.*]

WOMACLOWN [*wiping off* BABY's *lips*]: Oh! How dare he!

BROWN [*laughing*]: Come back Mr. Lee, I want me some too! You go on and get it Baby! He is FIIIINNNE!

SHADOW: How he gon' come up in yo'face and kiss you like that?

BROWN: I wish he'd come up in my face and kiss me like that!

BABY: How sick. How nasty? How disgusting!

WOMACLOWN: UUUGGGGGGGHHHHHHHH!

BROWN: Baby it ain't that bad!

SHADOW: It is when you been kissed by that fool!

BROWN: No it ain't! Unless you ain't neva been kissed befo'. Seventeen years ol' and ain't neva been kissed?

BABY: I been now-

WOMACLOWN: And I don't like it.

SHADOW: Lee runnin' off mean it must almost be time for class. 'Least the fool got some sense-

BROWN: OOH! Gotta do a run before seventh period, ya'll! See ya!

SHADOW: Yeah. See you later. Hope you make it back sometime.

BROWN: Just gotta hit ONE delivery to some guy who hangs out in the playground-

SHADOW: My mamma told me to always stay all the way away from any men who hang out lookin' at little kids, and you givin' him dope?

BABY: Shadow? You comin'?

SHADOW: Yeah, I'm comin'! Brown, you betta watch out. I ain't neva looked up in his face, but my mamma say-

BROWN: You and yo' damn mamma! Seventh period I'll be back. You ain't even gon' know I'm gone!

[BROWN *slaps* SHADOW *in the neck.*]

BROWN (cont-): Neck respect!

SHADOW: You betta quit hittin' me girl!

BROWN: You know you like it when a girl touch you anywhere! Peace!

[*Beat.*] [BROWN *exits.*]

SHADOW: Baby, you goin' straight to English?

BABY: Yup. I cain't wait to see what grade we got on them short stories we wrote last week.

SHADOW: We could walk together. Hold my hand.

BABY: We ain't goin' that far.

SHADOW: Oh. Okay- [*Beat.*] What you write on?

BABY: 'Member Tyronda Wilson?

SHADOW: Tyronda who?

BABY: You 'member. Way back in grammar school? That girl who-

SHADOW: Yeah! I neva forget how she beat me in the spellin' bee in front o' the whole damn school. You know that girl-

BABY: I wrote 'bout how she died. What you write 'bout?

SHADOW: 'Bout my daddy?

BABY: Yeah?

SHADOW: Well, my mama tol' me this story when I got ol' enough to listen cause she ain't neva want me feelin' sorry fo' myself cause I ain't neva knowed no daddy. She sat me down next to her, and wrapped this patchy quilt around me that been made with grease and baby clothes. She said to me- "Sharon. See this quilt? This patch here my mother's nursin' hat. This patch here? Her grandmother's favorite sock. This patch here is waitin' for your hands. All our mothers, all our daughters been quiltin' since we knowed how to love. But you not gonna fill this patch like we done filled it. Your hands-

[SHADOW *grabs* BABY'S *hands and interweaves them with hers*.]

Your hands gonna weave a diploma in there.   Listen to me, Sharon. 'Cause this spot right here is for your diploma. And I know you gonna fill it. So go on an' bust some ASS."

[SHADOW *holds* BABY'S *hand tightly, locks eyes with her. Beat*.]

BABY: Yo' mama said-

WOMACLOWN: "ASS?"

SHADOW: Naw. But the teacher don't got to know that, do he?

[SHADOW & BABY *exit*. BROWN *and* MR. CONN *enter*. WOMACLOWN *stands between them, becoming a tree*.]

BROWN: Hey, man. Here you go.

[BROWN *drops bag*. CONN *grabs it*.]

BROWN: You know how much it cost so come on wit it!

[CONN *reaches to give her money*.]

BROWN: Just drop it in front of you. I don't ever look you mo'fuckas in the face. Somebody tol' me that's...bad business. Nasty fuck.

[CONN *drops money*.]

BROWN: Now turn around-

[WOMACLOWN *begins a gentle breeze using arms & humming.* CONN *turns around.*]

BROWN (cont-): Good workin' wit you, Sir-

[*Abruptly*, WOMACLOWN'S *wind becomes extreme, turning around* CONN *staring* BROWN *straight in her eyes. Their eyes lock.* BROWN *trembles.*]

BROWN: Like...I...Said...Thank you. Sir...

[*Beat.* BROWN *breaks from his gaze and runs.* CONN, *looking at the tree and shivering, exits playground.* WOMACLOWN *appears, chants "love me, me in she. we are two, not she & you" throughout next scene. Enter* FIVE-OHH, LEE.]

LEE: Hey Five-ohh!

FIVE-OHH: What boy?

LEE: Come on over here, man. I got lots o'tips today workin' the bags.'

WOMACLOWN:
Love me.
Me in she.
We are two.
Not she and you.

FIVE-OHH: That mean you got lots o' quarters to pitch, Lee?

LEE: Yeah, man.

FIVE-OHH: Let me get out my change. Alright Boy, what yuh lookin' at now? Two dollars? Three? I only got uh dollar and seventy five hundredths of some cents.

LEE: You see that one?

FIVE-OHH: Which one?

LEE: This one right up in my hand ol' man-

FIVE-OHH: Yeah, boy.

LEE: UMMMM!

F IVE-OHH: You need to tell me what it is you see boy, cause I ain't got no eyes to mind read-

LEE: When I look up in this quarter, Five-Ohh, I see the most beautifulest, most exquisiteness, most wonderfulurifical young lady in the world-

WOMACLOWN:
Love me.
Me in she.
We are two.
Not she and you.

FIVE-OHH: I don't mean to be smart, but that ain't exactly a lady you be gazin' upon in that ol' quarter. He just got longish kinda hair.

LEE: Naw, Five-Ohh. I'm thinkin' 'bout that girl you made me walk home that day.

FIVE-OHH: Baby? That was just comin upon fo' years ago this spring when the chicks start hatchin' like yuhs done called them to the slaughtuh.

LEE: Yeah.

FIVE-OHH: Well. I mighta been wrong 'bout you walkin' her home. Now go on and pitch that quarter.

WOMACLOWN: We are two. Not she and you.

LEE: Naw, Ol' man. I been thinkin' 'bout her all this time. I be walkin' down the hall to class. She walk by. I be thinkin', "Damn she fine!" Only thing I wan' is her.

WOMACLOWN: We are two. Not she and you!

FIVE-OHH: Look, Lee. Baby ain't here for you to go and pluck her up out the ground and make her dirty like the Indy Five-Hundred on a Pelican's wings.

LEE: I ain't pluckin' out nothin-!

FIVE-OHH: You betta listen to me boy. I been at this battlin' all kinds o' devils for a lot o' years longer than you done knowed what a breathin' devil was. Don't waste any mo' o' huh beauty wit your juice-

LEE: Nevermind, nevermind. You just a old man anyway. A lot older now than you was then-

FIVE-OHH: I ain't old!

LEE: What you know about it now? It's now. Man, it's now. Hook me up with Baby!

WOMACLOWN:
Love me.
Me in she.
We are two.
Not she and you.

FIVE-OHH: Naw.

LEE: I want Baby.

WOMACLOWN:
Me and she
Not she and you!

FIVE-OHH: And I want to slide around in som' o' Sinclair's chocolate puddin' on my way to meetin' the Creator.

LEE: Didn't nobody say you couldn't do that-

FIVE-OHH: You don't even know her.

LEE: She got pretty legs. And her lips is luscious!

FIVE-OHH: Listen, boy- I know you been a dog wit my lil' niece like she just a piece of-

LEE: Dog? Who been a dog? I ain't been no dog.

FIVE-OHH: I know what you done did wit my niece!

WOMACLOWN:
Love me.
Me in she.
We are two.
Not she and you!

LEE: Man all I did was kiss her on the lips. And she didn't even know I was gon' do it!

FIVE-OHH: All you thinkin' 'bout is her pretty legs and luscious lips! You don' hurt huh once, and I took care of that fuh huh. You young spirits always just thinkin' 'bout biscuits, gravy, and boodie!

LEE: I ain't thinkin' 'bout Baby's boodie Five-Ohh! I swear!

FIVE-OHH: Good. Now if I got to conjure da spirits tuh keep yuh aways from huh, then I will. I an't gon' let her go thru what you don' already put huh thru!

LEE: Aw man, it was just a lil' kiss.

FIVE-OHH: Aw, man, nothin'.   It was mo'than a kiss and yuh know it.

LEE: I swear. All I did was kiss the girl. And she come up talkin' 'bout I'm a nasty boy. Ol' funky girl.

WOMACLOWN: Me and she.

FIVE-OHH: I don't blame huh after what yuh done did. She tired o'yuh lookin' at huh legs and huh luscious lips. Yuh callin' to huh, "Hey Baby, you is fine." Yuh wantin' to suck from huh peach and throw out the pit!

LEE: Eh, man. I ain't done none o'them things to that girl. I just threw a bag o'candy at her and gave her a kiss. I ain't do-!

FIVE-OHH: She just ain't here for you to drink her and throw her out wit the shit in yo' yard!

LEE: It was just a lil' kiss!

FIVE-OHH: A lil' kiss and then you tried to show huh how's to be a woman when she ain't even knowed she was startin' tuh let the spirit flow!

LEE: I don't know what you talkin' bout Five-Ohh so you betta shut up or I'm gon' have to shut you up!

FIVE-OHH: I done hel' muh tongue for go in on fo' years, Lee!   But I cain't hol' it no mo'!

[FIVE-OHH *pulls his cross from around his neck and points it at* LEE.]

FIVE-OHH (cont-): The devil done comed-!

LEE: No.

FIVE-OHH: And I got to make 'em leave! The devil done comed and I got to scoot his sleeve!

[FIVE-OHH *chants ancient African purification rhythm.* LEE'S *body shakes & vibrates.*]

LEE: Crazy ol' man. What you doin' to me?

FIVE-OHH: The devil done comed-!

LEE: NO!

FIVE-OHH: And I got to make 'em leave! The devil done comed and I got to scoot his sleeve!

LEE: STOP IT! STOP IT! STOP!!!

[LEE *freezes*. FIVE-OHH *begins to shake*. *Cross drops to the floor*. *Beat*.]

LEE [*slowly*]: Are you gon' pitch some of them quarters or what?

WOMACLOWN:

Love me.
Me in she.
We are two.
Not she and you.
Love me.
Me in she.
We are two.
Not she and you.

Not she and you.
Not she and you!
NOT SHE AND YOU!

[WOMACLOWN, FIVE-OHH, LEE *freeze*. FIVE-OHH & LEE *join company* (*except for* BROWN) as a class. MR. CONN *enters slowly, disguised*.]

SHADOW: Damn. Teacher ain't even here today. I wanna know what grade I got.

BABY: OOh. Look. Here come the sub.

SHADOW: He look kinda shady.

BABY: He look kinda familiar.

SHADOW: He probly subbed another class sometime.

MR. CONN: O.k. class. Settle down, settle down. Mr. Atkins is absent today. He has informed me of where you are in your readings of short stories, so I will conduct the class as usual. Is there anyone who can summarize the story you read last?

[SHADOW *raises her hand.*]

MR. CONN (cont-): Yes?

SHADOW: Mr-?

MR. CONN: Conn. My name is Mr. Conn.

SHADOW: Mr. Conn. We read Baby Fleming's story 'bout a little girl who committed suicide.

MR. CONN: Thank you, Miss. Where is the author of this story?

BABY: Right here.

MR. CONN: Can you stand please while the class critiques your writing?

BABY: Yes sir.

MR. CONN: Thank you, little one.

BABY: Little one-? My name is Baby.

MR. CONN: Excuse me. That's a pretty name for a pretty girl. [*Beat.*] Now, after you've just read aloud Baby Flemings' story, does anyone in the class have any feedback?

LEE: I 'member hearin' 'bout that girl. She went to my school-

SHADOW: That's that girl who beat me in the spellin' bee in the sixth grade. She was a whole year younger than us, and she still beat me.

LEE: I thought she was gon' get shot up by some dope dealers-

BABY: That's what everybody think happens-

MR. CONN: And indeed it does, class. But what is real and what is depicted in this story are clearly two different things.

WOMACLOWN: What?

MR. CONN: I have studied the African-American inner city culture extensively.

WOMACLOWN: Listen to me. My voice. Listen.

MR. CONN: According to the statistics, drugs and gang violence are the number one causes of death in their neighborhoods. So, as you can see class, Miss Flemings' story of a little girl committing suicide isn't believed to be one of the more widely accepted reasons the African-American community is being decimated.

[*A pause.*]

BABY: But I'm tellin' you what I saw-

MR. CONN: Please refrain from becoming hostile, Baby. Or I'm going to have to tell your mama.

[*The class laughs.*]

WOMACLOWN: Listen to me. My voice. Listen.

MR. CONN: Miss Flemings. What you saw is not what is recognized by the larger society.

BABY: But I'm tellin' you. When I was in eighth grade I saw it-

WOMACLOWN: Listen to me. My voice...

MR. CONN: However, Miss Flemings, I have done extensive research in African-American culture and I know-

[*Silence.*]

LEE: Well Mr. CONN. I thought Baby's story was hip.

WOMACLOWN: Love me. Me in she. We are two. Not she and you.

LEE: I thought her story showed a side of Black people that is not "recognized by the larger society."

WOMACLOWN: We are two. Not she and you.

LEE: In fact, Mr. Conn, SIR. I think your theories are bullshit.

[WOMACLOWN *covers* BABY'S *ears. The class snickers.*]

WOMACLOWN: Not she and you. [*To* BABY.] Listen to me. My voice. Listen!

MR. CONN: Excuse me, SIR. But this is an academic setting. I do not wish to be spoken

to as one of your "homeys", or "brothers" or any other ridiculous terminology your people use to identify themselves.

LEE: Excuse me, Mr. Conn, SIR. YOU people in the academic world have no understanding of what it means to be labeled in terms of the "ridiculous terminology" that YOUR people use to identify us.

MR. CONN: Please explicate your meaning.

LEE: Baby wrote this sensitive story. Now you tellin' us that that don't happen in Black America? It do. Obviously she see it when she walkin' down the street. So how you gonna tell Baby what goin' on in her own community?

MR. CONN: I merely stated that based on the research I have done-

BABY: Yo' research say that we all-

MR. CONN: My research states that African-Americans are most likely to die because of drug abuse and gang violence, that is what my research-

BABY: This yo' research! These people here. These people right up here in this classroom. We yo' research. We livin' proof!

LEE: You don't need to go to no encyclopedia of statistics on Black folk in America to see what is sittin' right up in your face!
WOMACLOWN:
My face. His eyes.
Listen to me. My voice.
Listen!

[*Silence.*]

MR. CONN: I see that you have very strong opinions about the matter. I am merely the substitute teacher. I have no answers. I am only here to serve as a catalyst in getting your creative processes in motion. That is all. [*Silence.*] I say that is all.

[*Company congratulates* LEE *and* BABY. *The company exits.* LEE, BABY, *and* WOMACLOWN *remain.*]

LEE: That teacher wished he could've tol' us what was up! You'd think that in this day folks is hip to the propaganda being propogated against us in this country.

BABY: Hmm.

LEE: What?

BABY: Nothin'. I ain't say nothin'.

LEE: You did. You said "hmmm."

BABY: So?

LEE: So what that mean?

BABY: It don't mean nothin'.

LEE: Y'all girls always be sayin' that!

BABY: You'd think that he'd understand that I ain't thinkin' 'bout what the "research" say.

[*Beat.*]

LEE: I really like your story, Baby.

WOMACLOWN: Liar!

[WOMACLOWN *crouches closer to* BABY.]

BABY [*mumbling*]: Thank you.

LEE: I cain't hear you.

WOMACLOWN: I said "THANK YOU!"

LEE: Naw, I mean, I really like your story. It got a depth and meanin' we cain't even understand.

BABY [*giggling*]: Quit it out!

LEE: It true. It deep. It goin' on.

BABY [*flattered*]: Shut up.

WOMACLOWN: Shut up!

LEE: Hey, would I lie? I keep tellin' you I be a man o' my word. You think I would stand up and risk my grade for you if I ain't believe that you are-

WOMACLOWN: What?

LEE: Beautiful. Yes.

BABY: "Yes" what?

LEE: Just yes.

[*He offers his   hand.* WOMACLOWN *reaches to touch* BABY, *but* BABY *moves and takes* LEE's *hand*.]

WOMACLOWN:
She leaves with him and I am left alone.
To be the little girl
who is left to die on the sidewalk on Rhodes Ave.
She must hold on to me, she must, she's not going on without me
in her--

[*Beat.* WOMACLOWN *is becoming increasingly angrier. Drumbeat.* LEE *is walking* BABY *home from school.*]

BABY: Walkin' wit you hand in hand-

LEE: Is scary. I cain't sleep at night cause I be thinkin' 'bout you-

WOMACLOWN: Mama I'm scared-

LEE: Scared-
BABY: That you ain't gon' love-

WOMACLOWN: Me.

BABY: Scared that gon' find somebody else who wanna eat now and laters-

LEE: Wit chico sticks-

WOMACLOWN: Scared-

BABY: That you or I gon' be at home at night and find we ain't thinkin' 'bout-

LEE: One 'nother no mo'.

BABY: And we don't wish-

LEE: To no mo'.

BABY: But oh-

WOMACLOWN: Faith.

LEE: Yes-

WOMACLOWN: Faith.

[*They motion slowly toward one another.* WOMACLOWN *continues to try and keep them apart.*]

BABY: Faith give me courage to-

WOMACLOWN [*to* BABY]:
Love Me!
Me in thee.
We are two.
Not thee and Lee!

LEE: Faith give me hope to be-

WOMACLOWN: In love. With me.

LEE: The moment I seent yo' face up in my thoughts-

BABY: I knew there was something about you-
LEE: That be too deep for me to ever understand.

[BABY *and* LEE *move closer.* WOMACLOWN *is in between them.*]

BABY: But I-

WOMACLOWN: Trust-

BABY: I learning to-

WOMACLOWN: Trust-

LEE: To have-

WOMACLOWN: Faith.

BABY: To know-

WOMACLOWN: Soul.

LEE: To trust-

BABY: You?

LEE: No.

BABY: To trust, who?

LEE: Yourself.

[WOMACLOWN *relaxes*.]

BABY: Myself?

LEE: Yourself.

BABY: I don't understand-

LEE: Understand this-

BABY: I'm listening. I'm waiting-

LEE: For answers. From who?-

BABY: From you. You my answer-

LEE: I-

BABY: Yes. You. You look inside me. You take my hand. You me-

WOMACLOWN: Love me! Love me!

LEE: I do.

BABY: I do, too.

WOMACLOWN: But your answer is me-

BABY: My answer?-

WOMACLOWN: Your answer.

LEE: You too deep fo' me to ever understand-

BABY [*to* LEE]: You my answer-

LEE: I cain't neva be yo answer-

BABY: You my answer!

WOMACLOWN/LEE: No!

BABY: YES!

LEE/WOMACLOWN: NO!!!!!

LEE: You too deep fo' me to ever understand-

WOMACLOWN [*to* Baby]: I LOVE YOU!

LEE: Love you. [*A pause.*] Love you. Good night, Baby girl.

[LEE *kisses* BABY *on lips. She struggles to keep him with her, but they've reached her home. He exits.*]

WOMACLOWN:
I am a box.
Inside me is my soul.
Look. Inside me!
[*Blackout.*]

[*Lights up.* BABY *is asleep in bed at home.*]

WOMACLOWN:
Bubble gum.
Bubble gum.
In a dish!
How many bubble gum
Do you wish?

[*Enter* CONN *in a mask to enter into* BABY's *dreamworld. During this scene,* CONN & WOMACLOWN *fight for* BABY's *attention in her dreamworld. Even when it is indicated in the script,* BABY *never wakes up until the dream is completely over.* BABY *never sees* CONN *during the dream. She only hears his voice.*]

CONN:
Bubble gum!
Bubble gum!
In a dish!
How many bubble gum
Do you wish?

Wake up, Baby!

Baby! Wake up!

[BABY *sits up, but she is still asleep.*]

BABY: What?

MR. CONN: C'mon-

Play!

Bubble gum! Bubble gum!
In a dish!
How many bubble gum!
Do you wish?

BABY: Three.

WOMACLOWN [*pushing* CONN *away from* BABY]: One two three spell three
So out you may go with the
Dirty Dirty Dish rag
On your left or right
Stinky Toe!

BABY: I'm gon' back to sleep.

MR. CONN: C'mon Baby. Stay with me. I love you.

BABY: What?

WOMACLOWN: I love you! Stay with me. Please? Please?

BABY: Alright. One more game. Then I gon' go back to sleep.

WOMACLOWN: O.k. Let's play "Miss Mary Mack."

BABY: I don't even know "Miss Mary Mack."

WOMACLOWN: That's o.k. I'll teach it to you. I love you.

BABY: We just play friends. That's all.

WOMACLOWN: But I love you.

BABY: Let's just play.

[CONN *edges toward* BABY. WOMACLOWN *snatches her away*.]

WOMACLOWN: Okay
Miss Mary Mack Mack Mack
All dressed in black black black
With silver buttons buttons buttons
All down her back back back-

BABY: I don't want to play anymore. I ain't a little girl. These be little girl games. I got a boyfriend now.

WOMACLOWN: You don't need him. C'mon. You promised you'd play with me til Mama got home!

BABY: Alright. C'mon. Only once through, then I'm gon' back to bed.

WOMACLOWN: Miss Mary Mack Mack Mack
All dressed in black black black
With silver buttons buttons buttons
All down her back back back!

Come on Baby! Keep playin-

[CONN *reaches for* BABY]
WOMACLOWN (cont-): he asked her mother mother mother
For fifteen cents cents cents
To see the elephant elephant elephant
Jump over the fence fence fence!

Keep yo' hands up!

MR. CONN: You know you like it.

WOMACLOWN: She jumped so high high high
Til she touched the sky sky sky
And she never came back back back
Til the fourth of July ly ly!

See? That wasn't so bad! Was it?

BABY: No. And now it time fo' you to go home and be wit yo' own Mamma.

WOMACLOWN: Yo' mama my mama.

BABY: No, she ain't. We just play sisters. You know. That's all. You go home now.

WOMACLOWN: We not just play sisters. We real sisters!

BABY: Play!

WOMACLOWN: Real!

BABY/MR. CONN: Play!

WOMACLOWN: Real!

BABY: When yo' gon' leave me alone?

WOMACLOWN: When you love me!

BABY: I love you... like my play sister.

WOMACLOWN: You should love me like you love yo' boyfriend and yo' play sister, and yo' mama!

BABY: That's it! I'm gon' to bed. Goodnight!

[BABY *cuts out the lights*. CONN *grabs* WOMACLOWN & *touches her ear*.]

WOMACLOWN: I can't-!

BABY: You can't what?

WOMACLOWN: See in the dark-

BABY: What?

WOMACLOWN: Darkness! All around my eyes. All throughout my heart-

BABY: I can fix that-

[BABY *reaches to* WOMACLOWN.]

WOMACLOWN: NO!

[CONN *pulls* WOMACLOWN *away from her, grabs milk, pours milk down* WOMACLOWN'S *forehead, watches it run, licks the milk*.]

BABY: What's wrong with you?

WOMACLOWN: Nothin'.

BABY: Nothin'? You crazy!

WOMACLOWN: Nothin' wrong wit me!

BABY: You always gotta play these games with me.

WOMACLOWN: You can't accept yourself!

BABY: I can!

WOMACLOWN: You can't!

[WOMACLOWN *breaks from* CONN, *pushes* BABY. CONN *sits back, crosses arms, smiles, exits slyly.*]
BABY: Don't push me!

WOMACLOWN: Yeah I'm a push you. [*Silence.*] Speak! [*Silence.*] Speak! [*Silence.*]
You a clown. You ain't even a clown. You- [*Motions to hit her.*] You killed me!
You killed me!

BABY: Don't. DON'T!

WOMACLOWN: I'm a do to you what you did to me!
BABY: What?

WOMACLOWN: You heard me!

BABY: I don't even know what you talkin' 'bout!

WOMACLOWN: Oh! You got something else to say to me, huh? You got
somethin' else to tell me?

BABY: Leave fo' I tell my mama!

[*Silence.*]

WOMACLOWN: What?

BABY: Yes!

WOMACLOWN: What? You killed me and you want ME to leave! Oh no, oh no. You gon' take me right back inside o' you!

Come here. Come here! Clown. Come here and feel me inside you!

BABY: I'll kill you first, I swear it!

WOMACLOWN: We'll see. You wanna play Miss Mary Mack now!

[WOMACLOWN *grabs* BABY. *They dance, violently.*]

WOMACLOWN (cont-): What you gonna do now? Huh? What you gon' do now! You gonna kill me? Huh? You gonna kill me! HUH! Come on Baby. Speak up! Speak up! Defend yourself!

BABY: AHH!

WOMACLOWN: Speak up! Speak up!

BABY: I can't-

WOMACLOWN: What you gon' do, huh? You a girl, or a woman? Huh? HUH?!

BABY: Ahh!

WOMACLOWN: I ain't even gon' waste my time wit you no mo'. I don't need you to love me!

[BABY *wakes up out of her nightmare in a cold sweat.* WOMACLOWN *hides.*]

BABY: God?! God. Promise me it'll go away-
[BABY, *wrapped in her bed sheet, begins to sway. We hear a drumbeat.*]

BABY (cont-): Promise me it'll go away-

[*She begins checking the exits, crevice, holes. She's looking for a peeking eye.*]

BABY (cont-): Please.

[*She settles into a spot near the black box with the empty purple milk glass. She tries to repeat her dance of sexual freedom, but she is disgusted. She is not beautiful anymore.*]

BABY (cont-): This ugly- I deserve-

[WOMACLOWN *rises and begins mirroring* BABY. *It is a touch of self-hate.*]

BABY (cont-): I- I-

[WOMACLOWN *begins to wrap the blanket around* BABY. *She wraps it faster and faster and tighter and tighter, and the drum pulse quickens.*]

BABY (cont-): Promise me!

[WOMACLOWN *wraps* BABY *while moving her back to the ladder.* WOMACLOWN *climbs the ladder pulling* BABY *with her. One of* BABY's *arms is free and together she and* WOMACLOWN *make a noose.* BABY *and* WOMACLOWN *put the noose hurriedly around* BABY's *neck. The drumpulse is at it's height, and it suddenly becomes the loud knocking on a door.*]

LEE: Baby! Baby! Are you in there!

FIVE-OHH: Baby! Open up this door!

[WOMACLOWN *panics.* BABY *is just about to jump/be pushed by* WOMACLOWN from the *ladder's top when* LEE *and* FIVE-OHH *burst into the room.*]

LEE: Baby! Baby!

FIVE-OHH: Grab her!

[LEE *and* FIVE-OHH *rush to the ladder and grab* BABY. *They uncover* BABY's *eyes and pull* BABY *down the ladder as* WOMACLOWN *watches defeatedly from the ladder's other side.*]

FIVE-OHH: Oh God! We got to call an ambulance quicker than she can say Tennessee peacock ten times backwards standin' on huh head!

LEE: Baby! What the hell are you doin-
BABY: Who's that?

LEE: What?

BABY: Who's that?

[WOMACLOWN *realizes* BABY *sees her. She rushes down the side of the ladder.*]

BABY: Who is she? Who is SHE!

LEE: Baby? Who are you talking about?

FIVE-OHH: She don' seent the spirit!

BABY: Who is she! WHO IS SHE!

LEE: Spirits? Ain't no spirits! Baby, ain't nobody there! Stop it! Ain't no body there!

BABY: I see her! She right there!

FIVE-OHH: Loosen that-

LEE: She ain't even thinkin' right!

BABY: Come back here! Come back here right now you!

[WOMACLOWN *absconds*. BABY *chases after her*. *Blackout*.]

[*Lights up. One month later*. BABY *is lying on a bed center stage with white sheets*. WOMACLOWN *is no where in sight*.]

BABY:

They tell me that it is crazy
to talk to the walls
to see and hear
ice cream oozing down the sides
of the t.v. set
and liquid thru
my fingertips
through my head's
cartoon characters
like lead
as the little girl takes her paw
and rubs
my teeth
to jump off the top
of the projects

I talk, sometimes.
To her.
I hear her.
Sometimes she talks back.
Sometimes she only nods.
Sometimes I see her laughing at
me.
Smashed potato head

against concrete soil.
Who are you?

[*Beat.*]

Answer me?

[*Beat.*]

What?

Now she wants to play hide and seek
from the exterminator-

No, I don't want to-! You're makin' me cough-!

[*Beat.*]

Where are you?

[*Beat.*]
Hey, get away from him!
He double-handed anyway.

[*Beat.*]

I'm coming
Is you here?

[*Beat.*]

I hear you
Mama!

[*Silence.*]

Taste-

[MR. CONN *slivers in* BABY'S *room.*]

MR. CONN: 'Scuse me. Ahem. 'Scuse me.

BABY: So much blood on my skirt!

MR. CONN: 'Scuse me. Baby?

BABY: And the blood stained my skirt-

MR. CONN: Baby?

BABY: And I got to school and Shadow asked me what the scabs was on my legs-

MR. CONN: Baby, I am your doctor-

BABY: What?

MR. CONN: I said I am your doctor-

BABY: No. I didn't hear the teacher say that-

MR. CONN: Baby, I don't know if you can hear me-

BABY: Nuh uh. Teacher didn't say that-

MR. CONN: But I done some thinking over the past few months, little one-

BABY: I knew she thought my daddy was white-

MR. CONN: I kept followin' you-

BABY: I told her my daddy was Black as Black is night-

MR. CONN: I kept watchin' you grow into a young woman-

BABY: I said I told her my daddy was Black-

MR. CONN: And when I saw you in your class that day I felt like this was all my fault-

BABY: My mama was, too-

MR. CONN: I didn't mean to put you here. I didn't think I was doing anything wrong little one. Forgive me?

BABY: Liar-!

MR. CONN: No. I didn't. Honestly.

BABY: Liar! Liar! You said you wouldn't tell-

MR. CONN: I didn't tell. I never told, Baby-

BABY: How do you know my name-

MR. CONN: Your name-

BABY: How you know my name-? [*Silence.*] GET AWAY FROM ME!

MR. CONN: Little one, listen to me. I been thinkin'. I made a mistake. If I give you a kiss will you forgive me?

BABY: Don't touch my face!

MR. CONN: I made a mistake. I ruined you, little one. If I give you a kiss with my tongue will you forgive me then?

BABY: Get that milk away from my face!

MR.CONN: Baby? You will forgive me.

[CONN *grabs* BABY'S *hands.*]

BABY: Let go o' my hands! Stop!

MR. CONN: Baby, I'm not touchin' you! You're hallucinating again, little one. Didn't your "other" doctor tell you about seeing people who aren't there?

BABY: Stop. Stop! STOP!

MR. CONN: Calm down. Listen to me. I love you.

[*She slaps him. Beat.*]

BABY: Please, mister. My mama is comin' home soon- PLEASE MISTER! GET OUT FO' MY MAMMA COME HOME! BLOOD! EVERYWHERE! GET OUT!

[*Knocking.* MR. CONN *attempts to leave. Enter* FIVE-OHH, LEE, & SHADOW.]

LEE: Are you the doctor?

MR. CONN: Yes. Yes. I am.

LEE: I feel like I seen you before. You ever had bags delivered from the A&P?

MR. CONN: Yes. Perhaps that's where you've seen me.

LEE: Hmm. I don't know-

SHADOW: You must be-

MR. CONN: Conn. Dr. Conn.

SHADOW: It say on her chart that Dr. Foley is her doctor.

MR. CONN: Uh. She had an emergency at another hospital. I'm her assistant. How are you all today?

FIVE-OHH: A betta question is how is Baby?

MR. CONN: Um. She's o.k. She's fine, actually. Just hearing voices. Seeing things, hallucinating. Some time on thorazine, and she'll be just fine.

BABY: I hear Baby. Where is you?

SHADOW: Baby? Baby? It's Shadow...And Five-Ohh. We's come to see you.

LEE: And Lee. I'm here too. Baby?

BABY: What do you want!

SHADOW: See? Boy always comin' around when she just wanna be wit her girl Shadow. She don't want you here!

BABY [*to* SHADOW]: What do you want!

[*Beat.*]

SHADOW: Here.

MR. CONN [*a pause*]: Looks like they brought you something to drink-

BABY: What is it?

FIVE-OHH: It milk, Baby. But it a special kinna milk. It the kind that is all mixed wit bubble eyes and cricket juice so you can see yo' spirits and make peace wit 'em.

BABY: I don't want no milk.

FIVE-OHH: Baby. You trust me. Yuh drink this milk. Yuh ain't gon' need no thoreau-zeen or whatever it is this here doctor tryin' tuh pump yuh full of.

SHADOW: Baby, drink your milk-

BABY: No!

SHADOW: Baby, you betta drink it-

LEE: Here. Sip this!

[*They try to force feed* BABY *the milk.* BABY *reluctantly drinks.*]

LEE (cont-): Now, that's better.

[LEE *kisses* BABY *on the forehead.* SHADOW *cringes. Instantly,* BROWN *bursts in the door. She is hyper on cocaine.*]

BROWN: Baby? I knew I'd fin' yo' room, girl! What up?

SHADOW: Brown! Calm down!

LEE: Dr. Conn? We cain't let Baby be seein' her best frien' as messed up as she is right now?

BROWN: I ain't messed up! I'm just livin' the HIGH life!

FIVE-OHH: Well yuh betta high-tail yo'self outta here fo' yuh upset Baby!

BROWN: I ain't gon' mess her up no way! She already messed up!

SHADOW: You the one who messed up! Get her outta here!

BROWN: I ain't messed up! She the one seein' ghosts, and talkin' to cartoon characters up in her head, and I'm messed up?

BABY: Who that?

BROWN: See? She glad to see me, ain'tcha Baby?

BABY: MAMMA! MAMMA! [BABY *screams frantically.*] I won't smoke no mo' pencil reefer! I swear!

MR. CONN: I'm gon' have to ask you to leave, Miss.

BROWN: Why don't you try and make me leave, BOY?

MR. CONN: I'm sorry Miss. But this is inappropriate behavior, and you are disturbing my patient!

BROWN: Inappropriate behavior? Motherfucker inappropriate behavior!

[BROWN & MR. CONN *lock eyes*. BROWN *starts to shake in fear.*]

[*Silence.*]

Brown (cont-):   Shadow?

SHADOW: Yeah.

BROWN: This...is...On the playground...-

SHADOW: Playground?

BROWN: This is the man we saw on the playground that day, 4 years ago, the same one I sell to all the time now-!

SHADOW [*whispering to* BROWN]: You really gon' overboard wit the drugs, Brown!

BROWN: Naw! It's him!

MR. CONN: I think you'd better leave now, Miss Brown.

FIVE-OHH: I think she'd betta stay. I think Brown don' seen the spirit!

[CONN *runs*. FIVE-OHH *pulls out his cross*. CONN *freezes by the power of the spirit.*]

FIVE-OHH:
The devil done comed up in her
And I got to make him leave
The devil done comed up in her
And I got to scoot his sleeve!

BABY: I am a box.

FIVE-OHH: The devil done comed up in her-

BABY: Inside me is my soul.

FIVE-OHH:
And I got to make him leave-
The devil done comed up in her-

BABY: Look.

FIVE-OHH: And I got to scoot his sleeve!

BABY: Inside me!

[FIVE-OHH *continues low chant*.]

BABY: Hard faced
Feel him
'Neath him
He become a locomotive
I become a field
Layin', just layin.
He cum along-

[*Enter* WOMACLOWN.]

WOMACLOWN: Cum along
and Grab me!
Cum along
and make me bleed
WOMACLOWN (cont-):some more on his blade!

BABY: I hurt!

WOMACLOWN: I hurt!

BABY: And all you see me as-

WOMACLOWN: Is a game!

[*Drumbeat builds.* FIVE-OHH's *chant and drums slam to a halt.* CONN's *body wiggles, shakes, collapses as* BABY *pours* FIVE-OHH's *milk over* MR. CONN's *body.*]

WOMACLOWN: I am a box. Inside me is my soul.

BABY: Look. Inside. Me….I see you girl, come here!

[BABY *jumps up and begins chasing after* WOMACLOWN. BROWN, LEE, SHADOW, *and* FIVE-OHH *disappear into background.* BABY *loses* WOMACLOWN *and suddenly stops.*]

Lord? Can you hear me lord? Where are you? There you are. I see you, hidin' from me. You can't hide no more. I see you. I see who you is. And I wanna take care of you.

WOMACLOWN: What?

BABY: That's right. You come over to me.

[WOMACLOWN *inches away from* BABY.]

BABY (cont-): I don't care if you run.

WOMACLOWN: No, No.

BABY: Umhmm.

WOMACLOWN: Nuh uh.

BABY: Oh yeah. Come here, Baby!

[BABY *chases* WOMACLOWN. *After an elaborate dance/chase, she catches the* WOMACLOWN.]

BABY (cont-): Now drink this. Go on. Drink it!

[WOMACLOWN *drinks*.]

BABY (cont-): That's it, Baby.

[BABY *holds* WOMACLOWN. WOMACLOWN *struggles.* BABY *holds her and soothes her until* WOMACLOWN *relaxes.* BABY *sets her down gently.*]

BABY: Now I lay she down to.

WOMACLOWN: Sleep I pray the lord my.
Soul to keep if I.

BABY: Should die.
Before I wake I pray.

WOMACLOWN: The lord my soul to take.

[*Beat.*]

BABY: I wanna play now.

WOMACLOWN: Yes.

BABY: I wanna play now.

WOMACLOWN: Okay

[*The women begin to play patty-cake.*]

BABY [*slowly*]: Miss Mary Mack Mack Mack-

WOMACLOWN: All dressed in black black black-

BABY: With silver buttons buttons buttons-

BABY/WOMACLOWN: All down her back back back…

[*The company enters one by one, slowing humming* "Miss Mary Mack" BABY *and* WOMACLOWN *continue playing while the company moves towards the two with outstretched arms. One by one company finish humming* "Miss Mary Mack". BABY *is the last voice we hear. Lights fade to black.*]

END OF PLAY

Fascia

by Shepsu Aakhu
World Premier 2001

For Daryl and Kelvin

Fascia
Director's Notes

Fascia was the second play in what is now a eight play partnership between myself and Shepsu Aakhu. It was with this play that his unique ability to structure a story in a way that allows an audience to look at familiar experiences through a new lens began to crystallize. His characters are all folks we know, shown to us in all their beautiful and frustrating complexity.

I credit my first theatre mentor, director Jonathan Wilson, with teaching me how to ingest a script, I credit my work with Shepsu with helping me to hone my ability to feel the intangibles in a script and bring them to life in a production. The work we did together on Fascia was the beginning of this process. We spent a lot of time in early rehearsals breaking down the play and getting comfortable with its symbolism and the style of associative storytelling employed by Aakhu. However, this only gave us the base from which to create. The real work was in helping my exceptional cast trust the story and themselves. In the end I think we succeeded in staging a production that increased the audiences appreciation of the beauty and fluidity of the storytelling.

Fascia is a play that challenges those of us lucky enough to encounter it, to look at our own choices in terms of their resonance throughout the history of our families and community. As I continue to live my life and make choices, and my family continues its journey, the characters, images and ideas of Fascia continue to surface in my thoughts. This to me, speaks to the power and relevance of this work

Fascia
Playwright's Statement

"Until you understand, everything that you thought you knew will only confuse you..."

I have long since forgotten who said this to me, but the expression still resounds in my mind. My family confuses me...frustrates me. I love them and yet I feel as if there are those who I can not reach, and those who can not reach me. As I age I realize that I am frustrated largely because I don't have a clear notion of what is really going on. Fascia is the struggle to understand a singular moment in the life of an entire family. The baggage that makes the seemingly simple -- so damn complicated. The many layers of living so densely packed together that it takes lifetimes to sort it out. But what a joy to discover the things you never knew you never knew.

Original Cast

Daryl Charisse...AIN'T MARIE
Tory Davis..MOSS/BROTHER
YvonneHuff..SNOW/ANTIONETTE
Charles Micheal Moore...............................UNCLE-ONE/UNCLE FRANKIE
Andre Teamer...RED
Demetria Thomas ....BLACK/PEACHES/ROSEMARY
Sati Word.. TURTLE
Tina Marie Wright..AIN'T VEE

Original Production Staff

Director ....Mignon McPherson Nance
Production Stage Manager ....Sharlet Webb
Music Composition & Live Performance..Poh'ro
Technical Director ....Sean R. Neron
Scenographic Design... Danjuma Gaskin
Lighting Design...Reginah Walton Ciss
Sound Design...Min. of the New Super Heavy Funk
Costume Design...Karen Nolan
Choreographer...Roxiana Fuqua
Properties...Reginald Lawrence
Producer...Reginald Lawrence

ROLE ASSIGNMENTS

PEACHES/BLACK/ROSEMARY
AIN'T VEE
MOSS/BROTHER
SNOW/ANTOINETTE
RED
TURTLE
UNCLE-ONE/UNCLE FRANKIE
AIN'T MARIE

Characters are doubled across generations and their likeness to previous generations is noted and embraced.

CAST OF CHARACTERS

STEVIE DOBSON/ RED
Youth : The oldest of the children. A leader, restless, struggling to comprehend his place in the world.
Adult: In self appointed exile. Struggling to balance the "two worlds" of his consciousness.

SNOW [RED's Sister]
Youth: The loud mouth know it all. She thinks being cute we get her out of anything.
Adult: Edgy. Sharp-tongued, loving at heart, but lacking any true sense of independence.

BLACK [RED's Mother]
Youth: Lonely and approval seeking. Relatively unambitious.
Adult: Classic "over-protective enabler". Her complaints thinly veil her need to be needed.

MOSS [RED's Cousin]
Youth: A follower prone to accepting whatever RED presents.
Adult: Well educated, ambitious, proud, but disconnected from much of the family. He wishes to do more for the family, but does not know how to accomplish this.

DEMETRIUS WATSON / TURTLE   [PEACHES' brother]
Youth: The baby of the bunch seeking attention from everyone.
Adult: Distant to the point of being secretive, Possessing a quiet but confident demeanor.

LISA WATSON / PEACHES [TURTLE's sister]
Youth: Edgy, Assertive, and self-assured. Knows that she has a "gift", and proud of it.
Adult: Battered but not broken, at peace with her circumstance.

VERONICA/ "AIN'T VEE" [Aunt to BLACK/Great Aunt to other children]
Young: Inquisitive, precocious, playful, free spirit- wants to see and know everything.
Adult: She most often feels "put upon". Her "responsibilities" isolate her from the living.

Uncle One [Married AIN'T VEE]
A tortured grouchy man. Intense in his emotions, and tough with his love.

AIN'T MARIE [VEE's Aunt]
Family Matriarch. "The Conjure Woman", crafty, wise old woman, who watches over the generations.
Teaches the subtleties to the "gifted".

Antoinette [VEE's Grandmother]
Adventurous, flamboyant, energized spirit, always looking for the next bit of excitement..

ROSEMARY: Caribbean Slave, as independent minded as time and convention would allow.
BROTHER: Caribbean Slave, Protective.

ACT 1
SCENE 1   *A Storm Is A Coming*

Period: Late 1950's

Lights gently fade up on a clothes line covered in the clothes of infants, pre-adolescents, and adults. The clothes reflect the period spanning the 1940-2001. The stage slowly darkens suggesting and approaching storm. The sound of wind increases in intensity. Enter AIN'T VEE. She looks at the clothes, then glances up at the sky, and finally her eyes fall down to the clothes again. She reaches out her hand to feel the fabric for moistness.

AIN'T VEE [*discovering the clothes are still damp*]: Damn!

[*She looks up again frustrated then calls out.*]

BLACK!! BLACK! ....get out here!

[*Enter BLACK, running.*]

BLACK: Yes AIN'T VEE...

AIN'T VEE [*indicating the clothes*]: Grab'em and go.

BLACK [*grabbing them, then retracting her arm*]: But they still wet.

AIN'T VEE [*returning her gaze skyward*]: I know.

BLACK [*insistent*]: I can't put wet clothes on my baby....

[*Low rumbling thunder startles the women.*]

AIN'T VEE: Grab'em 'for we be wet, too!

BLACK: But....

AIN'T VEE [*loading her up with clothes*]: Here.

BLACK [*sulking*]: It's too much, I can't carry ...

AIN'T VEE [*loading her down*]: Just a few more.

BLACK [*squirming and protesting*]: You're makin' twice the work for both of us....Why can't we just leave them out in the rain, the sun'll come out again later.

AIN'T VEE [*profound dissatisfaction*]: Just go.

BLACK turns, struggles with the clothes, and exits.

AIN'T VEE takes down the line and the remaining clothes and follows BLACK. Low rumbling thunder is heard in the distance. Exit AIN'T VEE. The lights slowly fade and the sound of rain comes rushing in.

End Scene.

ACT 1
SCENE 2
Flash

Period: Late 1990's

The rain and thunder provide a sound bridge from scene I. Crossfade up on MOSS, RED, *and* TURTLE, *in a one room basement apartment.* TURTLE *is unseen and unheard by* MOSS. *The room is unkempt. The walls rough and unfinished, are stained, hinting of the water damage from previous flooding. The lights are low and it is late in the evening.* MOSS *and* RED *are in mid- conversation.*

MOSS [MOSS *dragging his fingers across the water stains*]: You sure it ain't gonna flood down here?

[TURTLE *follows tracing the water marks with his fingertips.*]

RED: Sump-pump still working, but you never know.

MOSS [*concerned, mostly to himself*]: Water mark is pretty high. I'd hate to be down here when...

TURTLE [*to* MOSS]: Storms come and go, a little damage is to be expected don't you think?

RED [*interjecting*]: You want a beer?

MOSS: Huh?

RED: Beer, you want one? [*From a cooler, pulls out a six pack of canned beer*] It ain't imported.

MOSS: No whiskey?

RED: Black label is a bit out my price range of late. [*Holding out a beer*] ....You want one or not?

MOSS [*reluctantly taking the beer*]: Sure.

[RED *tosses a beer to* MOSS. MOSS *does not open it. The sound of the storm begins to subside.*]

MOSS: Sounds like it's lightening up.

RED [*to* MOSS]: So, you still into that paparazzi shit?

MOSS [*defensive*]: That is not what I do! I'm a photo-journalist.

RED [*self amused*]: You make a livin' pokin' your nose into other peoples business. [*Flippant*] I bet you got your fingers crossed that nobody figures out that you don't really do shit?

MOSS [*irritated*]: It's an honest day's work.

RED [*sarcastic*]: What you tryin' to say [*indicating the room*] that all of this splendor has come through some less than honorable means? ....Everybody didn't get to chase their dreams Moss.

TURTLE [*to* RED, *joking*]: For some, our dreams chased us.

MOSS [*apologetic*]: I didn't say nothin' 'bout you and your dreams RED. Lord knows my dreams feel like a nightmare from time to time.

RED [*sarcastic*]: Yea, you and the movie critics, complainin' bout shit that most would do for free.

MOSS: It ain't digging a ditch, but it's...

RED [*interjecting*]: An angle.

MOSS [*scanning the room*]: Somehow even the most unattractive things have their charms. The world is a beautiful place when you see it through the lens. Once you get hooked, ...it's better than...

RED [*interjecting*]: What? Alcohol, women?

MOSS [*looking in TURTLE's general direction*]: Some things look better frozen in two dimensions.

TURTLE [*to MOSS*]: Problem is most of us need three to be, and four for a little more.

[TURTLE *repositions himself*, RED's *eyes track him as he moves across the room.* MOSS' *eyes in turn follow* RED's *but he does not see* TURTLE.]

MOSS [*to RED, still preoccupied with tracking what RED sees.*]: SNOW falls and train wrecks, through the lens, it's your own little piece of heaven.

RED [*returning his focus to MOSS, dismissive*]: Your heaven, my hell.

MOSS: What's that supposed to mean?

RED: If them pictures mean so much to you.. If they're meant to replace the family you tryin' to forget, don't cut corners...thoroughly indulge your delusion. [*Lighting a cigarette*] You want one?

MOSS [*uncomfortable*]: That shit'll kill you.

RED: Now that wouldn't be so bad would it?

MOSS [*condescending*]: It's your poison.

RED [*interjecting*]: You juice carrots this morning? Passion fruit, kiwi, celery, avocados and shit? [*self amused*] What the fuck is a kiwi Moss? Huh? You drinkin' shit that's meant to be eaten....

MOSS [*interjecting*]: ...And you're smoking....

RED [*interjecting*]: ...Shit that's meant to be smoked.

MOSS [*surrendering*]: I just stopped by to ....

RED [*dismissive*]: Yeah yeah, snowfalls and train wrecks. ...When I look through a camera you know what I see? [*Taking a long drag from the cigarette*] Not a damn thing [*exhaling*] ...I don't own no camera.

MOSS [*rising, exasperated, heading toward the stairs*]: Fine by me.

[TURTLE *crosses to the stairs and sits in front of the door blocking* MOSS' *exit.*]

RED: What you catch in your little box of light, they print that in newspapers and magazines?

MOSS [*stopping at the stairs*]: More or less.

RED [*pondering*]: Yeah, well, ...Me, when I see a train wreck, cousin it's a train wreck. ...Twisted metal, grieving families... You see falling snow. ...I see that my engine ain't gonna turn over. That ain't exactly no little piece of heaven.

MOSS [*still holding the unopened beer he moves up the stairs to exit*]: Well like I said, I just thought I'd stick my head in the door and see how you're doin'.

RED: Marking time cousin, ...marking time.

MOSS: Yea, well ..okay.

RED [*mocking* MOSS]: That's it huh?   ... you roll a brew around in ya hand for a few, ...never crack the top, ...then, "damn look at where all the time went"?

[TURTLE *stands up obstructing* MOSS' *exit.* MOSS *pauses.* TURTLE *looks him the eye, then whispers something unheard by the audience. A cascade of indecipherable whispering voices seeps into the room.* MOSS *returns to the room.*]

Crossfade to Scene 3.

End Scene.
ACT 1
SCENE 3 *Whispers And Wishes*

Period: Middle 1940's

The indecipherable whispers provide a sound bridge into the scene. Crossfade in on MARIE *and* VEE *in a Mississippi town, they are seated on the steps of a rickety shack.*

AIN'T MARIE [*to* VEE]: There is more power in a whisper than a wish. To give power to a thought is to speak it in a hush. To free it from your mind and allow it to take root in the world. Not so free as to be heard by everyone, and not so hidden as to be known only by you.

VEE: Who am I gonna tell?

AIN'T MARIE: What I say is for you to hear 'cause you ask. Ain't no recipes forth comin'. If you wanna bake cake, brown pie crust, or set mint jelly, it's best you ask ya mama.

VEE: Ain't no cake bakin' for me Ain't Marie. I wanna know from you all what there is to know.

AIN'T MARIE: I'll show you what they show'd me, and do you one better. I won't show you that what won't work no good. Won't be showin' you how to call for money, or for a man. I won't be showin' you how to fix those what wanna fix you. I won't show how to break no hearts, or mend old fences. You won't be flyin' through the air, or speakin' in tongues.

VEE: What's the fun in bein' a conjure woman if I ain't gonna learn none a that?

AIN'T MARIE: You don't need conjure for that. Any girl with a loose skirt and tail to boot can do most of that.

VEE: Any girl in a loose skirt can't call spirits.

AIN'T MARIE [*amused*]: Oh yes indeed she can, probably better than you or me. [*Concerned*] Why you wanna know 'bout callin' spirits?

VEE: You got a list from here to Sunday 'bout what you ain't gonna teach me. I gotta learn somethin' useful.

AIN'T MARIE [*reflective*]: Trick ain't in callin'em, it's in callin' the right ones. You got some family, what you wouldn't never wanna lay eyes on, livin' or dead.

VEE [*disappointed*]: Family is family.

AIN'T MARIE: Some wasn't pretty folk when I was a little girl, and time ain't done them no favors.

VEE: So you gone teach me or not?

AIN'T MARIE: I'll teach ya how to make what's wrong right. And if not right, at least betta' than you found it. [*In a stage whisper, to* VEE] To see them, is to see yourself... and everyone yet to come ...seein' ten thousand summer nights in Yazoo City, chasin' billowing clouds of white smoke spewing from....

[MARIE *holds out her hand and summons* PEACHES *onto the stage.*]

VEE & PEACHES [*in near whisper*]: ...D.D.T. trucks ...We inhaled mosquito death like a fragrant flower, ...forget-me-nots like those that line...

PEACHES: ...My great aunt's house. Five cousins from seven to fourteen, ...the fruit of one great-great-great grandmothers womb.

[RED, MOSS, SNOW, *and* TURTLE *come running by.* PEACHES *joins the other children.*]

AIN'T MARIE [*to* VEE]: Don't stay to play for too long... we gotta get supper going.

VEE: Okay Ain't Marie.

Exit Marie.

Crossfade into scene 4.

End scene.
ACT 1
  SCENE 4 *Photo-Op*

Period: Middle 1970's

Crossfade to MOSS *preparing to take a photograph.* RED, PEACHES, TURTLE, & SNOW, *are posed next to the house.* VEE *interacts with the children throughout much of the scene but does not speak. Only* PEACHES *is aware of her presence.*

RED: Uncle-One gonna get you if he find out you got his camera.

MOSS: He said I could.

PEACHES [*to* MOSS]: Stop lying!

MOSS [*insistent*]: He did.

SNOW [*to* MOSS]: Gimme a dollar and I won't tell.

PEACHES [*to* MOSS]: Any film in there?

MOSS: Nope.

RED [*stern*]: Betta not be.

SNOW [*to* MOSS, *her hand stuck out*]: My silence ...ONLY one dollar.

MOSS [*to* SNOW]: Why I'm gon' pay you if I ain't done nothin' wrong?

PEACHES [*taunting/laughing with* VEE]: If ain't no film in it, then press the button.

MOSS [*to* PEACHES] Shoot Peaches, ...I'm just practicin'.

TURTLE: He scared!

MOSS: Ain't neither.

SNOW: Then do it! I dare you.

[*Everybody poses including* VEE. *The flash goes off /everybody freezes, terrified.* VEE *runs into the house startled.*]

PEACHES [*to* VEE *as she exits*]: Where you goin'....

TURTLE [*to* MOSS]: OOOOOOO I thought you said...

RED [*taking the camera/to* MOSS]: You see them numbers!

MOSS [*scared*]: Yeah ...

RED [*to* MOSS] That's the counter.

MOSS [*clueless*]: So.

RED [*insistent*]: The film counter.

MOSS [*realizing his error*]: But it can't be no film in there cuz....

TURTLE [laughing]: Uncle-One gonna whip you.

MOSS [*to* TURTLE, *threatening*]: Ain't like you ain't in the picture.

SNOW [*to* MOSS *with her hand stuck out*]: Five dollars not to tell.

MOSS [*to* SNOW, *threatening*]: He gone get you too.

SNOW: I'm too cute. 'Sides, once I tell it, you gone be the one he come lookin' for.

RED: Shut up Snow!

PEACHES [*to* RED]: He gone be lookin' for you too, ...You the oldest.

TURTLE [*to* RED *taunting*]: You the one sp'osed to be keepin' us outta trouble.

RED [*to* SNOW, *pulling her aside*]: I'll give you a dollar not to tell.

SNOW [*defiant*]: Five!

TURTLE [*to* RED, *with his hand stuck out*]: Give me something too.

RED [*balling up his fist*]: I'll give you somethin' alright...

PEACHES [*to* RED, *interjecting*]: Don't hit him!

MOSS [*to* RED]: Ain't nobody gonna hit nobody, [*to* SNOW]... and ain't nobody gonna give you five dollars?

SNOW [*probing*]: Three then?

PEACHES [*to* MOSS, *consoling*]: We'll be back home before he develops it anyway.

SNOW [*to* RED]: Okay give me the dollar.

[RED *reaches into his pocket for the dollar,* SNOW *excited takes the dollar and stares at it satisfied.*]

MOSS [*to* SNOW]: I'll tell Uncle-One myself.

[RED *snatches the dollar,* SNOW *stands stunned.*]

TURTLE [*to* MOSS]: That's just stupid . Why you gonna tell on yourself ?

MOSS [*to* RED, *indicating* TURTLE]: Go ahead, ...hit him.

[RED *smiles, and smacks his hand into his fist threatening* TURTLE. TURTLE *takes off running,* RED *gives chase.*]

PEACHES [*chasing after* RED, *calling*]: Don't hit my brother!!

SNOW [*pleading to* MOSS]: Fifty cents?

[RED *catches* TURTLE *wrestles him to the ground and pens down his arms.*]

RED [*threatening to hit* TURTLE]: Say it.

[RED *punches* TURTLE *in his chest.* TURTLE *wails out in pain.*]

TURTLE [*through the tears*]: Uncle!!!!

[TURTLE's *wails provide a sound bridge which merges with the sound of the crying infant. Each child freezes and* PEACHES *is isolated in a beam of bright light. Exit* MOSS *and* TURTLE. RED *and* SNOW *remove [or add] a layer of clothing from* PEACHES *thus transforming her into* BLACK. *Exit* RED *and* SNOW.]

Crossfade into Scene 5.

End Scene.

ACT 1
SCENE 5 *Let's Dance*

Period: Late 1950's

The sound of an infant crying is audible. Lights up on a room cast in dim light and long shadows. A baby is laying in a waist high bassinet. BLACK *peers into the bassinet concerned. She begins to dance about in hopes of quieting the child. The infant's wails lessen. She continues her dance, intent upon comforting her child. What develops is an elaborate dance pleading for quiet, and consolation. Enter* AIN'T VEE*, the infant still crying. She watches for a moment, then turns on the light.*

AIN'T VEE: BLACK!

BLACK [*abruptly ending the dance*]: Huh?!

AIN'T VEE [*half asleep*]: Baby what you doin'?

BLACK [*ashamed*]: Nothin'...

AIN'T VEE: Pick him up.

BLACK: Ma'am?

AIN'T VEE [*consoling*]: It's a pretty dance baby, really it is, but it won't stop him from cryin'.

BLACK: I was just...

AIN'T VEE: I know, but now you gotta pick him up. You check his diaper?

BLACK: No ma'am.

AIN'T VEE: You feed him?

BLACK: No ma'am.

AIN'T VEE: Gas?

BLACK: I don't know.

AIN'T VEE: Is he cold?

BLACK: I don't think so.

AIN'T VEE: Sleepy?

BLACK: If he was sleepy, wouldn't he be asleep?

AIN'T VEE: Not always.

BLACK: Why you askin' me all these questions?

AIN'T VEE [*picking up the baby and quieting him*]: 'Cause I wanna get some rest. ... At my age I don't wanna be tendin' nobody's newborn...Not even yours.

BLACK [*sincere*]: What you want me to do?

AIN'T VEE [*comforting*]: Stop being so scared.

BLACK [*timid*]: I ain't scared.

AIN'T VEE: Mother's first instinct is to go to her child. If you dancin' stead'a tendin' to him, girl that's what scared looks like.

BLACK: Sometimes when I do that, ...dance I mean, he quiets down a lil' bit.

AIN'T VEE: A wet diaper won't dry, cold bones don't warm, a belly won't fill, and gas don't pass, just cause you dance. That chile got needs. Tend to'em, or you won't get no peace, and I won't get no rest.

[AIN'T VEE *returns the baby to the bassinet. The infant resumes crying.*]

[*Displeased*] He's turnin' more shades of red then I thought a body could.

BLACK: But....

AIN'T VEE [*turning to go, interjecting*]: Yeah wipe his butt too. You don't want him getting no diaper rash. Slap a lil' talc on him to keep'em dry...

BLACK [*pleading timid*]: Help.

AIN'T VEE [*turning back, to the infant*]: Don't worry RED, she'll figure it out in due time. 'Till then won't nobody be gettin' any rest I guess.

[*Exit* AIN'T VEE. BLACK *exasperated by the crying drops her head, then reaches out and begins to add* [*or remove*] *a layer of clothes, thereby transforming into an older version of herself.*]

Crossfade into scene 6.
End Scene.

ACT 1
SCENE 6 *Lock With No Key*

Period : Late 1990's

Crossfade up on BLACK *standing by the bassinet. The sound of a child crying is now heard off in the distance.* SNOW *runs into the room.*

SNOW [*pleading*]: Mama pick me up some diapers while you're out.

BLACK [*indicating the crying*]: Why's ya baby cryin' like that? What'd you do, stow her under some pillows?

SNOW [*flippant*]: Diapers mama, will you get me some?

BLACK [annoyed]: You got any money?

SNOW: My check'll be here Friday, can't you spot me 'til then?

BLACK: Can I ? Yes. ...will I?   ...NO.

SNOW: What you want me to do mama, let them "go" all over the house?

BLACK [*upset*]: Your children cut loose on my furniture, you gonna have more problems then how you gonna cover their behinds.

SNOW [*pleading*]: I promise I'll pay you back.

BLACK: My sister gotta bury her son in three days, any little bit I got is gonna go to her.

SNOW: Six dollars ain't gonna bring TURTLE back.

BLACK: It ain't gonna get you no diapers either.

SNOW [*bluffing*]: Maybe I'll steal 'em then, is that what you want?

BLACK [*dismissive*]: Don't waste your one phone call on me.

SNOW: Mama you act like I'm askin' for the world, it's only a few dollars.

BLACK: Come on and get your things outta my room, I gotta lock up.

SNOW: If you lock it, I can't get to the phone.

BLACK [*sarcastic*]: You don't say?

SNOW: What if something happens to one of my kids?

BLACK: You suffocatin' Veronica right now and it don't seem to bother you none.

SNOW: I can hear her, I know she fine.

BLACK [*turning to lock the room*]: Last chance.

SNOW [*pleading*]: Mammmaaaaaa.

BLACK [*stopping, annoyed*]: What?

SNOW [*angry*]: What about RED? ...you know how he is....

BLACK: Don't you be usin' your brother's problems tryin' to work me.

SNOW [*discovering the thought*]: I'll get him and the kids out the house for a little bit after you get back.... give you a break... help you pull things together.

BLACK: You got three babies to watch. That sticky fingered boyfriend of yours be comin' and going like he got a key, I'm barely keepin' the phone on as it is, and your brother ain't hardly got a mind for this world no more...You wanna do me a favor? Take care of yourself and your kids.

[BLACK *pad locks the door to her bedroom.*]

SNOW: You won't forgive yourself if something happens.

BLACK [*to herself*]: I don't hardly forgive myself now.

SNOW [*holding out her hand for the key*]: I'll ONLY use the phone in an emergency, and I'll lock the door when I ain't in there.

BLACK [*on the verge of tears*]: SNOW, I gotta get some groceries, pick up some new shoes, and get us some train tickets to..... [*losing the thought*]

SNOW [*finishing the thought*]: Atlanta ...for the service.

BLACK [*surrendering the key/ turning to exit*]: Stay off the phone and don't let that boy at my things. I can't afford to be replacing anything else.

SNOW [*calling to BLACK as she exits*]: Huggies with leak protection. ...stage three.

Exit BLACK.

Fade to black.

End Scene.
ACT 1
SCENE 7 *Ìwóri Wotúrá*

Period: 1940's

Crossfade up on AIN'T MARIE *and* VEE *seated on the rickety steps of the Mississippi shack.*

AIN'T MARIE: Fetch me a couple of stones.

VEE: How many?

AIN'T MARIE: A hand full.

[VEE *picks up a few rocks from around the yard and delivers them to* AIN'T MARIE, *who then sorts through them and discards the unwanted stones.* MARIE *bends over and scoops up a handful of dirt. Then let's it pass through her fingers and onto the ground. She drops the remaining rocks onto the loose dirt, then studies it intensely.*]

VEE: What?

AIN'T MARIE: Ìwóri Wotúrá

VEE [*looking over the stones, pondering*]: Give me a second, I'll get it...

[*Beat.*]

Crooked wood scatters the flame.   ....A madman scatters his own home.

AIN'T MARIE: This was the sign seen for the father snake and his children. He was told that his children would never agree to come together to ward off an attack.

VEE: If he, the father snake, wants them to band together, he must make an offering:

AIN'T MARIE: Which?

VEE: Sixteen snails, pigeons, poison, and sixteen polished shells....

AIN'T MARIE: But?

VEE: They refuse to sacrifice.

[AIN'T MARIE *picks up a stick and slowly drags patterns in the dirt.*]

AIN'T MARIE [*to* VEE]: No matter how some try to hold down the fallen as examples of what NOT to be, ...The babies keep comin'. Most carried on hips too young and suckled on breasts too new. A tiny badge of shame that grows each day, soon to need new shoes, fresh diapers, and a pressed Easter Sunday outfit.

VEE [*to* AIN'T MARIE]: Somewhere between then and now we stopped being happy that a young old spirit would be rejoining the family. Stopped helpin' them make their transition.

AIN'T MARIE [*to* VEE]: Down deep, the spirits know. So they come in abundance.

VEE: Givin' each of us one more chance to maybe, this time, ...get it right.

AIN'T MARIE [*glancing down at the stones once more*]: Father snake...He refused the sacrifice?

VEE: Yes ma'am.

AIN'T MARIE [*indicating the stones*]: What do you see?

VEE: We are having problems with our children, whether we realize it or not.

End Scene.

Seamless transition to scene 8.

ACT 1
SCENE 8 *Blockbusters, Firebombs, And The Split Atom.*

Period: Early 1980's

Enter UNCLE-ONE, RED, *and* MOSS. AIN'T VEE *circles* UNCLE-ONE *staring longingly into his eyes. The three men sit on the rickety steps of the Mississippi shack unaware of* MARIE *and* VEE.

MARIE [*to* VEE]: Chile, get that man out your mind. This ain't your time to be together.

[UNCLE-ONE *opens a bottle of whiskey, then places three shot glasses on the steps.* MARIE *and* VEE *linger.* VEE *is still captivated.*]

UNCLE-ONE [*pouring the shots*]: Here.

MOSS [*skeptical*]: You gonna let us drink it?

UNCLE-ONE: Yea.

RED [*interjecting*]: But it's whiskey.

UNCLE-ONE [*to* RED]: I know.

VEE [*to* UNCLE-ONE, *longingly*]:   I miss you....

MARIE [*to* VEE, *disappointed*]:   If you can't behave, then we gotta go.

[*Exit* MARIE *dragging* VEE *behind her.*]

RED [*to* UNCLE-ONE]: You got any beer?

[UNCLE-ONE *dismisses* RED's *request, then hands the boys their shots glasses.*]

UNCLE-ONE: Bottoms up.

[RED *and* UNCLE-ONE *drink their shots and wince,* MOSS *smells his shot.*]

RED [*ordering* MOSS]: Do it.

UNCLE-ONE: You ain't gotta if you don't wanna.

RED [*ordering* MOSS]: Do it!

[MOSS *sniffs the shot again and then sips it.*]

UNCLE-ONE: Single grain ain't meant to be sniffed Moss.

[UNCLE-ONE *pours a shot and demonstrates the proper technique.* MOSS *follows suit and coughs.*]

RED [*to* MOSS, *enthusiastic*]:   See, it ain't so bad.

MOSS [*to* UNCLE-ONE, *clearing his throat*]: You like this stuff?

UNCLE-ONE: Drink it enough, you learn to like it.

RED [*to* MOSS]: I can't believe you, we got a Uncle that lets us do whiskey shots and you're whinin'.

MOSS [*defensive*]: I ain't whinin'...

UNCLE-ONE [*correcting* RED]: TODAY I let you do whiskey shots.

RED [*holding out his shot glass, pleased*]: Yes sir, TODAY sir.

UNCLE-ONE [*refilling his glass*]:   You sure about this one Red?

RED [*military fashion*]: Yes sir, I would like another shot please sir. [*He chuckles.*]

UNCLE-ONE [*serious*]:   Not the whiskey.

RED [*souring*]:   How sure do I need to be?

UNCLE-ONE: Ya mama say she don't want you to do it.

RED: I don't need her permission.

MOSS [*interjecting*]: You didn't need her permission to drop outta school neither.

RED [*to* MOSS]: I got a right to do what I want, the way that I want. [To UNCLE-ONE] It ain't like she can tell me what to do for the rest of my life.

UNCLE-ONE: No, probably not.

RED: I'm gonna get a G.E.D. while I' m there.

[*Enter* TURTLE.]

TURTLE: What's a G.E.D.?

MOSS [*taunting* RED]: Good enough diploma.

UNCLE-ONE [*to* TURTLE]: What you doing up?

TURTLE: Can't rest.

RED [*to* TURTLE, *irritated*]: Go back where you come from, ain't nobody ask you here.

TURTLE [*innocent*]: I gotta ask first? A got as much right to be here... [*His volume trailing off into a mumble.*]

UNCLE-ONE [*to* RED]: ... a quitter that can go to class for a few weeks on how to pass a test, ain't really accomplished nothin'. Now let's say that you got up outta bed every day for four years and went to class. Let' s say in all that time you only made C's. You know what that tells people?

RED [*defiant*]: It says I'm ordinary.

UNCLE-ONE: Ordinary... ...or a quitter, which is more impressive?

[*Beat.*]

RED [*to* UNCLE-ONE, *annoyed*]: Can I have another shot?

TURTLE [*to* UNCLE-ONE]: Me too.

MOSS [*to* TURTLE]: No, [*confidential*] ...and be quiet 'for they send you back inside.

UNCLE-ONE [*pouring another*]: It ain't a regular job Red.

[TURTLE *reaches for a shot glass*, MOSS *covers the glass with his palm*. MOSS, RED, *and* UNCLE-ONE *each do their shot, they all wince.*]

RED [*to* UNCLE-ONE]: You tryin' to stop me before I even get goin'.

TURTLE [*to* UNCLE-ONE]: Tell 'em 'bout Uncle Frankie... and I bet he won't wanna join up then.

MOSS: Yea, tell 'notha' one of them stories 'bout how he used to fight with the white...

RED [*interjecting, annoyed*]: Don't nobody wanna hear 'bout that no more. That was a long ass time ago.

TURTLE [*to* RED]: Why you cursin' in front of Uncle-One?

UNCLE-ONE [*sarcastic*]: He's grown now, Red can say what he please.

RED [*to* MOSS *excited*]: Man, I will probably be flying attack helicopters and stuff.

UNCLE-ONE [*to* RED, *dismissive*]: Infantry most likely.

MOSS [*to* RED, *balancing the ideas on each hand*]: Flight school, aeronautics, engineering, ...G.E.D.

RED [*hitting* MOSS]: Shut up!!

MOSS: You'll be catchin' bullets with your chest.

RED [*to* MOSS]: You'll just be catching hell. [*To* UNCLE-ONE] Tell him how the service is a wonderful place to become a man.

UNCLE-ONE [*to* MOSS, *dispassionate*]: The service is a wonderful place to become a man.

RED [*to* MOSS]: I'm gonna see the world, know women from exotic places. I'll have money, and everything... You need to sign up with me.

TURTLE [*to* RED]: For what?

RED [*to* TURTLE, *threatening*]: If you don't be quiet so help me God.

MOSS [*to* RED, *resolute*]: I got a job.

RED [*laughing*]: Making fries? The only thing you learn makin' fries is how to make more fries. Tell'em UNCLE-ONE. Management don't come from side orders.

UNCLE-ONE [*dispassionate, to* MOSS]: Management don't come from side orders.

RED [*to* UNCLE-ONE, *annoyed*]: Why you mockin' me?

UNCLE-ONE: Just want you to hear what you sound like.

[RED *responds in disappointment and frustration.* TURTLE *sniffs an empty shot glass, then sticks his tongue in the up-turned glass.*]

UNCLE-ONE [*to* TURTLE, *laughing*]: Boy, get away from that.

TURTLE: Can I have a taste?

MOSS: No.

TURTLE [*to* MOSS, *pouting*]: I ain't gotta listen to you.

UNCLE-ONE [*to* TURTLE, *amused*]: That's my medicine Turtle, what you got inside you that hurt so bad you need to seek treatment from that bottle?

TURTLE [*to* RED, *discovering the thought*]: Whatever Red and Moss got.

RED [*to* UNCLE-ONE, *half serious*]: Give him some if he want it.

TURTLE [*enthusiastic*]: Yeah gimme some!

UNCLE-ONE [*to* TURTLE, *returning the cap to the bottle*]: I don't think so.

TURTLE [*to* UNCLE-ONE]: I ain't that much younger than Moss. How come he can have it and I can't?

MOSS: You can't do everything that we do. Them years are like dog years.

[MOSS *and* RED *share a laugh at* TURTLE's *expense*.]

RED [*to* MOSS, *cajoling*]: Come on an up with me.

UNCLE-ONE [*dismissing the thought*]: Can't --he's only sixteen.

MOSS: Mama gotta sign off on it.

RED [*mocking* MOSS]: Fat chance of that huh?

UNCLE-ONE [*to* RED]: Enough people in this family been in wars.

RED: It's peacetime Uncle-One.

MOSS [*interjecting*]: War could break out anytime... meanwhile you just gonna be peelin' potatoes.

RED: I'll peel potatoes, scrub floors with a tooth brush, dig ditches, and shovel shit if I have to, just as long as I get be something without everybody tellin' me what I can't do.

UNCLE-ONE [*to* RED]: Uncle Sam's gonna chime in on o'cassion 'bout what you can't do. Count on that.

[*Low rumbling thunder*, TURTLE *searches the sky*.]

RED [*to* MOSS]: The recruiter say I got the college fund goin' for me, and the G.I. bill.... [*to* UNCLE-ONE] Ain't you always takin' 'bout how you got your house with the G.I. bill?

UNCLE-ONE [*to* RED]: ...You gotta be willin' to do what you're told. You gotta be willing not to think.

TURTLE [to UNCLE-ONE]: That won't be hard for him.

[RED *balls up his fist and silently threatens* TURTLE.]

TURTLE [*To* RED, *standing his ground*] Hit me, I dare you.

[MOSS *grabs* TURTLE *by the mouth and moves him away from* RED. TURTLE *struggles*.]

UNCLE-ONE [*to* RED]: You ever ask yourself how it is that we could drop two A-bombs on Japan?

RED [*chuckling*]: They didn't have sense enough to surrender after the first one.

[*Low rumbling thunder*.]

UNCLE-ONE: A good serviceman is in lock step with his orders. The brass decided it was okay to start firebombin' civilians. -- after that it didn't matter much if we did it in steps or all at once. Planes come in at first light and they drop blockbusters. :...High explosives that punch holes in brick and mortar, shatter glass and shake foundations.

[*The thunder transforms into the sound of bombs dropping and exploding. This builds in intensity.*]

UNCLE-ONE: A fire bomb is just that, ...a bomb of fire. When it hits it screams out that it is here to burn. While a blockbuster hits with a flash and then goes dark with dust, a fire-bomb will light up the sky brighter than the sun. And it stays lit. Make you think the sun will never set. --That flame she runs to anything that she can hold on to, and there's plenty 'cause the blockbuster will have opened everything up. And that's when the real dying starts, 'cause them ain't bases that's ablaze, ...them's peoples houses, and businesses, and the people are still inside, some in their beds dreamin' their last dreams.

RED [*detached*]: It's war Uncle-One. That's what people do in war.

UNCLE-ONE: The planes fly off and the people, they come out in their little trucks with their hoses and buckets and they fight the fires, ...and that's when the next wave of firebombs is dropped.

TURTLE [*shocked*]: They burn up the firemen?

UNCLE-ONE: Naturally.

TURTLE: Who'll be left to fight the fire?

MOSS: Nobody.

UNCLE-ONE [*to RED*]: Once you can firebomb civilians, --dropping an A-bomb --second nature. Only three weeks past between the first test of the atom bomb and Hiroshima?

RED: They did start Pearl Harbor, Uncle-One, and you got to bring some to get some.

[*The exploding bombs subtly transform to low rumbling thunder.*]

UNCLE-ONE [*to RED*]: If they make them, it's a safe bet that they plan to use them, and where they lead, you are expected to follow, ...in lock step.

[RED, *irritated by* UNCLE-ONE's, *remarks begins to walk off.*]

RED [*calling back to* MOSS]: Com'on.

[MOSS *silently and reluctantly follows* RED.]

UNCLE-ONE [*to* RED *and* MOSS]: Where you boys going?

RED: We'll be back.

TURTLE [*to RED, pleading*]: Can I come?

RED [*emphatic*]: No.

TURTLE [*whining*]: Why not?

[*Fade down on* UNCLE-ONE *and* TURTLE *at the porch stairs. Low rumbling thunder is heard in the distance.*]

UNCLE-ONE [*calling*]: You two least have sense enough to come in outta the rain.

End Scene.

Crossfade into scene 9.
ACT 1
SCENE 9 *Powder Burns*

Period: Late 1990's

Crossfade up on the basement apartment . The low rumbling thunder provides a sound bridge into the scene. RED *is supine on the floor with* TURTLE *on top of him penning his arms down.*

TURTLE [*to* RED, *threatening*]: Say it!

MOSS [*concerned*]: RED, you okay?

TURTLE [*threatening to hit* RED]: Say it!!

MOSS [*to* RED, *concerned*]: Can you get up?!

[TURTLE *hits* RED *in the chest with force.* RED *recoils from the blow.*]

TURTLE: Next one's gone really hurt!

MOSS [*raising his voice, worried*]: Red, are you okay?

RED [*to* MOSS *shaking off the effect of the punch*]: Yea, just give me a second! [*Reaching up, trying to dislodge* TURTLE] Come on now, let me up.

[TURTLE *hits* RED *in the chest, with greater force.*]

TURTLE [threatening]: I got all day!

RED [*coughing and laughing from the blow*]: Alright, Uncle.....Uncle.

[TURTLE, *deeply satisfied, climbs off of* RED.]

RED [*To* TURTLE, *confidential*]: Damn.... you still hit like a girl!

TURTLE: You still cry like one.

[TURTLE *retreats into the shadows.* MOSS *paces holding an unopened beer can in his hand.*]

MOSS [*to* RED, *concerned*]: What the hell was that? I thought you were having a heart attack, or a stroke or something.

RED [*dusting himself off, amused*]: It's good to know that if I am ever really stroking out, you'll stand over me and scream like a bitch?

RED gets out another beer from the cooler.

MOSS [*serious*]: That ain't funny.

RED: I ain't heard nobody sound that scared since Rodney Cooper shot himself in the eye with one of them top rifles we used to make.

MOSS: How long you been like this?

RED [*clicking the cap on his beer*]: Remember when we were little they had the pull off kind?

MOSS: You been to see a doctor?

TURTLE [*laughing from the shadows*]: He don't need no doctor..

RED [*opening the beer and taking a large gulp*]: It's just a little anxiety attack. They come and go.

MOSS [*unconvinced*]: Yeah? ...Okay.

RED [*reflective*]: A clothes pin...The spring action kind... A hunk of two by four, some rubber bands, and a nail. ...Double barrel were the best. [Reliving the moment] You snap off them two cap loops, ...Slide'em into the rubber bands, then pull each one back taunt, and ever so gently clasp'em with the clothes pins. [*Aiming and firing*] Pow.....Pow...

MOSS [*remembering fondly*]: Rodney got one stitch. ...One damn stitch.

RED: Cut wasn't even deep, but it bled like it was never gonna stop.

MOSS: Mrs. Cooper should'a just held the cut closed for a few minutes and he would'a been fine.

RED [*to* MOSS]: You, Rodney, [*to* TURTLE] and Turtle ...all scream like sissies.

TURTLE [*teasing, to* RED]: Don't make me get Uncle Frankie....

RED [*to* TURTLE, *confidential*]: Get him then, ...I ain't afraid no more.

MOSS: The next day.... his mama was not happy to see us.

RED [*more to* TURTLE *then to* MOSS]: Ain't nobody ever been happy to see us?

TURTLE [*comforting*]: I know...

MOSS [*to* RED]: She thought we were thugs corruptin' her sweet little boy... We all had toy guns but... [*imitating her*] She couldn't abide by symbols of violence. [*Beat.*]

 ...What ever happened to him?

RED [*matter of factly*]: The joint.

MOSS [*surprised*]: You kiddin'.

RED: Just dumb luck... Somebody tried to take his leather jacket over on a hundred and nineteenth. He pulled out a gun, fired it at the ground, and the ricochet caught one of 'em in the head.

MOSS [*disbelief*]: Damn.

RED: Yea well, shit happens. You gotta bring some to get some.

MOSS: You been over to see his mama?

RED [*mildly amused*]: ...Mrs. Cooper? ...No Moss I have not darkened her door.

MOSS: Why not?

RED [*to MOSS*]: I have seen that look too many times, from too many people. I don't need it from her.

MOSS: She might be glad to see you, ...to know that you thinkin' 'bout her and Rodney.

RED: Ain't nobody ever been happy to see me?

MOSS [*half-sincere*]: I am.

RED [*chuckling*]: You can't hardly sit down, and that beer has got to be 98 point 6 by now.

MOSS [*looking at the beer*]: I ain't never been much with liquor.

RED: You remember your first girlfriend? I don't mean the little girls you was sniffing 'round on Magnolia, but your first real girlfriend? The girl you was with when you first got some sense of yourself. Some sense of what you could be?

MOSS [*smiling*]: Brenda.

RED: You remember the first time she brought you home?

MOSS [*smiling brighter*]: Yea...

RED: Her daddy. [MOSS' *smile abruptly turns*] Wasn't happy to see you was he?

MOSS [*uncomfortable*]: Naw, not really.

RED: Did he smile? Ever look at you and see the potential in you?

MOSS: No.

RED: He had his mind made up already ...Before you could extend your firmest grip to his rough hand he knew.   ...he was imaginin' the day when his little girl would wise up and move on to someone better.

MOSS: I suppose.

RED: They still look at me that way. ...that Mrs. Cynthia Cooper look, comin' right back at me. Bleeding through forced smiles and polite nods...

MOSS: They who?

RED: All of you.

TURTLE [*to* RED & MOSS]: The same way most of you look at us.

RED [*to* MOSS]: My spirit ain't never been fully connected to my body. ...and lately I feel like I'm drifting farther away from it.

MOSS [cracking open the beer, unsettled]: ...Yea.

[MOSS *takes a gulp of beer.*]

Low rumbling thunder is heard.

Transition into scene 10.

End Scene.
ACT 1
SCENE 10   *Help with the chores*

Period: Late 1950's

Lights up on AIN'T VEE *and* BLACK *carrying out the laundry. It is sunrise. Each takes an end of the clothes line and ties it off on the post.*

AIN'T VEE: Reach over there and get the pail full of clothes pins.

[BLACK *retrieves the pins and examines them.*]

AIN'T VEE [*continued*]: Now ain't this better than leavin' the clothes out in the rain?

BLACK: They still wet. -- they woulda been dry if we'd left 'em, then we could still be sleepin'.

[BLACK *picks up each article of clothing shakes it hard once, and then hands it to* AIN'T VEE, *who pins it to the line. This action continues throughout the scene.*]

AIN'T VEE: Your babies woulda had us up anyway.... Just be glad that pale little daughter of yours ain't stir your Uncle, ...You know how he get when he don't feel rested.

BLACK: Like a grouch.

AIN'T VEE: Mind what you say now. Red and Snow flake ease him, just be grateful for that.

BLACK [*holding a damaged clothes pin*]: These look 'bout ready to be tossed out.

AIN'T VEE: They got some life left in'em yet.

BLACK [*examining and addressing the clothes pin*]: ...Mr. clothes pin my family thanks you for your years of dutiful service.   You are now free to go on to your great reward.

AIN'T VEE: You should show as much reverence for us as you do that clothes pin.

BLACK [*joking*]: I love you at least as much as I do Mr. Clothes Pin. [Beat] [To AIN'T VEE] Do you love me?

AIN'T VEE [*without hesitation*]: Certainly.

BLACK [*tentative*]: You still angry?

AIN'T VEE [*dismissive*]: What's past is past. A few heated words ought not keep you from comin' down here.

BLACK: You ever think about leavin' this place?

[BLACK *hands* VEE *a wet shirt.*]

AIN'T VEE [*drawing back her hand*]: That shirt will be hangin'out here for a week before it dries.

BLACK [*wringing the shirt*]: Ain't Marie didn't leave either did she?

[*Enter* MARIE, *she joins* BLACK *and* AIN'T VEE *in hanging laundry.*]

AIN'T MARIE [*to* AIN'T VEE]: You touch water to ground and call us down?

AIN'T VEE [*to* Marie, *displeased*]: She don't know...

BLACK [*to* AIN'T VEE]: Know what?

AIN'T VEE [*to* BLACK *irritated*]: ...You have no idea what you set in motion.

BLACK [*defensive*]: It's just a question.

AIN'T MARIE [*to* BLACK]: I stayed. [*Indicating* AIN'T VEE] Who you think looked after this one after her Mama pass?

AIN'T VEE [*to* BLACK, *apologetic*] Just be more careful what you say okay?

AIN'T MARIE [*to* AIN'T VEE]: If you don't teach her, you got no right to be mad for what she say?

AIN'T VEE [*to* Marie, *confidential*]: She ain't ready... May never be!

BLACK [*confused*]: What did I say?

AIN'T VEE [*holding out her hand*]: Just hand me the shirt baby.

AIN'T MARIE [*coaxing, to* VEE]: Tell her why you won't leave.

AIN'T VEE [*to* Marie]: ...I like where I am. [To BLACK] Why do I need to go someplace else?

AIN'T MARIE [*whispering to* BLACK]: Progress.

BLACK: Progress.

AIN'T VEE [*more to* MARIE *than to* BLACK]: What you know 'bout progress?

BLACK: There are places where people don't have to wash clothes by hand.

AIN'T VEE: And that's progress?

BLACK: Ain't it?

AIN'T VEE [*to* BLACK]: Your idea of progress sounds a lot like your great-grandmothers.

BLACK [*picking up another wet shirt*]: Why?

AIN'T VEE: We was walked over here from South Carolina.   ..everybody 'cept for my grandma Antoinette who had other aspirations. She left South Carolina for Philadelphia. Folk say she was trying to pass.

[BLACK *wrings out the shirt and the water seeps into the ground.*]

BLACK: Antoinette? Really?

AIN'T VEE [*to* BLACK]: Baby you gotta know your power. You just can't be callin' on people like that.

AIN'T MARIE [*to* VEE *joyful*]: Oh the more the merrier.

[*Enter* ANTOINETTE *she begins to hang laundry with the other women.*]

ANTOINETTE [*to* BLACK]: Folks think being able to pass means living easy. But for everything you get, you gotta give something up. ...And I had to give up dark men all together. Truth is they where my favorites. Thick lips that cradle you like you nestled in a bed a cotton. Skin so pretty it move you to tears. [*To* MARIE] White fella, ...he white everywhere. It's quite a fright seein' ya most favorite parts bleached pale, 'stead'a kissed by the sun.

[MARIE *and* ANTOINETTE *laugh.*]

AIN'T VEE [*to* ANTOINETTE *and* MARIE]: Quit that cackling.

BLACK: I wasn't...

ANTOINETTE [*discovering* BLACK *does not sense her presence*]: You can't see yet?

AIN'T MARIE [*to* ANTOINETTE]: Not even a peek..

ANTOINETTE [*to* BLACK]: You got me wasting a good tale.

AIN'T VEE [*to* BLACK/ANTOINETTE *growing irritated*]: My grandmother found the price of progress too high and soon made her way back to South Carolina.   ...but we was gone.

ANTOINETTE [*dismissive, to* MARIE]: We wasn't separated all that long.

AIN'T MARIE [*to* ANTOINETTE]: Long enough, that we missed you...

AIN'T VEE [*to* ANTOINETTE, *accusatory/confidential*]: Maybe somebody needs to stay put to hold things togetha'.

ANTOINETTE [*to* BLACK] Ain't nothing wrong with seekin' a little adventure and a better way in this world.

BLACK [*to* VEE]: So even if everybody left here, you would still stay?

AIN'T VEE [*to* MARIE *and* ANTOINETTE]: That's the problem, everybody ain't left, and what's more they think they can drop in whenever the mood strikes them.

AIN'T MARIE [*to* AIN'T VEE]: We don't come unless we asked..

AIN'T VEE [*to* MARIE]: I ain't ask.

BLACK [*to* AIN'T VEE]: Ask what?

AIN'T MARIE [*indicating* BLACK]: Sugar, you ask, she ask, it don't make no nevermind.

ANTOINETTE [*to* VEE]: We can't hardly go no place else you ask us here so much.

AIN'T VEE [*to* BLACK]: To be the one keep this place for the rest.

AIN'T MARIE [*to* VEE, *holding up pants*]: This is a heap of laundry to hang. [*Smelling them*] ...And sour. VEE, you need to hang this right away, you can't just let it sit...

ANTOINETTE [*to* AIN'T VEE, *indicating* BLACK]: Child got two kids and ain't even eighteen. She don't have no man. And she don't know the hush. When you gonna teach her better?

AIN'T MARIE [*to* VEE]: Ain't I show you a better way?

AIN'T VEE [*to* ANTOINETTE, *confidential*]: What you want me to do? ...She don't believe in it, so she don't seek it. If she don't seek it, she won't see it.

ANTOINETTE [*to* VEE]: Get her to ask.

AIN'T VEE [*to* ANTOINETTE, *confidential*]: Ain't nobody have to GET me to ask.

AIN'T MARIE [*to* VEE]: When it's done right, you could live forty or fifty years believin' that it was really your idea.

BLACK [*to* VEE]: You act like its punishment.

AIN'T VEE [*distracted*]: What?

BLACK: Being here.

AIN'T VEE: Being part time anyplace is punishment.

ANTOINETTE [*to* VEE]: Then quit being part time.

BLACK [*to* AIN'T VEE, *sensing that something is amiss/looking around*]: You okay?

AIN'T VEE [*to* BLACK]: I'm fine.

BLACK: You wanna go in the house and I'll get you a little something?

AIN'T VEE [*picking up another item*]: Let's just finish with the laundry.

BLACK [*concerned*]: You need some help around here... or at least a little company. Three kids and a grumpy old man ain't....

AIN'T VEE [*looking to* ANTOINETTE *and* MARIE]: Baby, I got plenty of company... More than I need most days.

[ANTOINETTE & BLACK *peel off a layer of clothing from* AIN'T VEE *returning the scene to the 1940's*.]

Exit ANTOINETTE & BLACK.

End Scene.

Seamless transition to scene 11.

ACT 1
SCENE 11 *Òtúrúpòn-Sé*

Period 1940's

The radio streams in a 1940's tune. MARIE and VEE begin taking down the wall of clothes that hang from the clothes line.

AIN'T MARIE: They dry on that side?

VEE: Pretty much.

AIN'T MARIE: Then put them in the basket and come here.

VEE [*putting down the clothes*]: Ma'am.

AIN'T MARIE: Fetch me a couple of stones.

VEE: Okay?

[VEE *reaches into her pocket an pulls out a cloth with the rocks wrapped inside.*]

VEE [*continued*]: Here.

AIN'T MARIE [*pleased*]: Very nice.

[MARIE *scoops up a handful of dirt. She lets the dirt pass through her fingers and onto the ground. She drops the rocks onto the fresh dirt then studies it intensely.*]

VEE: Òtúrúpòn-Sé?

AIN'T MARIE: Òtúrúpòn-Sé.

VEE [*pondering*]: This world is not sweet enough to live in forever. Only a child believes otherwise.

AIN'T MARIE: A child eats what he earns, though the father must first earn what the child is to eat.

VEE: The wisest of the wise obey and sacrifice.

AIN'T MARIE: We were told to make sacrifice on our own behalf ....but only a few did as asked.

VEE: Òtúrúpòn-Sé is seen in the pepper tree, which had a new baby. It is said that both the mother and baby would suffer from want. They did not sacrifice and now each burns.

AIN'T MARIE: Nothing worth having comes without sacrifice. Only the young believe otherwise.

[AIN'T MARIE *reaches down she picks up the stones one by one and returns them to the wrapping. She takes a stick and scatters the dirt, then looks upon VEE with pride.*]

AIN'T MARIE [*continued*] Very, nice. [*Indicating the clothes & the line*] I'll take care of the rest of these. You go on and play.

[RED, SNOW, TURTLE, MOSS, *and* PEACHES *run in and sit in a semi-circle.*]

VEE: Ain't my game Ain't Marie -- them's my grand-babies at play.

AIN'T MARIE: Them's ya sister's grand-kids.

VEE: They mine too.

AIN'T MARIE: Don't you wanna play with them?

VEE: Better not... we gotta finish the wash, ...sides I think they okay for now.

End of Scene.

Seamless transition into Act 1 Scene 12.
ACT 1
SCENE 12 *Lisa, Michelle, Antoinette, Rosemary, Veronica, Marie, Watson*

Period: Middle 1970's

Crossfade up on the children engaged in the name game ritual. Marie and VEE continue to take down the laundry. Eventually exiting when it is done.

SNOW: Lisa.

RED: Michelle.

MOSS: Antoinette.

TURTLE: Rosemary.

RED: Veronica.

PEACHES: Marie.

SNOW: Watson.

PEACHES [*to the other kids*]: Word is we part French.

TURTLE: And Indian...

VEE [*to the kids*]: Family split so many ways, we could claim just 'bout anything we want.

AIN'T MARIE [*to VEE, scolding*]: You said you didn't wanna play.

VEE: But they callin' my name...

AIN'T MARIE: They callin' a lot of us, but that don't mean we rush in.

PEACHES: I know for a fact that we got Choctaw,

MOSS: Black Creek,

VEE [*to MARIE*]: When they call ain't we supposed to answer.

SNOW: Turtle Clan.

AIN'T MARIE [*to* VEE]: Not always.

MOSS: Irish.

RED: English.

PEACHES: African by way of Senegal,

SNOW: That's how we got the French.

VEE [*calling out*]: Nigerian too!

TURTLE: And Nigerian.

AIN'T MARIE [*to* VEE, *scolding*]: Hush now...

PEACHES: Got some Caribbean islander though nobody seams to know exactly which island, and any other variety of hodge-podge Geechy line you care to mention.

TURTLE: Lisa

RED: Michelle

MOSS: Antoinette.

SNOW: Rosemary.

RED: Veronica.

PEACHES: Marie.

SNOW: Watson.

VEE [*to* MARIE, *resolute*]: I changed my mind, -- I wanna play.

AIN'T MARIE [*to* VEE]: Just remember which place is yours and which you visit. And never visit too long.

PEACHES [*to the kids*]: Watson is my family name. I get it from my daddy and he from his, and he from the man what raised him. [*To* MOSS *indicating he should start the cascade of names*] The rest...

MOSS: Lisa.

TURTLE: Michelle.

RED: Antoinette.

SNOW: Rosemary.

MOSS: Veronica.

SNOW: ... and Marie.

PEACHES: Them names come through my mother. And to her they come through women speaking in a hush. Each passin' on some of what they remember. And for some them names is there only connection.

VEE [*to the others scolding*]: Tell it right.

TURTLE: I am!

RED [*to* TURTLE]: You're what?

TURTLE [*to* RED]: Tellin' it right.

PEACHES [*to* TURTLE, *confidential*]: Just cause you hear'em, don't mean you gotta answer.

AIN'T MARIE [*to* VEE, *admonishing*]: You see the child can hear you, so be quiet.

PEACHES [*to* TURTLE, *encouraging*]: Go on and say your part.

TURTLE [*more to* VEE *than the children*]: My sister says we got us a slave ship flowin' through our veins.

PEACHES [*to* RED]: All them people from all them places, cramped up inside each and every one of us.

TURTLE [*to the kids*]: None of 'em hardly speak the same language. They speak, African...

SNOW: Creole.

RED: Indian.

PEACHES: French, English, Irish.

TURTLE: Geechy, Boukra Swamp.

MOSS: Patwa and Pigeon.

PEACHES: And they all tryin' to speak through me.

VEE [*to* MARIE, *confidential*]: Black turned them stories all inside out. I ain't teach them all that...

AIN'T MARIE [*to* VEE]: You all up in there too. Sides, who taught Black?

VEE [*to* MARIE]: Peaches is the only one really trying to get it, Black never cared one way or the other.

[*The delivery of the names overlap so as to create a cascade of names.*]

PEACHES [*rolling the names from his tongue lightning fast*]: Lisa, Michelle, Antoinette, Rosemary, Veronica, Marie, Watson

MOSS, SNOW, & TURTLE [*lightning fast*]: Lisa, Michelle, Antoinette, Rosemary, Veronica, Marie, Watson

RED [*stumbling through*]: Lisa, Marie, Michelle, Rosemary, Veronica, Antoinette, Watson.

SNOW [*to* RED, *scolding*]: Wrong!

RED [*surrendering*]: There's too many of them, I can't keep them straight.

TURTLE [*taunting*]: It's easy.   ...you just give up all the time.

RED [*hitting him in the arm*]: Shut up.

[VEE *and* MARIE *finish taking down the clothes and the clothes line.*]

AIN'T MARIE [*to* VEE]: Teach it right... you got no idea what you set in motion.

[MARIE *turns to exit.*]

VEE [*to* Marie]: Can't we just stay on for another minute or two.

AIN'T MARIE: You can't spend every minute of the day at play with spirits.

[*Exit* AIN'T MARIE *forcing* AIN'T VEE *to leave.* PEACHES *senses their departure.*]

PEACHES: One at a time.

PEACHES *points to* MOSS *as if testing him.*

MOSS: Lisa...

[PEACHES *points to* SNOW *indicating it's her turn.*]

SNOW [*to* PEACHES]: Our great aunt, that you was named after.

[PEACHES *points to* TURTLE *indicating it's his turn.*]

TURTLE: Michelle.

[PEACHES *points to* RED *indicating it's his turn.*]

RED: That's mama.

TURTLE [*interjecting/teasing*]: ... Ain't Black, ...as in black magic....

[SNOW *bristles at the notion.*]

RED [*to* TURTLE *balling up his fist, threatening*]: As in black yo' eye!

MOSS: She's our great-great grandma's sister.

PEACHES [*to* MOSS, *correcting*]: Only one great.

MOSS: Our great-grandma's sister.

[PEACHES *points to* RED *indicating it's his turn.*]

RED: Antoinette.

[PEACHES *points to* TURTLE *indicating it's his turn.*]

TURTLE: My mama and my great-great grandma.

SNOW [*interjecting*]: The one that passed for white.

[PEACHES *points to* MOSS *indicating it's her turn.*]

MOSS: Rosemary.

[PEACHES *points to* TURTLE *indicating it's his turn.*]

TURTLE: Slave woman, Antoinette's mother.... she the one walk here all the way from South Carolina.

SNOW: No she ain't, Rosemary was dead by the time they walked from South Carolina.

MOSS: Rosemary is the one that dropped the baby in the middle of the cane ain't she?

RED: Yea... I think.

PEACHES [*to* MOSS]: And she was from one of them Caribbean Islands. Either Jamaica or St. Thomas or something like that.

TURTLE [to MOSS]: What else?

MOSS *looks to* RED *for the answer.*

RED [*annoyed*]: Don't look at me.

PEACHES: Rosemary was our great-great-great-grandmother who started it all. Slave woman from Senegal.

TURTLE: Nigeria!

PEACHES: Senegal!

TURTLE [*emphatic*]: Nigeria!!

MOSS: Grandma's name was Rosemary too...

SNOW: Mine too...

TURTLE [*antagonizing* SNOW]: We know your name, just don't nobody care.

PEACHES: Next!

[PEACHES *points to* SNOW *indicating it's her turn.*]

SNOW: Veronica.

TURTLE: Ain't Vee?

RED: Yea, our great- Ain't Vee who was named after our great grandmother.

PEACHES:...who was herself a conjure woman.

SNOW [*to* RED]: She helped take care of mama when she was pregnant with you.

RED [*to* SNOW]: Like she lets me forget it.

TURTLE [*to* SNOW *teasing*]: Conjure woman raise your mama. ...That makes her a conjure woman too.

SNOW [*hitting* TURTLE]: Do not!
TURTLE [*to* SNOW]: You ain't gotta hit me just cause yo' mama's a witch.

SNOW [*angry, trying to hit* TURTLE *again*]: Is not!

TURTLE [*taunting*]: Yo' supposed to be proud.

PEACHES [*to* SNOW & TURTLE]: Quit it.

[PEACHES *points to* RED *indicating it's his turn.*]

RED: I forget.

TURTLE [*interjecting*]: Marie

MOSS [*to* RED]: ...My mama.   You forgot my mama?!

RED: This game is stupid!

PEACHES: Not just your mama Moss, -- Marie is also THE Conjure woman!

SNOW: What do you mean THE Conjure woman?

MOSS [*laughing to* PEACHES]: The woman that taught your mama?

PEACHES [*to* MOSS]: Why you gotta be so silly?

TURTLE: Marie taught Vee, and Vee taught Black...

PEACHES: VEE taught all the sisters... She just didn't teach them all the same.

SNOW [*to* PEACHES, *angry*]: Ain't Vee ain't no conjure woman!

TURTLE [*taunting*]: Is too!   And she taught all y'all mama's to be witch sisters!

SNOW: Did not!!

TURTLE [*emphatic*]: Did too.

SNOW [*to* TURTLE *angry*]: Say that again and I'm gonna fat yo' lip.

TURTLE: Of the three, my mama the only one ain't no witch.

PEACHES [*to* TURTLE, *cautioning*]: Conjure woman, ...not witch.

TURTLE: Fine.

PEACHES: Lisa, Michelle, Antoinette, Rosemary, Veronica, Marie, Watson. I got a name as long as a city block.

nd my brother like   *ter them, pleading*] Come on ya'll. ...Let's tell it again,

est single grain... I

rom now, that's when

on the stairs. UNCLE-ONE *spots* RED *and* MOSS

e a while?

t.

happy. In time, ...you
ow I need to mind my

urself.

out of it okay.

our tour will be over,
hen your life just be

o different.
ied 'bout
even ove

orty

UNC hol. You'll be on ya knees, and it won't be for worship.

RED on't you worry.

MOSS [e]: I ain't hardly touched it.

UNCLE RED]: Got one cause he got one huh?

RED [de ake him do nothin'.

UNCLE-O er was a lot like the two of you.

TURTLE: U

MOSS: Twins

TURTLE: Identical?

UNCLE-ONE: No, but we favored much.

RED: How we supposed to be like you and your dead brother?

UNCLE-ONE [*to* RED, *taken aback*]: I do somethin' to you make you disrespect me that?

RED [*insincere*]: No sir.

UNCLE-ONE: We all supposed to be men here tonight ain't we? I got some of the fir try to tell what I know of your days ahead and you....

MOSS: He didn't mean nothin' by it Uncle-One really.

UNCLE-ONE [*to* RED, *raising the bottle*]: Have another. [*Pouring*] Five, ten years I get to be the mo-fuckers and some-bitches.

RED & MOSS [*Surprised*]: What?

[TURTLE *laughs. Low rumbling thunder is heard.*]

UNCLE-ONE [*to* RED]: Nights like this will haunt you more than they'll make you won't hardly speak ...maybe you mumble some hateful shit under your breath 'bout h own business and leave you the fuck alone. ...right?

RED [*cold*]: Why you trippin'? Ain't nobody steppin' all over what you want for yo

UNCLE-ONE [*to* RED]: Funny thing about the service. You turn around twice and y your pockets will be empty, and you start talkin' 'bout being a lifer. [*Remorseful*] T cut short.

RED [*resolute*]: I'm going Uncle-one, and you can't talk me out of it.

UNCLE-ONE: Fine. Some shit you just gotta learn the hard way.... Frankie wasn't n so he up'ed. We figured it would be an easy way to get away from here. Wasn't wor cause they wasn't lettin' niggah's no where near the fightin'... Rope, that they got ....

RED [*frustrated*]: I don't wanna hear 'bout no mistakes you and your brother made

UNCLE-ONE [*grabbing* RED *by the collar*]: That's my flesh and blood boy! Any my lips to speaks on him....

MOSS [*interjecting /trying to part the men*]: Come on now Uncle, everybody's had

[UNCLE-ONE, *while holding* RED *in one hand, pushes* MOSS *to the ground with th*

UNCLE-ONE [*to* RED]: Know your place. You won't last ten minutes otherwise. Frankie dead. ...Sitting up underneath them French women....

RED [*demanding, trying to break free*]: Let me go!

UNCLE-ONE: He couldn't be still long enough to listen either.

MOSS [*pleading trying again to part them*]: Come on let him go!

UNCLE-ONE [*to* RED]: What kinda heart you got boy? 'Cause where you goin' ya mama can't help you.

RED [*to* UNCLE-ONE, *angry*]: Hit me then!!

[UNCLE-ONE, *balling up his fist and drawing back.*]

RED [*continued*] [*to* UNCLE-ONE, *angry*]: Do it!! Cause once you knock me down I'll bounce right back up.

UNCLE-ONE: I been waitin' seventeen years for you to do that.

TURTLE [*pleading to* UNCLE-ONE]: Don't hit my cousin.

[UNCLE-ONE, *suddenly aware of* TURTLE's *presence, releases* RED]

UNCLE-ONE [*to* RED, *simmering*]: Always be certain of your footing.

[*Beat.*]

TURTLE [*to* RED, *distraught*]: Why you gotta go?

RED [*indicating* UNCLE-ONE]: 'Cause of shit like that!

MOSS [*to* RED, *confidential*]: You overstepped. Just say you sorry ...

[*Beat.*]

RED [*to* UNCLE-ONE]: Is Frankie's memory more important than your flesh and blood?

UNCLE-ONE [*to* RED]: He's still my flesh and blood.

RED [*insistent*]: I'm alive... I'm right here.

UNCLE-ONE: You spend a lifetime with someone... You eat every meal with them. Every step I take he be right...

UNCLE-ONE [*continued*]: there wedging his soul under mine so I can't hardly feel the ground. Then he's gone and don't nobody mourn his loss. Smart ass little boys wanna tell me I can't speak on him. Don't nobody wanna break bread, see that he well fed. What he supposed to do if he ain't got us to be there for him. We're lost.... and don't nobody care.

MOSS [*to* UNCLE-ONE]: Ain't Vee over there with him ain't she?

UNCLE-ONE: ... she got so many babies to look after, ... I know she fed.

TURTLE: Uncle Frankie ain't got that?

RED [*to* UNCLE-ONE]: I'm dying a little bit everyday and ain't nobody mourin' me.

MOSS: Everybody dies a little bit each day.

RED: No they don't! Most folk livin' one day and then dead the next. Their dying comes all at once.

Heart attack... boom! Mack truck ....boom!...Lights out . [To Uncle One] My life, ...It just leaks away at the seems... And you don't care.

UNCLE-ONE [*disgusted, to* RED]: Boy, you just marking time, waiting for the real madness to begin.

RED: Now you gonna tell me that what I feel ain't real?

UNCLE-ONE: Some things you fall into... and only discover their value after the fact. It don't make'em less real... Dumb luck is as real as anything else I suppose.

MOSS [*to himself*]: Being stuck here is dumb, but it ain't lucky.

UNCLE-ONE: Everything happens for a reason.... Even Single grain whiskey.

[UNCLE-ONE *looks into his empty glass, pours, then downs another shot.* UNCLE-ONE *then pours* RED *another shot.*]

MOSS [*to* RED & UNCLE-ONE]: Don't you think it's time the we push back from the table?

UNCLE-ONE: Somebody had to drink the first whiskey before there was ever such a thing as whiskey. Somebody had to decide to gulp down some dingy water that was left to sit for days, weeks even, with old moldy grain floating in it.   ...then he boiled down the water to make the potion stronger. Now dumb luck is what saved his life... Gave us this sweet ambrosia. Without it, I'd be toasting you with a coke-a-cola.

[UNCLE-ONE *fills two shot glasses. He hands one to* MOSS *then hesitates for a moment.*]

UNCLE-ONE [*continued*] [*Handing* TURTLE *the shot glass*]: Here boy.

TURTLE [*smiling with satisfaction*]: Yeeeah

UNCLE-ONE [*toasting*]: To the man who drank dingy water and my great nephew who joined the Army. Bottoms up.

[UNCLE-ONE *drinks from the bottle.* MOSS, TURTLE, *and* RED, *drink from their glasses. They all wince.* TURTLE *yells in disgust. Low rumbling thunder is heard in the distance.*]

Fade to black.

The sound of rain pours in.

End scene.

End Act I
ACT 2
SCENE 1 *A Bug's Life*

Period: Middle 1940's

Lights up on Marie and VEE at the front stairs of the Mississippi shack.

AIN'T MARIE: Some stories need a hundred years or more to be told propa'. They say yo' great-great-grandmother Rosemary was working cane, standing next to her brother when Bug came?
VEE: Bug ?

AIN'T MARIE: Antoinette.

[*Crossfade up on two characters in field clothes circa 1860's. A woman is crouched over in the field giving birth. Her brother looms over her as she labors.*]

BROTHER: C'mon Rosemary you can't very well drop the baby right'here.

ROSEMARY: I can't have her no-place where she can be seen by...

BROTHER [*interjecting*]: She?

ROSEMARY: For certain.

BROTHER: How you know?

ROSEMARY: She tell me when I was a lil'un that she'd see me on this day.

BROTHER: Did she tell ya that if you ain't careful you'll lose ya baby and ya self.

ROSEMARY: We fine!

BROTHER: But for how long, 'fore the life drain right out cha'. Trust me Rosemary, my love ain't enough to hold ya in this place. If we could just find one of the women to...

ROSEMARY: If you so worry, then leave me be.

[*Fade up on MARIE and VEE, their dialog is delivered as ROSEMARY and her brother deliver the baby. The baby is symbolized in the body of a spirit who re-enters the world as a child. This dynamic is conveyed through stylized movement between the spirit/ANTOINETTE, ROSEMARY, and her brother. Other Spirits aid in the delivery.*]

AIN'T MARIE [*to VEE*]: Most believe that the work, is in the labor. Truth is your body knows what to do, and if you let it, it will do it's job. The pain will peak but the body will accommodate. It's the moments afterward which trouble a soul. All your work is done, but ya baby ain't with you yet? How long it take befor' the first breath is drawn? The centuries that pass while you wait for ya baby to pull it in. Story goes that Rosemary stop breathin' while she watched. That she held her breath waitin' for first breath from Bug. She turn blue to match her hue and then her air give out. In a rush, she let wail to the heavens and start to will the life into'er. Callin' on every good deed, and sweet thought, every kind word and soft heart. She call on God, and spirits alike, she call on love, and her darkest fright. Haints from heaven and down below, all with a will to draw that breath slow.

VEE [*concerned*]: She breathe it in right?

AIN'T MARIE: Three minutes she wait for one breath. Three minutes of faith, balanced against death. ROSEMARY will it so... And Bug pull it in slow and strong. Your great grandmother there in the cane. She conjure the greatest conjure there is...... She conjure life.

VEE: Bug?

AIN'T MARIE: All of us.

Fade to BLACK.

End Scene.

ACT 2
SCENE 2 *Six Inches, Four Times.*

Period: Late 1980's

Lights up on BLACK & SNOW tidying the basement apartment. Enter TURTLE from atop the stairs.

TURTLE [*whispering*]: Quiet now he's at the front door with Uncle-One.

UNCLE-ONE [*off-stage to* RED]: I don't know where your mama could be.

RED [*off-stage, to* UNCLE-ONE] She said she'd be here when I got back.

BLACK [*calling to* RED]: I'm down here baby.

[*Enter* RED *and* UNCLE-ONE. RED *is immaculately dressed in an Army dress uniform.*]

ALL: Surprise!!

UNCLE-ONE [*disappointed*]: It woulda been a surprise if your mama coulda kept her mouth shut.

SNOW [*to* RED, *embracing/teasing*]: Welcome home red neck.

BLACK [*dusting herself*]: We just wanted a place for you that was suited to your needs.

RED: Mama you didn't have to....

UNCLE-ONE [*interjecting, disapproving*]: Don't no grown man need to be movin' into his mama's basement. When I was a young fella that kinda nonsense...

BLACK [*to* UNCLE-ONE, *scolding*] Hush up now... [*to* RED] Come here and let mama look at you.

RED [*to* BLACK, *stepping over smiling*]: Give me a hug. [*They embrace*] I missed you mama.

BLACK [*proud*]: I missed you too, Corporal Stephen Dobson.

RED [*to* BLACK]: It's only two stripes, don't make a big deal outta it.

UNCLE-ONE: Thought you was gonna be a Lifer?

RED: It's a job, ...I got up every mornin' and at the end of the month I got a check...

UNCLE-ONE [*to* RED]: You sure you alright boy?

RED [*uneasy*]: As well as can be expected.

BLACK [*comforting*]: Everything looks better after a little home cookin' and a night in your own bed.

TURTLE [*to* RED]: Moss said he tried, but he couldn't get a flight in from D.C.

SNOW [*to* RED, *consoling*] He woulda been here if he could have.

RED [*unconvinced*]: Yea. --I bet.

SNOW: It's his first big assignment.

UNCLE-ONE [*to* RED]: He can't just pick up and run on a whim. He's got responsibilities.

RED [*shaking off his disappointment, to* TURTLE]: So lil'man how you doing?

TURTLE: I'm good, -- I'm in Atlanta now.

RED: So I hear.

BLACK [*teasing*]: He say it's for school, but his mama and me think he's got him a woman down there.

SNOW [*surprised*]: Turtle? --a woman? Don't nobody want that scrawny boy.

RED [*amused*]: That it Turtle? ...You got you a woman down there?

TURTLE [*emphatic*]: How old do I have to be before I get to be called by my given name?

SNOW: Is dead old enough Demetrius?

RED [*to* TURTLE]: A.T.L. huh?

TURTLE: Ain't no worse than Yazoo City.

SNOW: It couldn't be...

UNCLE-ONE [*interjecting*]: I know ya'll ain't complainin' about no weather. It's so damn much snow outside that a body can't hardly drive. [*To* BLACK] Do you know how hard it was to get to the airport?

BLACK: And I appreciate it Uncle-One, I do.

RED [*to* UNCLE-ONE]: Yes sir, thank you sir.

UNCLE-ONE [*rambling*]: Rain fallin' on top of snow... roads slick.. Then it will freeze up and the stupid motherf...

BLACK [*interjecting*]: Uncle-one!

UNCLE-ONE [*rambling on*]: ...Damn fools in such a hurry, -- slip sliding all over the place. -- And it 'bout look like it's gonna storm to boot.

TURTLE [*to* UNCLE-ONE]: Ain't much chance of an electrical storm this time of year.

UNCLE-ONE: I thought you was gonna be an engineer not a damn meteorologist.

RED [*to* UNCLE- ONE, *amused*]: They got many things in the Army, but they don't have one of you.

TURTLE [*to* RED]: You oughta think about comin' down to Atlanta. You never know what might turn up.

RED: Maybe, ...if I can't get nothin' goin' here.

BLACK [*to* TURTLE, *teasing*]: When the wedding bells ring we'll be on the first thing movin'.

TURTLE: Ya'll need to quit. I got classes, a room, and a few friends, but I'm ain't keepin' company.

RED: Ya'll think maybe he can get out of his first year before you get out the shot gun?

UNCLE-ONE: Snowflake.

SNOW: Huh?

UNCLE-ONE: .... get my medicine would you sugar?

RED [*to* UNCLE-ONE, *amused*]: Same prescription?

BLACK [*disapproving*]: From Dr. Johnny Walker.

SNOW [*to* UNCLE-ONE]: Hold on a second and I'll...

UNCLE-ONE [*insistent*]: Now honey...

SNOW [*reluctant*]: Alright.   .....[*to* RED] I'll be right back...don't say nothin' good till then.

Exit SNOW.

RED [*to* TURTLE]: How's Lisa?

BLACK [*pulling* RED *aside*]: Baby, do you want me to fix you something to eat?

TURTLE [*to* RED, *matter of factly*]: She's in the joint.

UNCLE-ONE [*to* BLACK]: Quit pullin' on the boy.

RED [*pulling away from* BLACK, *to* TURTLE]: For what?

TURTLE: Poor judgement.

UNCLE-ONE: That ain't what the judge called it.

BLACK [*to* RED, *tugging on his sleeve*]: Let me show you how I fixed up the place.

RED [*to* UNCLE-ONE]: What'd she do?

BLACK [*to* RED]: ...We still need a fresh coat of paint...

UNCLE-ONE [*to* RED]: Six inches, four times, just as hard as she could.

RED: Who?

TURTLE: Justin.

RED [*to* TURTLE]: What happened to Charles?

TURTLE: He was kicked a long time ago.

BLACK [*to* RED] I got a bed set up for you and a television over here.

RED [*digesting the thought*]: Jason huh?

[*Re-enter* SNOW *with the whiskey and a shot glass.*]

TURTLE: No, Justin.

SNOW [*to* TURTLE, *disappointed*]: You told him! ...man why ya'll gotta take all the fun outta everything? I was gonna tell him myself.

BLACK [*to* SNOW, *upset*]: Ain't no fun in the misfortune of your family.

UNCLE-ONE [*to* SNOW]: You ain't bring but one glass.... You disrespecting the corporal and the engineer.

RED: I'm fine Uncle-One.

TURTLE: Me too...

RED: Maybe later we kick back and slam a few.

UNCLE-ONE [*pouring himself a shot*]: Your loss.

RED [*to* TURTLE]: What did Justin do?

SNOW: Whatever he wanted.

RED: And so she...

SNOW [*interjecting*]: Cut him!

RED: She kill him?

UNCLE-ONE: Damn near.

TURTLE [*dismissive*]: He's fine.

SNOW: A hundred and seventy two stitches. And six weeks laid up.

BLACK [*to* RED]: I'm gonna get you a refrigerator down here just as soon as I can find one on sale.

RED [*to* BLACK]: Why you go through all this trouble?

BLACK: They can't send you home if you ain't got a home to come home to.

RED: I can't stay but a few weeks mama...

UNCLE-ONE: It's a medical discharge Black, ...the boy ain't bein' committed.

BLACK [*to* UNCLE-ONE, *becoming unnerved*]: Later! [*Composing herself*] This is a day for rejoicing....

SNOW [*to* RED]: Peaches is in County 'till they process her and move her to a woman's facility.

RED [*to* TURTLE]: How long?

SNOW [*still excited*]: Get this, four times she stuck him right, guess what she got?

RED: What?

SNOW: Aggravated battery.

UNCLE-ONE: I guess if a Black woman take a knife to her man, it's just 'cause she aggravated.

SNOW [*to* UNCLE-ONE]: She had good reason!

TURTLE [*to* RED]: She'll be out in a few years on good behavior.

UNCLE-ONE: Damn near forever if she true to her nature.

SNOW: Maybe she be back home by next Christmas.

[*Loud thunder clap.*]

UNCLE-ONE: Must be that none to frequent electrical storm Mr. Engineer say we ain't gonna get.

TURTLE [*playful*]: Why you pickin' at me Uncle...

BLACK [*upset*]: I have worked too hard for you all to spoil my baby's home-comin' with all this foolishness. Will somebody please come upstairs and help me get supper on the table.

[BLACK *storms up the stairs, one by one they follow, leaving* RED *behind.*]

Fade to BLACK.

The sound of a gentle rain transports us into the next scene.

ACT 2
SCENE 3 *Chicken, Greens, and Babies*

Period: Early 1990's

Lights slowly fade up on the basement apartment, suggesting the passage of time. The rain continues from the previous scene. RED is slouched in a chair watching T.V. He is wearing his dress uniform from the previous scene [minus the tie]. Enter SNOW from the top of the stairs.

RED [*irritated by her presence*]: What'chu want?

SNOW: Mama say dinner's ready.

RED: Okay.

[RED *doesn't move.*]

SNOW: You gonna come up or what?

RED: I ain't hungry.

SNOW: Fine.

[SNOW *turns to leave.*]

RED: What'd she cook?

SNOW [*sarcastic*]: Dinner.

RED: Funny.

SNOW: I try. [*Turning to go again, joking*] See ya, wouldn't wanna be ya!

RED [*serious*]: Why not?

SNOW: What?

RED: What's wrong with me?

SNOW: Dem jus' jokes dude...

[*Beat.*]

SNOW [*concerned*]: You alright, ...you're sweatin?

RED [*wiping his brow*]: ...It's just damp down here from the rain.

SNOW [*skeptical*]: Ain't that damp.

RED [*insistent*]: Why wouldn't you wanna be me?

SNOW [*laughing*]: Look at you, ...every couple days you put on that uniform.   It's been four years.

RED: Gotta see if it still fits.

SNOW: You see, that's why I wouldn't wanna be ya.   --I got enough problems. I don't need yours.

RED [*defensive*]: I don't need yours either.

SNOW [*flippant, turning to exit*]: Later.

RED [*pointed*]: Why do you keep having babies?

SNOW [*taken aback*]: Excuse me?

RED: I just wanna know.

SNOW [*sarcastic*]: Me, too.

RED [*earnest*]: You don't?

SNOW [*attacking*]: Don't you wanna do more than stay here and sponge off of mama?

RED: I work. I help.

SNOW [*defensive*]: So do I?

RED: You ain't answered my question.

SNOW: You ain't asked nothin' worth answerin'. Why don't you just mind your own business and leave me the fuck alone?

RED: You're in my space!

SNOW: You're in my face!

RED [*retreating*]: Was. --ain't no more.

SNOW: The time for big-brotherin' is over Red. You been back for four years now, and out of the clear blue sky, you've got something to say?   I'm grown, I got responsibilities. You wanna pick up behind somebody, --do that for yourself.

[*Beat.*]

RED: Did she make chicken?   I gotta taste for chicken.

SNOW: Greens and cornbread.

RED: You wanna walk up to Popeye's with me?

SNOW: It's raining.

RED: So. Your clothes will dry.

SNOW: I would, --but --If I walk out the door without my kids, mama would have my throat in a noose.

RED [*sincere*]: Hey, -- I'm sorry.

SNOW: We cool. Don't sweat it.

RED: Could you bring me down a plate?

SNOW: Maybe. Might even batter you up a few wings. If you can act right.

RED: Thanks.

SNOW: Yea, [*turning to exit, then turning back.*] It's cause I want them!

RED: Want what?

SNOW: Kids. I want them. --so I have them. --simple as that.

Exit SNOW.

Thunder claps transition into the next scene.

Fade to black.

End Scene.

ACT 2
 SCENE 4 *Thunder and Lightning*

Period: Middle 1970's

Lights up inside the Mississippi shack. Late in the evening, the kids are asleep on the floor [except RED*], wrapped snug on top of blankets and quilts. Lighting flashes, followed by distant thunder. A loud thunder clap is heard.*

TURTLE [*shaking her, agitated*]: Peaches, wake up.

PEACHES [*drowsy*]: What.

TURTLE [*worried*]: Storm.

PEACHES [*agitated*]: Go back to sleep.

TURTLE: I can't.

PEACHES: Why you gotta be scared all the time?

SNOW [*moaning from underneath her pillow*]: Shut uuuuuppp!

[*Lighting flash followed by a loud thunder clap.*]

TURTLE [*to* SNOW *trying to whisper*]: It's gettin' closer.

SNOW [*removing her pillow/to* TURTLE]: I said shut up!

MOSS [*waking, to* TURTLE]: Come crawl in with me.

[TURTLE *crosses and curls up next to* MOSS.]

SNOW [*to* RED]: Why you always gotta baby him?

[*Lighting flash followed by a loud thunder clap,* TURTLE *cowers. Enter* RED, *carrying a sandwich and bottle of cola.*]

PEACHES [*to* TURTLE, *comforting*]: It ain't gonna do nothin' to you. It's like I told you, thunder is just God bowling.

MOSS *and* SNOW *struggle to fight back the urge to laugh.*

PEACHES [*to* MOSS *and* PEACHES. *Also fighting the urge to laugh.*] Shhhhhh.

RED [*to* TURTLE, *trying to scare him*]: Thunder is the sound of the dead comin' back, and lighting is the light they need to find you! [*Discovering the thought*] ...and the rain melts you together so that you can't ever get away from them.

[TURTLE *whimpers.*]

PEACHES [*to* RED, *irritated*]: Why you wanna go and do that?

RED [*to* PEACHES, *disappointed*]: Why you gotta lie to him?

PEACHES [*to* RED]: Ain't like you helpin'.

RED [*to* TURTLE, *flippant*]: If the lightnin's gonna get you, it's gonna come fast and you gonna die fast. And if you die you know what that means?

TURTLE [*unconvinced*]: No?

RED: You get to be with Uncle Frankie, and all the rest of the untimely departed.

[TURTLE *puts his head under a pillow and cowers.*]

PEACHES [*to* RED, *sarcastic*]: Thanks. [*To* TURTLE] Just ignore him. Ain't nothin' gonna happen to you, ...And even if it did, why would RED know anything about what's waitin' for you?

[*Lighting and thunder clap*, SNOW *is startled.*]

MOSS [*To* SNOW, *laughing*]: You scared too ain't you?

SNOW [*covering with her pillow*]: I'm sleepy!

RED [*removing* TURTLE's *pillow*]: If the lightin' wants you, you can't stop it no how. Anything that's supposed to find you, sooner or later it will.

TURTLE: Even when it ain't stormin'?

RED [*tormenting* TURTLE]: Next week, next year, clear sky, or downpour ...you just never know.

[TURTLE *cowers and* RED *laughs.*]

MOSS [*to* RED]: No fair Red, he's only seven.

RED [*to* MOSS]: He needs to toughen up.

PEACHES [*to* TURTLE]: Did you go to the bathroom before you laid down?

TURTLE: No.

MOSS [*pushing him over, annoyed*]: Boy you better go then! You can't sleep next to me if you gonna....

TURTLE [*to* MOSS, *whining*]: Come and go with me. I can't go out there by myself.

MOSS: I'ain't.

RED [*imitating* MOSS]: No fair, he's only seven.

TURTLE [*to* MOSS]: Pleeeeeaaassse. A water snake or somethin' could be hidin' in the grass.

SNOW [*rising, to* TURTLE]: Come on, I'll take you. ... go put your shoes on.

RED: Ain't you sweet?

SNOW: Anything if ya'll will just be quiet.

RED [*taunting* TURTLE]: You better watch out, sometimes snakes work their way down into the shit hole, when you least expect it, ...they bite you on your bare ass...

TURTLE: Ooooooo.

SNOW: Unlike you, I guess he'll have to pee standing up.

[*Lightning flashes and* TURTLE *takes off running.* SNOW *follows him off stage.*]

PEACHES [*to* MOSS]: You really believe that, "you gonna die quick so it don't matter" stuff?

MOSS: I guess.

RED [*munching his sandwich, to* PEACHES]: You don't?

PEACHES: AIN'T VEE once told me, ...everything's got it's fit, but that don't mean it's stuck.

RED: The woman was practically out her mind when she pass.

PEACHES: No she wasn't, ...this family just gotta have somebody to talk about.

MOSS [*to* PEACHES]: She wasn't all there and you know it. Mama said she was talkin' to spirits and goin' on about playin' in the yard with her great grandchildren. ...She ain't even got no kids.

PEACHES: She gave me these.
[PEACHES *pulls out a set of carefully wrapped stones.*]

MOSS: A handful of rocks in a nasty old rag?

RED [*indicating the rag*]: Thought you said she WASN'T crazy.

MOSS: UNCLE-ONE, ...he had to sit by and watch his wife loose touch altogether.

PEACHES [*spilling them onto the floor*]: She was showin' me how to "see" just before she pass.

RED [*confused*]: The rocks?

PEACHES: No. --us.

RED [*growing uneasy*]: Alright put that away.

MOSS [*taunting*]: Why? You scared?

RED: It's stupid, ...put it away.

MOSS [*to* RED, *dismissive*]: Dude, -- they're rocks.

PEACHES [*to* RED, *reading the stones*]: It say here, Uncle Frankie's gonna get you for the way you treat Turtle.

RED [*half-believing*]: Does not!

MOSS [*to* PEACHES]: Can you really read them things?

PEACHES: Sometimes.

MOSS: Then what it really say?

[*Enter* AIN'T VEE *unseen by* MOSS & RED.]

AIN'T VEE [*to* PEACHES]: Go on, just like I showed you.

RED: She don't know nothing.

[PEACHES *picks up the stones and drops them again then looks at them intensely.*]

AIN'T VEE: Òkànràn-Ìwòrì

PEACHES [*to* AIN'T VEE] The Lizard?

AIN'T VEE [*reassuring*]: The Lizard.
RED [*to* PEACHES]: Is that a question or a statement?

AIN'T VEE & PEACHES: This was seen for the lizard and all other reptiles.

MOSS [*to* RED, *laughing*]: She callin' you a reptile.

AIN'T VEE & PEACHES: The lizard said he would not tell his problem to anyone.

PEACHES: He struck his head against the willow tree and the wall.

[*Enter* AIN'T MARIE.]

AIN'T MARIE & AIN'T VEE: But none would feel sorry for him.

MOSS [*excited*]:   And!!!

PEACHES [*disappointed*]: I can't remember the rest.

RED: That's cause you just makin' it up... goin' on 'bout lizards and shit. [Mocking her] What kinda help is "seeing" a lizard gonna give somebody?

PEACHES, AIN'T MARIE, & AIN'T VEE [*to* RED]: Sacrifice a he-goat, a cock, a pigeon, and money.

RED: What the fuck!

MOSS [*to* PEACHES, *fascinated*]: Tell the rest.

PEACHES [*to* MARIE *and* VEE]: He refused to sacrifice...

AIN'T MARIE & AIN'T VEE: Then a lizard he shall remain.

RED [*to* PEACHES, *laughing*]: Sacrifice what? ...A Yack, a billy goat?

PEACHES: I did not say that!

RED [*to* MOSS, *laughing*] What else she say?

MOSS: Money.

RED: Givin' up money ain't no sacrifice that's bonafide hardship.

[*Lighting flash followed by a loud thunder clap. Enter* SNOW *with* TURTLE *running from the thunder.*]

Exit AIN'T VEE *and* AIN'T MARIE.

RED [*scattering the stones*]: Cut out that conjure woman shit.

PEACHES: Why?

[TURTLE *stops dead in his tracks when he hears* RED *swear.*]

TURTLE: Oooooh you said shit... I'm gon' tell...

RED: You said it too.

TURTLE: No I didn't.

SNOW [*to* TURTLE]: Yea you did.

TURTLE [*to* SNOW] Fo'get'chu.

SNOW [*to* TURTLE *awestruck*]: Fo'get me?

MOSS [*to* TURTLE]: Take off your shoes and crawl in...

SNOW [*to* TURTLE, *irritated*]: Next time go to the out house by your damn self, or better yet, pee in the bed again.

TURTLE: Oooooo you said damn.

PEACHES [*to* TURTLE]: Just crawl in and be quiet.

[*Lighting flash followed by a loud thunder clap,* TURTLE *jumps under the blanket next to* MOSS.]

MOSS [*looking to* TURTLE]: You didn't drink no water or nothin' did you?

Fade to black.

Lighting flash followed by an extremely loud thunder clap. TURTLE *screams out in terror.*

End Scene.

Exit SNOW *and* PEACHES.

ACT II
SCENE V
Five steps to daylight

Period: Late 1990's

The sound of children running and crying is heard. Lights up on MOSS and RED in the basement.
TURTLE is still under a blanket. As the scene progresses he crawls out and begins to change into funeral clothes.

MOSS: How can you stand all that racket?

RED: You got a kid, you tell me.

TURTLE [*to* MOSS]: They just my babies, ...more like music than noise.

MOSS: He don't cut up like Snow's kids do.

RED [*proud*]: ...Yea, everybody always thought you would make good daddy.

MOSS: I try.

RED: Scary huh?

MOSS [*reflective*]: Three times a night he wakes and screams the cry of life and death. It's the kinda wail that cuts right through you. That's when it's the most terrifying. ...If you don't provide, he won't eat. I used to think that it was the size of them, ... how tiny the fingers, and frail the neck...but that ain't it... It's that cry, ...that I can't live without you cry ....the feed me or I'll die cry... 'cause if you don't, he just might.

TURTLE [*smiling knowingly*]: I know what you mean.

MOSS: Uncle-One said he was gonna stop by before he left for Atlanta. ...You still mad at him?

RED: I ain't mad at him, but he's always had a problem with me.

[*Crossfade up on* UNCLE-ONE *circa 1980.*]

UNCLE-ONE: Folk 'round here ain't gonna take no dog to the doctor. Look at Gray. What do I feed him?

[RED *crosses to* UNCLE-ONE.]

RED: Table scraps.

UNCLE-ONE: Grits, greens, cornbread, beef fat, it don't matter.   Whatever I don't eat, that what I still don't want, that's what Gray gets. You seen that commercial where the dog is runnin' through the house chasin' after a covered wagon?

RED [*uncertain*]: Yea.

UNCLE-ONE: That's the first problem right there, why is the dog rippin' through the house?

RED [*speculative*]: To catch the wagon?

UNCLE-ONE [*emphatic*]: To get me to buy dog food. You catch my meanin'?

RED [*apologetic*]: No sir.

UNCLE-ONE: I ain't gotta spend no money on feedin' a dog. ...and I damn well ain't gonna pay for the dog to have his own doctor.

RED: What do you do when the dog gets sick ?

UNCLE-ONE: He will eat whatever herbs it needs.

RED: And if he don't get any better?

UNCLE-ONE [*resolute*]: Then he will die.

RED: Man that's harsh.

UNCLE-ONE: Trouble enough gettin' money if I take sick, or one a you kids. Ain't like ya mama's got anything to send down here if one'a ya come up wantin'. You think I should spend it on a dog instead?

RED [*perplexed*]: Well... A dog's s'posed to be man's best friend ain't he?

UNCLE-ONE: You got six foot ideas trapped in a four foot body.

RED [*resolute*]: I wanna be a vet.

UNCLE-ONE: Enough people in this family been in wars.

RED [*interjecting*]: A veterinarian!

UNCLE-ONE: If you wanna be something, be a baby doctor. Lords knows this family could use one of those.

RED: Don't you care 'bout what I want to be?

UNCLE-ONE: Half of what you get, come from what you already got. The other half come from you workin' hard and bein' lucky. The half you already got, -- a world full of po' Black folk, that can't use no dog doctor. You understands me?

RED [*walking away angry*]: Yea sir, I understand. [*To himself*] You don't want me to be shit?

[*Fade out on* UNCLE-ONE, RED *crosses back into the basement.*]

MOSS: He just doin' his best to help us through... He meant well.

RED: You ran around the whole summer worryin' 'bout his camera, and instead a whippin' yo' ass like he should'a. He gave it to you. Me, -- I just got another kick in the teeth.

MOSS: I still have it .

RED: That old Range-Finder?

MOSS: It's in a box on the shelf, -- pulled it out when my son was born -- took pictures of him in the incubator. I wanted him to be able to see his first struggles. ... know what he's been through, so he'll know what kinda fight he has in him.

RED [*concerned*]: I didn't know.

MOSS: Yea well, --he's fine now. [*Beat.*] Your mama used to talk about the magic a newborn could conjure just to fight it's way into the world. ...You still believe in conjure women?

RED: If my mama could work magic, I'd be livin' someplace else. [*Probing*] You?

MOSS: If there is such a thing...maybe it's only the newborns that have it, The rest of us? I can't see it.

[*Beat.*]

So why is Uncle-One angry at you?

RED: Difference of opinion. ...I told him something and he said I was full of shit.

MOSS: Really? What'd you tell him?

RED: I went to see Peaches a few weeks ago.

MOSS [*uncomfortable*]: I been meaning to get over to see her but... Probably go by in the mornin'. Take her a few pictures of the baby,...see how she's holdin' up.

[*Fade up on* PEACHES *seated, wearing a bright orange jump suit. She is aged well beyond her years. An empty chair faces her.* RED *crosses and sits.* MOSS *continues to watch* RED.]

RED: You okay?

PEACHES: Sure.

RED: Lonely?

PEACHES: Not so much.

RED: I'm sorry don't nobody get by here much. People be livin' their lives I guess.

PEACHES: I got plenty company.

RED: Who Mama?

PEACHES: Older people mostly, and the grand babies. They just come by to play.

RED [*looking her over*]: They feeding you okay?

PEACHES: Ain't Vee and Ain't Marie was just by this morning.

RED: Ain't Vee?

PEACHES: Antoinette stops by less frequent. She say institutional gray gives her the willies.

RED [*humoring her*]: You don't say.

PEACHES [*serious*]: I asked them to come and keep me company.

RED [*attempting levity*]: Where did you address the invitation?

PEACHES [*piercing*]: How's Uncle Frankie?

RED [*abrupt*]: What?

PEACHES [*comforting*]: Ain't Vee told me.

RED [upset]: Cut it out!

PEACHES: She say you called on him while you was in the Philippines and that he ain't left you since.

RED [*angry*]: I ain't call nobody!!

PEACHES: Ain't what I heard.

RED [*nervous*]: How much could you hear locked up in here anyway?

PEACHES: You started seeing him in the barracks, ...later he just show up whenever he wants.

RED [*surrendering*]: Yea.

PEACHES: And that's why you got sent home?

[RED sits despondent.]

PEACHES [*continued*] [*Consoling*]: You don't ever have to be alone.... unless that's what you want. I'll show you. He'll only come to see you when you want him to.

RED [*uncomfortable*]:   I don't think so.

PEACHES: Everybody only gettin' pieces now.

[PEACHES *waves her hand and the sound of a infant crying seeps in. The room is cast in dim light and long shadows. The child is laying in a crib.* PEACHES *rises, peels off the jump suit, thus transforming into* BLACK. *She peers into the crib concerned, then begins to dance about the crib in hopes of quieting the child. The wails intensify. She abandons the dance and stares hopelessly at the child.*]

BLACK: I can't think with you and that noise. Sometimes I wish...

[*Enter* AIN'T VEE.]

AIN'T VEE: BLACK! [*Crossing and comforting the child*] ...As they grow, they require a little more attention. The old life fades... [*Taking the child*] Ain't enough to just fed 'em, clean'em, burb'em, and dream'em.   They start to get a sense of themselves in this new place and next they want to get a sense of you.

BLACK: He's just a baby.

AIN'T VEE: He'll crawl today, walk tomorrow, and in a week he'll be gone.

BLACK: You still thinking I'm that little girl that used to spend summers at your house. That ain't me no more-- I'm somebody different now.

AIN'T VEE [*pointed*]: Who are you?

BLACK [*pondering/pensive*]: I'm older...

AIN'T VEE [*dismissive*]: So is dirt.

BLACK: I got responsibilities now.

AIN'T VEE: You always had'em.

BLACK [*exasperated*]: Fine Ain't Vee, I ain't nobody different then, -- I'm just a ten year old ghetto child still passin' my summers in Mississippi. And you still givin' mama a break from her own children. [*Beat.*] Do I ever get to be grown?

AIN'T VEE: We'll always be older.

BLACK: One day you'll all be dead too.

AIN'T VEE [*wounded*]: True.

BLACK [*bitter*]: I ain't ask ya'll for nothin'.

AIN'T VEE: We family, we do that what ain't asked for, -- and on o'cassion withhold that which is.

BLACK: All my life I been hearin 'bout conjure women. How it is that you know the ways of whispers. How you can shape peoples lives, turn hearts and heads with simple words. [*Emphatic*] I don't believe it! Cause if you could, you'd have a better life than this.

AIN'T VEE [*indicating* RED]: He's gonna fall more than a few times. And when his soft butt hit that hard earth, he gonna stop and take account of himself. He'll look for you... and if he sees you there big and protective, that's when he'll let wail.... Not 'cause his bottom hurts, but 'cause he know you'll come a runnin'. That's when you get a measure of yourself. Can you just let him cry?

BLACK: If you don't want us here we can catch the next train back to Chicago.

AIN'T VEE: If you wrap all your magic in him, what you got once he's gone?

BLACK [*angry*]: You don't have no kids and you wishin' your misery on me.   My son and me'll be fine. We got each other.

AIN'T VEE [*collecting herself, resolute*]: Whistle stop is at six a.m. --Be on it.

[BLACK *transforms into* PEACHES *and takes her seat next to* RED, *fade out on* AIN'T VEE.]

PEACHES [*to* RED]: Ain't Vee never bothered to teach Black the ways after that. Yo' mama come down the next year with you and Snow in tow, but never did Ain't Vee try again.   Not with her heart and soul. Instead she wait for me to come. That what I got ain't enough -- 'Cause Ain't Vee chose to leave us, -- to be with the others.

RED: What about Uncle Frankie?

[*Enter* UNCLE FRANKIE.]

UNCLE FRANKIE: What about me?

[RED *jumps up scared and retreats.*]

PEACHES: You spent how many years with him comin' to see you and you pretending he ain't there.

UNCLE FRANKIE: You wasn't never happy to see me.

PEACHES: If we won't recognize'em, what is there for them to do? The time between lives is made for workin'.

[RED *and* UNCLE FRANKIE *tentatively negotiate the distance between each other.*]

UNCLE FRANKIE [*to* RED]: Three times a night he wakes and screams the cry of life and death. It's the kinda wail that cuts right through you.

RED: That's when it's the most terrifying.

UNCLE FRANKIE: If I don't provide, he won't eat.

RED: The size of them, -- the tiny fingers, the frail neck...but that ain't it...

UNCLE FRANKIE: It's that cry he has...

RED:...that I can't live without you cry .

UNCLE FRANKIE...the feed me or I'll die cry.

RED: 'Cause if you don't, we just might. [*Embracing* UNCLE FRANKIE] I'm sorry.....

UNCLE FRANKIE [*comforting*]: It's alright...

RED: I just ain't been able to tell nobody.

UNCLE FRANKIE: You coulda told him.

RED: Uncle-One?

UNCLE FRANKIE: I go to see him too. ...Not so much now, but when we were younger...

RED: Why'd you stop?

UNCLE FRANKIE: Didn't ....just don't let him know I'm there anymore.

RED: And I deny you more than Peter did Christ... but you're still there pullin' at the frayed edges of my life. Why not your brother?

UNCLE FRANKIE: 'Cause you -- in your heart still want me here. And so the door is opened. It don't matter what I did wrong before. For him -- shame is branded deep. He can't separate my wrong from his, --so he can't let himself ---see me, --or feel me. His door ain't open anymore. He got hurt enough for both of us -- but there ain't room enough for much else.

RED: What you want me to do?

UNCLE FRANKIE: Tell him I ain't never far from him ...or from you.

[RED *crosses and returns to the basement with* MOSS *and* TURTLE. *Fade out on* PEACHES *and* UNCLE FRANKIE.]

RED [*to* MOSS]: I ain't believe Peaches at first, but she showed me all kinds of things... she showed me how to call'em here to be with me when I want them here.... and when Turtle passed, I guess I missed him more than I thought I would.... so I call him to be here with me too....

MOSS: Here?

RED: In and out for the past two days.

[TURTLE *emerges from the shadows dressed in funeral attire, unseen by* MOSS.]

TURTLE [*to* RED]: I have a few things to see about.... I'll be back after a awhile.

[TURTLE *crosses to* PEACHES, *she happily welcomes him and they sit and begin to chat. The light lingers upon their reunion.*]

Fade to black.

End scene.
ACT 2
SCENE 6 *Divination*

Period 1940's

Lights up on AIN'T MARIE *and* VEE *seated on the steps of the Mississippi shack. The stones are cast upon the ground and* VEE *begins to collect the scattered stones.*

VEE: So it don't really matter what we use?

AIN'T MARIE: Way back we used palm nuts. But you gotta make do with what you got, ..bones, guts, shells, cards, pan drippins, petals, leaves. What matters is what you see, not how you see it.

VEE: So you really believe, in your heart of hearts, that we are predicting the future?

AIN'T MARIE: No.

VEE: Then why am I memorizing all these old stories?

AIN'T MARIE: 'Cause you asked.

VEE: How do you know they're true?

AIN'T MARIE: Where's the sun gonna come up at tomorrow?

VEE [*pointing East*]: Over there, -- right between them willows.

AIN'T MARIE: How you know?

VEE [*assured*]: It was there yesterday.

AIN'T MARIE [*skeptical*]: Really?

VEE: I get up to pump the water every mornin' and it's always right there. I stand over there and pump, [*demonstrating*] like this here. And then the sky gets all golden and orange like a pie crust. Then it peeks out right between them willows.

AIN'T MARIE [*pointing North*]: Tomorrow how you know it ain't gonna be over there?

VEE: It's gonna be where it's supposed to be.

AIN'T MARIE: Maybe.

VEE: I see it all the time, you gonna tell me it ain't there?

AIN'T MARIE: Maybe you just wanna see it.

VEE: I know what I know.

AIN'T MARIE: Even if it ain't happened yet?

VEE: The sun come up where it's supposed to. -- Tomorrow just like yesterday.

AIN'T MARIE: If I say I KNOW there ain't no sun -- then what?

VEE: Then you lying.

AIN'T MARIE [*in mock outrage*]: Ain't your mama ever tell you not to call no elder a liar?

VEE: If it's there with me everyday of my life, -- you can't tell me...

AIN'T MARIE [*intercepting the thought*]: Same way for me.

VEE: The Sun?

AIN'T MARIE: Seein'.

VEE: You can't tell me how you know, you just know huh?

AIN'T MARIE: What I know is this, -- everything that can possibly happen to a person, will happen, sooner or later, to somebody. ...And to that, add that all that can happen, already has and will again.

VEE: So you know what's comin' and when?

AIN'T MARIE: It's all coming... The chore is in seein' what you need , and how to avoid the rest.

VEE: Finding the trouble and making sure it don't trouble you?

AIN'T MARIE: Something like that.

VEE: And that's what seeing is?

AIN'T MARIE: We ain't so much predicting the future, as we're telling the past. We know what tomorrow holds 'cause it's got the same set of rules as yesterday. If I look inside you and see that you need some sunshine in your life, then I just tell you to stand 'tween them willows at first light, and sure enough, you'll get what you need.

Fade to black.
End Scene.

ACT II
SCENE VII
All Tight in His Shell

Period: Late 1990's

Crossfade up on MOSS, and RED, in the basement.. The scene opens upon the two men in mid conversation.

MOSS [reflective]: I wonder if it hurt.

[*Enter TURTLE still unseen by MOSS.*]

TURTLE [*to RED*]: A little...

MOSS: They say he went in feelin' pretty decent, more or less, but then...   He gave up.

TURTLE: That what you think?

RED [*to TURTLE, confidential*]: If you wanted to stay you could have.

TURTLE [*to RED, indicating his own body*]: I gotta have a place to stay.

RED [*to MOSS*]: Seems kinda silly ...everybody makin' a fuss over when he was gonna get married huh?

MOSS: .... Ain't like he told anybody.

TURTLE [*sarcastic*]: You wanted to listen?

RED [*to MOSS*]: They know where he got it from?

TURTLE: Yea.

MOSS: No.

RED [*to MOSS*]: His friend, is he okay?

TURTLE: No.

MOSS: Near as anyone can tell.

RED [*to MOSS*]: You going?

MOSS [*to RED*]: If I can get enough together for both of us you gonna come?

RED: Probably better if I don't. His mama ain't told hardly nobody about him. Things could get ugly and I don't need to see no more ugly.

TURTLE [*to RED*]: Mama will tell in her own time.

MOSS [*to RED*]: Lisa can't be there, ...we need to go.

RED: You walk in with your wife on your arm, baby pictures in the wallet. You're the consummate family man. Me...

MOSS: By right you supposed to be there too. We're family Red, we're supposed to stick together.

RED [*to* TURTLE *and* MOSS]: For most of my life you been runnin' up underneath me. For every step I take, my foot can't hardly touch the ground for you wedging your soul underneath mine.

MOSS [*comforting*]: We need to say our goodbyes.

TURTLE: We can all say those right here.

[MOSS *looks in* TURTLE *general direction as if he heard* TURTLE's *remark.*]

MOSS [*to* TURTLE *as reflex*]: Turtle?

RED [*to* MOSS, *hopeful*]: You hear him?

MOSS [*unnerved, shaking off the feeling*]: What? [*Shaking off the feeling*] No nothin'.

RED: Every time we lay somebody to rest the people tell us how the body in gone but the spirit live on. They won't hardly say that somebody is even dead, just that they pass on. To what?

TURTLE [*to* RED]: Tell him.

RED: ...I asked him here Moss. ...and he come. I spend eighteen years of my life tryin' to shake him and the rest of you off of me. Like I done stepped in a pile of shit, I scrape my soul on the side of the curb, and then poke at it with a stick to work the grooves. ...but when it counts...

TURTLE: You miss me.

RED [*to* TURTLE *and* MOSS]: I miss us!

TURTLE: We're still here.

MOSS [*dismissive*]: You been down here too long and you don't talk to nobody hardly but your self.

TURTLE: ...And me.

RED [*to* TURTLE *smiling*]: Yeah..... [*to* MOSS] You scraped him off too.

MOSS: Who?

RED: Turtle.

MOSS [*defensive*]: I did no such thing!

RED: Ain't nobody here 'cept us. Ain't no reason to lie!

MOSS: That's your problem right there. You got too much time to sit and fixate on the insignificant.

RED [*sarcastic*]: Yea, something's gotta be wrong with me.

MOSS: People grow cousin, and to do that ...some things gotta be put aside.

TURTLE [*to* RED]: You can't make him see just cause you want him too. Just like you couldn't make Uncle-One open places he don't wanna..... [*Yelling and clapping his hands*] Moss you-who.... Moss!

MOSS: I'm trying to help you Red, ...but you gotta meet me half way okay?

RED: You miss it?

MOSS: What?

RED: Being connected.

MOSS: To what?

RED: Us.

MOSS: I am connected.

RED: Really?

MOSS: Whatchu want me to say Red? You're thirty eight years old... You spend your time locked away in your mama's basement drinkin' shit beer and watching T. V.   ...Now you say you're talkin' with spirits. You tell me that Lisa's in the joint seein' the same shit that you are. You're wallowing in your own delusions and you want me to join you. I got a sick baby upstairs, a tired wife, a heart-broken aunt, and a cousin to bury. What the fuck do you think I can do with what you're tellin' me?

RED: Me and Turtle ain't said two words to each other in nearly ten years Moss. You, I ain't seen more than once a year in the same period, and only then when somebody is near to life or near to death.

TURTLE: If you ain't on assignment.

MOSS: I got responsibilities cousin. Shit you wouldn't know nothin' about. I got mouths to feed, my son's education to pay for. I got a life to live.... [*Laughing in frustration*] [*Checking his watch*] Look, I gotta be getting back upstairs.

RED [*to MOSS & TURTLE*]: I got no reason' to go to Atlanta.

MOSS: Funerals are for the living.

RED: All the more reason to stay at home.

TURTLE [*to RED*]: Either way --I'll be --close by

[*Exit* TURTLE. *Beat.*]

MOSS: Then just come upstairs for a minute.

RED: I'm fine right here.

MOSS [MOSS *crosses/then stops at the foot of the stairs*]: You can come out if you really want to.

RED: You gotta remember which place is yours and which you visit. And never stay too long.

[MOSS *exits.* RED *rises from his chair, reaches into the cooler for a beer. He hesitates for a moment, then crosses to the rural front porch... He ascends the stairs and sits down.*]

Fade down on RED *to a gentle pool of light. Low rumbling thunder is heard,* RED *looks skyward, then holds out his palm to test for rain.*

End Scene.

Seamless transition.

Crossfade into next scene.
Act 2
Scene 8 *Òsé-Òtúrúpòn*

Period: Now and Then

The stage is dark except for RED . *Lights slowly fade in to suggest the twilight.* AIN'T VEE *enters carrying her wrapped stones. She sits quietly with stones between her legs.* AIN'T MARIE *enters, she sits next to* VEE. *The low rumbling thunder is heard and continues to build [draw nearer] as the scene progresses.*

AIN'T MARIE: The first time you call'em.... Start slow and feel the power grow within you. Feel your heart and let it call out for the spirits...

VEE [*uneasy*]: Okay.

AIN'T MARIE: They tried to take the drum away from us back in slavery times.... Didn't understand that you got one inside callin' out a rhythm everyday that can call spirits from here to heaven and back again.

[*Gentle percussion builds keeping the rhythm of her heart and calling spirits for her.*]

VEE: Okay, I can feel it now....

AIN'T MARIE: The rhythm?

VEE: Yeah, ...now what do I do?

AIN'T MARIE: Just feel for a moment...

[*Accents are added to the percussion rhythm adding to the complexity of the sound.*]

VEE [*smiling, and beginning to sway with the rhythm*]: Can you hear that?

AIN'T MARIE: Everybody's got a heart.

VEE: Teach me more...

AIN'T MARIE: This ain't really somethin' you teach outright.   ...more like somethin' you choose to learn.

VEE [*she stops swaying*]: Huh?

AIN'T MARIE [*taking her by the hips and swaying them*]: Can't let anything pull you out.   [*Indicating the rhythm*] You got it again?

VEE [*nervous*]: Yeah. ...Sorry, ...I mean ...yeah, ...okay,   ...Ready

[*The percussion is embellished by other instruments one by one creating the full lush sound of a festival.*]

AIN'T MARIE [*to the Audience*]: Don't let no man, No God, nobody, keep you from your loved ones..... Living, or dead! You can call'em forward and backward. ...them what's here, and them what's on their way back.

[UNCLE FRANKIE, TURTLE, ANTOINETTE, ROSEMARY's *brother, and* PEACHES *enter one at a time. VEE shows each a simple movement that complements the rhythm of her heart. What results is a growing collection of generational family dancing to VEE's rhythm. MARIE scoops up a handful of dirt. She lets the dirt pass through her fingers and onto the ground. She picks up VEE's bag of wrapped stones, opens it, and then drops the rocks onto the fresh dirt then studies it intensely.*]

AIN'T MARIE [*calling out*]: Òsé-Òtúrúpòn!

All: Òsé-Òtúrúpòn!

AIN'T MARIE [*proclaiming*]: Òsé-Òtúrúpòn! This has been seen for a woman. They said a man she is about to marry will make her poor and make her often unhappy, though she would bear children.

VEE [*stepping forward from the family*]: She asked what to sacrifice to prevent this:

ALL EXCEPT RED: Two snails, kitchen cloth, a jar of cottonseed oil, eighteen thousand polished shells...

VEE: She heard, -- but did not sacrifice.

THE FAMILY: You have said we will have children, --and that is enough.

[*Each character then exits one by one leaving* MARIE, VEE, TURTLE, *and* RED *on stage. The music slowly fades out and the lights fade down.* RED & TURTLE *move to the stairs and sit.*]

AIN'T MARIE: Pretty good for your first try...

[PEACHES *runs in and gathers up her stones and wraps them in the cloth.*]

VEE [*smiling*]: Yeah, pretty good.

[MARIE *and* VEE *pick up the clothes line and re-hangs it.* PEACHES *carries in the laundry. And the three women begin to hang it on the line.*]

AIN'T MARIE [*to* RED *and* TURTLE]: You fella's gonna lend us a hand or not.

[*The sound of thunder intensifies. Gentle percussion drifts in complementing the sound of the approaching storm.*]

Fade to Black.

Fade out the percussion leaving only the sound of rain and thunder.

End Scene.

The End.

She Calls Up The Sun
by Addae Moon
World Premier 2002

She Calls Up The Sun
Director's Notes

She Calls Up The Sun emphasizes the importance of family relationships in the African-American community, a subject frequenty explored in Afrikan Centered Theater. Some relationships are loving, nurturing, and extremely functional. Others are bitter, contentious or emotionally empty. Let's not forget those that are non-existent, as well as ones that, to some degree, are a mixture of these qualities. But all of these relationships have some importance. Few people have no reaction to their mother's or father's passing, despite what the relationship was or wasn't. If nothing else, they reflect upon what it could or should have been. Often, the "voices" of our family are not silent, even after they've left this plane of existence and their physical manifestations have dissolved. They still speak to us, warn us, counsel us, scold us, and even comfort us. Then there are the voices and bodies of those who are still here, and our issues with them cry out to be addressed whether we can resolve them to our satisfaction or not.

The symbols and customs which often play a part in Black theatre are quite present here. They figure most prominently in the making of the dolls, which is a tradition of the "coastal women" such as Marie's mother, Claire, and many of their relatives and friends. This doll making is depicted as a rite of passage with which Marie is now trying to grapple. It is most difficult because she is now beset by loss, regret, anger, and the feeling she is not understood by those who love her. But gradually, Marie begins to realize the truth of Claire's observation that "we ain't nothin' but the sum total of all the folks that came before us". And from there, she is able to continue. Hopefully, the understanding will come.

I found this play moving and poignant. I suspect the same will be true for the reader.

She Calls Up The Sun
Playwright's Statement

It began with an image of a woman sitting in a rocking chair, facing a large open window, a child in her arms. All of my work begins with an image or a song. My challenge is to find the clues that will lead me to the story. I usually have no idea where it will end up. The paintings of John Biggers, the myth of Orpheus, the ideas of Paul Carter Harrison and Southern matriarchal culture were somehow woven into the final tapestry of this play. But I didn't realize any of this until *after* the play was completed.

On a conscious level, I wanted to tap into the complex struggles in black families and romantic relationships. As a man, I wanted to explore the mystery of womanhood, which will always excite and frustrate me.

She Calls Up The Sun
Original Cast

Darryl Charisse.. CLAIRE
Earl Fox...OLIVER
Ethan Henry...FELIX
Sean Nix ....ISHMEAL
Taylar...MARIE

Production Staff

Director ....Terry Cullers
Production Stage Manager ....Carla Stillwell
Technical Director ....Sean R. Neron
Scenographic Design... Shepsu Aakhu
Lighting Design...Shepsu Aakhu
Sound Design..Min. of the New Super Heavy Funk
Costume Design...Kanika Sago
Properties...Reginald Lawrence
Producer..Reginald Lawrence

Characters

CHARACTERS:

MARIE   Late 20's. A doll maker and schoolteacher.

ISHMAEL   Early 30's. A musician and schoolteacher. Marie's fiancé.

OLIVER   Early 50's. A wandering singer.

CLAIRE   Late 50's. The neighborhood elder.

FELIX   Late 20's. Marie's old friend.

SETTING
The Present. A small costal town in Northern Florida.

The stage is separated into two sections. There is a bench at a bus stop the intersection of Nostalgia Court and Cassandra Lane. The remainder of the stage suggests a modest living room. The room is without walls only a doorframe, sofa, loveseat, old rocking chair, coffee table, and bar area. The rest of the space has an "open-air" feel to it an open stormy sky near the ocean, which shifts in color and tone as the play progresses. A large sepia colored photograph hangs from ceiling to floor in the upstage area…it resembles a watercolor. There is a blurred image of a woman standing on a beach, facing the ocean. She has a parasol in one hand and the hand of a little girl in the other. There are pages of sheet music on the sofa and coffee table. Fluid movement occurs between the two sections of the space suggesting a malleable treatment of time from one scene to the next.

ACT 1
SCENE 1

The shadow of a window pane is cast across the floor ISHMAEL *is seen in the shadow. He is dressed in a black suit, sitting in the rocking chair, playing guitar. The song is simple and melancholy with a mournful tone.* MARIE *opens the door. She is dressed in black and standing in the doorway holding a parasol. She folds the parasol before entering – she doesn't notice* ISHMAEL *playing. The lights come up in the living area.* MARIE *walks towards the bar and begins pour two drinks, she offers one to* ISHMAEL.

ISHMAEL: No, thank you. Is it gonna be like this forever?

MARIE: Like what?

[ISHMAEL *stops and stares at her a moment.*]

ISHMAEL: The weather.

MARIE: I'm *not* a meteorologist.

ISHMAEL: You walking around with a parasol...Thought maybe you knew something I didn't.

MARIE: It's like that sometimes. The weather seems appropriate, considering.

ISHMAEL: It's been this way for months, Marie. Sky's keeping all the emotion inside.

MARIE: You're exaggerating.

ISHMAEL: Tension. Knotted with clouds. [*Pause. Beat.*] I can't keep going like this. Don't think I've seen the sun since I've been here. Nothin' but grey skies, like a hurricane's gonna strike at any moment.

MARIE: It's Florida. Have a drink…It'll make you feel better.

ISHMAEL: But it doesn't rain. It's like we're... stuck.

MARIE: Stuck? Here, Ish.

ISHMAEL: I don't want it.

[MARIE *swallows his drink in one gulp.*]

ISHMAEL: You shouldn't be drinking.

MARIE: Why not?

ISHMAEL: Doesn't seem right.

MARIE: Don't care much for appearances. When I'm thirsty, I drink.

[MARIE *walks back to the bar…Beat.*]

MARIE [cont'd]: Besides, she would do the same.

ISHMAEL: I doubt

MARIE: Mamma would pour a little rum for everyone. Invite some of the guys from Pete's over to play music…some soft blues…that's what I'd want if it was my funeral.

ISHMAEL: Please.

MARIE: Put on some old records…send off the dead in a proper fashion.

ISHMAEL: We've had enough of that…nothing but food, rum, and music the past three days.

MARIE: Death is a celebration.

ISHMAEL: You'd think it was carnival.

MARIE: A transition from one stage to the next.

ISHMAEL: You don't seem convinced.

MARIE: It's what she wanted.

ISHMAEL: What are we gonna do?

MARIE: Can't pull back the clouds, baby.

ISHMAEL: It was different in the city.

MARIE: This is not the city.

ISHMAEL: Could always go back.

MARIE: This is home.

ISHMAEL: Happier times.

MARIE: As long as you're here with me. Come on, have a drink.

ISHMAEL: Put that down.

MARIE: Sip those blues away.

ISHMAEL: [*Beat.*] What was it your mother said…after we lost the baby?

MARIE: I don't want to talk about the baby.

ISHMAEL: What did she say?

MARIE: Said she should've been the one to die first, spare us that pain.

ISHMAEL: She also said, "while we're here…among the living…we should cherish and *respect* each other."

[ISHMAEL *removes the glass from* MARIE'S *hand and places it on the coffee table.*]

ISHMAEL: You need to rest.

[MARIE *picks up the glass from the table.*]

MARIE: I'm not tired. I don't have time to sleep.

ISHMAEL: You haven't slept in weeks.

MARIE: I've got worked to do.

ISHMAEL: Dolls.

MARIE: I promised her it would be done weeks ago. I haven't even started.

ISHMAEL: You can start tomorrow.

MARIE: I have to start tonight. It's already; we've already put her in the ground.

ISHMAEL: She'd want you to rest.

MARIE: There is no rest. Then, there's school tomorrow.

ISHMAEL: We've already talked about this

MARIE: I'm not gonna sit around the house

ISHMAEL: You're getting some rest tonight

MARIE: I'M NOT TIRED.

ISHMAEL: Get school and that doll shit out of your mind. [MARIE *ignores him and sips some more rum.*] Would you just

MARIE: What's the problem?

ISHMAEL: NOTHING.

MARIE: Maybe you need some sleep?

ISHMAEL: Could you put that down?

MARIE: It's helping me RELAX!

ISHMAEL: Jesus Christ!

MARIE: You should try some. Come on.

[MARIE *straddles* ISHMAEL.]

MARIE: You know how horny this stuff makes me...last summer. The little wooden church in Guyana. Stained glass in the moonlight....Rum on our tongues.

ISHMAEL: STOP IT!

MARIE: WHAT IS WRONG WITH YOU?

ISHMAEL: What? The question is, "what's wrong with *you*!?"

MARIE: You're the one walking around like a corpse.

ISHMAEL: Ever heard of mourning?!

MARIE: What are you expecting, tears and a veil? That's not how we do things around here.

ISHMAEL: You just lost your mother.

MARIE: You don't have to tell me that. I WAS THERE! I watched it.

ISHMAEL: I know.

MARIE: Saw it with my own eyes.

ISHMAEL: I understand.

MARIE: And you expect me to be some wilting flower crying on your shoulder? That's not who I am.

ISHMAEL: You gotta let go, gotta release it somehow.

MARIE: I gotta keep living, keep moving.

ISHMAEL: You didn't shed one tear at the funeral.

MARIE: I cried for her a long time ago. We've got oceans of tears between us. But Ish, I'm still alive. I can still taste the liquor on my tongue. There is breath coming in and out of my body. On the way home, I counted the date trees along the way. They were all orange and plump. It may be grey outside, but those dates, bundles of warm sun.... I'm gonna be fine.

ISHMAEL: You need to talk about your feelings.

MARIE: Talk about my *feelings*?

ISHMAEL: I'm serious.

[MARIE *plays in* ISHMAEL'S *hair.*]

MARIE: Don't wanna *talk* about anything.

ISHMAEL: You're crazy, you know that?

MARIE: Sanity is overrated. Let's just say I want to walk on the beach with my arms open wide.

ISHMAEL: On a dreary day.

MARIE: With a dark eyed man who will hold my hand and walk *with* me.

ISHMAEL: I 'm worried about you.

MARIE: You shouldn't be.

ISHMAEL: Can't help it. So much has changed.

MARIE: Just be patient. We've got our whole lives together.

[MARIE *hands* ISHMAEL *the glass of rum*.]

ISHMAEL: Mad. Mad woman. I'm not sure why I love you so much.

MARIE: I'm irresistible.

[*She drinks then kisses him. They laugh. They both drink. At the bus stop*, CLAIRE *approaches the intersection. She is carrying a fabric bag.* OLIVER *approaches the intersection and is in the process of crossing the street.* CLAIRE *blocks his path.*]

OLIVER: Pardon me.

[CLAIRE *stares at* OLIVER *and does not move.*]

OLIVER: I...I need to cross the street. You're in my way.

CLAIRE: *Your* way? What? You own this street or something? This street belong to you?

OLIVER: No, it's just would you let me by, please?

[CLAIRE *steps out of* OLIVER'S *way.*]

CLAIRE: Oh, you wanna walk. Go 'head.....WALK.

[CLAIRE *walks over to the bench and sits. She begins working on a quilt.* OLIVER *tries to cross the street but is unable to.*]

OLIVER: My knees....must be getting a little stiff.

CLAIRE: Yeah....stiff.... Not sure why you standin' there. You ain't got the guts to move.

OLIVER: Excuse me?

CLAIRE: Standing there ain't gonna make it any easier

OLIVER: Not sure what you mean

CLAIRE: You got three options... left, right, or straight-ahead. Then again you can always turn around and go back where you came from.

OLIVER: Well I don't

CLAIRE: Decisions.

OLIVER: I'm looking for a friend of mine.

CLAIRE: Yeah.... I bet.

OLIVER: Haven't seen them in a while.

CLAIRE: I don't think you got any "friends".

OLIVER: ....Do I know you?

CLAIRE: I know you.

OLIVER: Tate. Oliver D.

CLAIRE: Pretty boy.

OLIVER: So, you do know me. Must be an old fan.

CLAIRE: Just 'cause I know you don't make me a fan

OLIVER: That's true

CLAIRE: As for "old". You damn sure ain't no spring chicken.

ISHMAEL: I just thought....Well, it's been awhile since I been in swamp country. Figured you know me cause of the music.

CLAIRE: Too far north to be "swamp country" as you say.

OLIVER: Any place on this here peninsular is swamp country to me.

CLAIRE: Only gators I've seen is at the shoe store.

OLIVER: I see.... Well, I'll just leave you be Ms. I'm sorry I didn't get your name.

CLAIRE: Ain't give it.

OLIVER: I figure since you know mine, I might

CLAIRE: I know a lot about you Mr. Tate…. And ain't none of it good.

OLIVER: Oh.....Well, I'll be damned…Ain't this something… Genuine. In the flesh....Thought y'all was a dying breed. Still sprouting up like cane stalks around these parts.

CLAIRE: Hmmmm.

OLIVER: Oh, you had me fooled for a second... Course you know my name…. Your kind usually does

CLAIRE: I beg your pardon

OLIVER: Apologize for my brashness...sister. If I'd known who I was talking to…Well... So, what's the going rate these days? Ain't got no cash on me. You take credit?

CLAIRE: There must be some mistake

OLIVER: Oh, no mistake. I know a two headed lady when I see one. What else you got in that bag besides fabric?

[OLIVER *holds out an empty palm.*]

CLAIRE: Mr. Tate!

OLIVER: Go head. Tell me what you see

CLAIRE: I'll have you know that I am a god-fearing woman

OLIVER: Don't care who you fear, sister.... just tell me what you see.

[CLAIRE *briefly studies his palm.*]

CLAIRE: Ain't nothing to see.

OLIVER: Am I gonna find my friend?

CLAIRE: Already told you... You ain't got no friends.

OLIVER: Well, you lying then.

[OLIVER *walks back to the intersection. He tries to cross it, but is still unable to.*]

CLAIRE: You know that girl dead.

OLIVER: ...Yeah... I heard...folks being rather tight lipped about it.

CLAIRE: Good...there was another one too...a grandchild....left before its time

OLIVER: ....Oh God....Didn't know about no baby

CLAIRE: 'Rather peculiar how haints from the past always show up too late for the wake.

OLIVER: Ain't come here for judgment

CLAIRE: Then what you come here for?

OLIVER: I come for what's mine.

CLAIRE: Yours? You don't even exist!

OLIVER: What? You blind now?

CLAIRE: Prove it.

OLIVER: I'm standing right here.

CLAIRE: Prove to me that you exist!

OLIVER: Look, I ain't got time

CLAIRE: All I'm asking for is proof. What? 'Cause you talking to me? That could easily be the wind, or a bee flying near somebody's ear. The breath in your lungs and the hot air from you lips don't mean a thing. What kind of proof you got?

OLIVER: I got what belongs to me!

CLAIRE: What's that? Love?

OLIVER: Yes.

CLAIRE: Sure that's all?   It's been...what....fifteen years?...15 years and you suddenly feel love pulling you back.... Pulling you down that road again....I see your eyes Tate. You're tired....Ain't love you looking for

OLIVER: You don't know what you talkin' bout

CLAIRE: And ain't nobody here to love you.... if nobody love you…Well... I reckon you don't exist.

OLIVER: What about the love I got in me, huh?

CLAIRE: Like I said...it ain't love you looking for. Whatchu want comes with a price

OLIVER: I've paid enough

CLAIRE: Rest...Peace of mind... a haint's paradise.

OLIVER: ...I got me a little brown child.... with pretty brown eyes just like mine. And a voice as strong and sweet as cane syrup. I came back for that voice and the vessel that holds it.

CLAIRE: Ain't no "voice" Mr. Tate. Memory makes folk mute... and even syrup don't stay sweet forever... The voice that *binds* you is gone and the little one, she ain't found hers yet so she can't set you free… You looking for forgiveness. Ain't no forgiving a dead man.

OLIVER: Specially one that's alive!

CLAIRE: I'm a Christian woman Mr. Tate.... and I'm not sure what demon you made a bargain with that allowed your sorry ass to prance out of hell's gate in one piece, but heed my words what's above ground ain't no prettier. If you looking for something to ease your spirit.... you done come to the wrong place. Heartache floats in the air around here…smells sweet like a summer breeze… but it's deadly. So, for your own safety… it would be best if you just walk on back down that road….otherwise...well… lets just say I ain't too fond of games.

OLIVER: Listen, I done played spades with the devil himself and that motherfucka always reneges. I never loose. Ain't a damn thing you got to say gonna keep me from what's mine.

[OLIVER *reaches in his pocket and pulls out two dates.*]

OLIVER: Here....dates....Take one.

[CLAIRE *takes a date from his palm. She looks him straight in the eye. The both eat.*]

OLIVER: Sweeter than a sunrise.

ACT 1
SCENE 2

[*Later that evening….*MARIE *walks towards the intersection; she is followed by* FELIX *carrying two large bags.*]

MARIE: Hurry up!

FELIX: Don't think these bags are in a hurry…they appear to be patient.

MARIE: …Told Ishmael I'd be back by nine.   It's nine thirty, he's probably worried

FELIX: Paranoid…the nigga sounds paranoid.

MARIE: He worries about me.

FELIX: This ain't the big city. The things you need to be worrying about don't come with pistols and gold teeth. Besides…You got me to protect you.

MARIE: I'm sure he would find that reassuring.

FELIX: What you been telling him bad things about me?

MARIE: No, he saw us talking at the wake and after the funeral…I could tell by the look on his face.

FELIX: That's why he didn't shake my hand.

MARIE: He doesn't know you... give him time.

FELIX: The green eyed monster… an ugly beast

MARIE: And why would he be jealous of you?

FELIX: …You're not married yet….I'm the zombie lurking in the shadows...

MARIE: I don't like monsters.

FELIX: You should.

MARIE: …Give me the bags, I gotta get going.

FELIX: Wait…   Two blocks is a long way to walk caring this heavy bag.

MARIE: It's fabric.

FELIX: Feels like a bag of bricks…Think I need to rest my knees.

MARIE: Alright…what do you want?

FELIX: All this walking and lifting got me feeling mighty hungry.   Now I might be able to postpone my raging appetite ….if you agree to have dinner with me.

MARIE: Give me the bag

FELIX: Think I'll hold it hostage… What we got here….Lace…..Silk…. unfortunately none of these lovely materials are eatable.

MARIE: I've got a lot of work to do….

[MARIE *grabs the bag.* FELIX *won't let go.*]

MARIE: Marie is grounded…. She can't come out and play!

FELIX: DINNER. Even doll makers gotta eat.

MARIE: I can't. Before you leave town…I promise.

FELIX: Uhuh…let go...stand back… I'll scream!!… Help! Police!

MARIE: Shut up fool…!

FELIX: Don't touch my bag lady! I've worked hard for my fabrics!

MARIE: Gimmie!

FELIX: I have mumu's to make!

MARIE: Mumu's?

FELIX: ….Charity work….The Obese Transvestite's Shelter.

MARIE: You have serious problems.

FELIX: I'm willing to postpone my moral obligation to fat shemen…if you have dinner with me?

MARIE: I told

FELIX: I want definite plans. I'm only here for a couple of days.

MARIE: I'm busy!

FELIX: Dolls, dolls, dolls!

MARIE: This is important.

FELIX: You…you're so damn country.

MARIE: I know *you* ain't calling me country

FELIX: Just like the rest of these ole swamp niggas around here. I guess you gonna shave your head and start fishing ...maybe work some roots on folk

MARIE: It's my duty

FELIX: It's a doll.

MARIE: I made a promise to my mother, I want her to rest. This is the only way I know how.

FELIX: Marie, come on you can't tell me you believe in all that.

MARIE: I don't know what I believe anymore…ever since I came back here it's been one disaster after another.

FELIX: I heard about your baby.

MARIE: Damn…this town.

FELIX: Can't keep nothing private.

MARIE: Yeah.

FELIX: I'm sorry.

MARIE: Thank you…and thanks for

FELIX: No problem. Couldn't let a lovely lady carry such a heavy bag.

MARIE: Not that…thanks for coming.

FELIX: Wish I could have been here sooner…When my grandmother told me what happened, I hopped on the plane didn't think twice about it.

MARIE: I never thought I'd see you back here again.

FELIX: Never thought I'd come back…but you're here.

[*There's an awkward silence.*]

MARIE: …I was here before you left.

FELIX: …Yeah.

MARIE: …That was a long time ago.

FELIX: A long time.

[*Another awkward silence.*]

FELIX: So, you going back to Atlanta?

MARIE: Ishmael wants to…he thinks going back to the city is the answer…. Some magic cure all. But this brown soil, salty air, seashells and memories… it belongs to me…all of it, the sweetness and the pain I can't walk away from it.

FELIX: I'm taking you to dinner…. You are loosing your mind

MARIE: Oh God

FELIX: I'm serious, Marie. "The salty air" has infected your brain.

MARIE: Oh please…you keep going on and on about the "perfect beaches of Martinique"

FELIX: They are perfect

MARIE: And you say it with the "haughty tinge" of some transcontinental Negro

FELIX: "The *perfect* beaches of Martinique"

MARIE: Exactly and I keep thinking. "This is the same nigga that flunked French in high school."

FELIX: The only way to learn is to commune with the natives.

MARIE: *Commune*…I bet.

FELIX: …And the beaches really are perfect.

MARIE: *Perfect.*

FELIX: If you don't believe me …you should come

MARIE: I wouldn't want to disrupt your communion with the natives.

FELIX: Only one costal woman has my heart.

MARIE: I find that hard to believe.

FELIX: I'm serious. [*Beat.*] Let me take you to dinner…maybe I can convince you…I'll even bring a gift.

MARIE: Bribery.

FELIX: You bet.

MARIE: ….Bigger than a breadbox?

FELIX: Nope. Smaller.

MARIE: …Any clues.

FELIX: You'll have to wait.

MARIE: Alright…dinner it is day after tomorrow. [*Beat.*] So…can I have my bag?

[FELIX *steps up close to her.*]

FELIX: Only if I get a good night kiss.

[MARIE *moves closer to him as if she's about to kiss she grabs her bag instead and starts to walk away.*]

FELIX: Tease.

MARIE: You love it.

[MARIE *crosses the street. Lights fade.* ISHMAEL *begins to play…and begins to sing the opening refrain to* *MARIES THEME *in the transition…*]

ACT 1
SCENE 3

[*The living room.* MARIE *enters carrying the big bag as* ISHMAEL *continues sing a few more verses. She stops at the door and listens to him.*]

MARIE: Beautiful.

ISHMAEL: Thanks….

MARIE: Is that new?

ISHMAEL: Yeah…still working on it... Hard to find the words.

MARIE: I miss your music.

ISHMAEL: ... I'm always playing.

MARIE: Not for me.

ISHMAEL: Can't practice in the house for too long….the mind drifts.   You can always come to Pete's.

MARIE: No self respecting woman would be caught dead in Pete's.

ISHMAEL: There are plenty of women at Pete's.

MARIE: Looking for "customers".

ISHMAEL: Oh.

MARIE: You are so green.

[MARIE *kisses* ISHMAEL.]

ISHMAEL: So…Where you been?

MARIE: Well "father" let me see….

ISHMAEL: You know I can't sleep until you get home.

MARIE: Needn't worry so much.   I'm a big girl.   Ran into Felix on my way.

ISHMAEL: Oh. Joy.

MARIE: He's leaving town soon… wants to go out for dinner.   You're welcome to come.

ISHMAEL: I'd rather give myself an enema… with battery acid.

MARIE: Give him a chance, Ishmael.

ISHMAEL: How you gonna trust a nigga named "Felix"?

MARIE: He's a wonderful person

ISHMAEL: FELIX! What kinda crack was his mamma smoking?

MARIE: The name fits him

ISHMAEL: Perfect for a punk

MARIE: He's slick…. like a cat

ISHMAEL: Is that a euphemism for "bitch made"?

MARIE: I won't have you insulting my friends

ISHMAEL: You should pick a better class of people to pal around with.

MARIE: …Funny. That's what my girlfriends used to say when we started dating.

ISHMAEL: ….Never liked them hoes anyway.

MARIE: Charming.

[MARIE *pulls out pieces of fabric.*]

ISHMAEL: Here we go. You just don't let up.

MARIE: I told you I was gonna get started on this.

ISHMAEL: I don't see what the big deal is.

MARIE: Mamma was trying to show me how to do this for the past two weeks.

ISHMAEL: Do you even know how to sew?

MARIE: We'll see…You could help me?

ISHMAEL: No.

MARIE: Come on.

ISHMAEL: I would be of no use.

MARIE: Here, just hold that end while I cut it.

ISHMAEL: …So…is this a normal thing?

MARIE: What?

ISHMAEL: When some dies…you make dolls for them?

MARIE: …It's my first one.

ISHMAEL: You can't even cut a straight line.

MARIE: Shut up… you're making me nervous.

ISHMAEL: So what is this supposed to do?

MARIE: It's a tradition. When a child is born a doll is made…for protection and when a mother dies another doll is made to continue the bloodline

ISHMAEL: What about the fathers?

MARIE: Few fathers stuck around long enough…maybe they've got their own traditions… Nanna would make the dolls for all of the births and deaths in town

ISHMAEL: That's a lot of damn dolls

MARIE: When she passed momma took over…now …I guess it's me.

ISHMAEL: Couldn't y'all just go to the toy store and pick up a Black Barbie?

MARIE: Barbie?

ISHMAEL: Don't they got a Moesha doll or something?

MARIE: Ishmael….never mind.

ISHMAEL: What? I'm just joking baby.

MARIE: You're makin' fun of me.

ISHMAEL: Naw… It's just… y'all some different folk.

MARIE: Don't start

ISHMAEL: No, I'm just saying. Since I've been here…well… I've gotten quite the education.

MARIE: You're not funny.

ISHMAEL: As soon as I got here first thing your momma had me doing I mean, I'd just gotten off the bus… walked three blocks didn't even get a chance to put down my bags before she put a broom in my hand

MARIE: She wanted you to feel at home

ISHMAEL: Yeah right. But I was cool, you know "respect your elders" especially one that's about to be your mother in-law

MARIE: How hospitable

ISHMAEL: But I didn't complain. "Yes Ms. Dianne, I will gladly sweep your front porch". Then… she gives it to me…a bag of dust

MARIE: You should have seen the look on your face

ISHMAEL: "What am I suppose to do with this"?

MARIE: "Sweep the porch with it"

ISHMAEL: "…I thought the goal was to get the porch clean"

MARIE: "Brick dust is the only way to clean it."

ISHMAEL: She looked at me like I was a damn fool.

MARIE: How were you supposed to know? It keeps the bad energy out of your house.

ISHMAEL: Like taking off your shoes

MARIE: Yeah

ISHMAEL: Another stupid superstition.

MARIE: "Yea of so little faith."

ISHMAEL: You don't actually believe that stuff.

MARIE: I don't know. I spent my whole life making fun of these people and their ways. Didn't make much sense to me…I mean, I understood the richness of it, the "poetry" of it, but that didn't mean it mattered. Mamma and Nanna with their doll making and stories of fisherwomen what did any of that have to do with me? But when I came back to take care of her …I don't know… Maybe it's because I hadn't been home in long time…I was older…came back to this town a *woman*…a woman carrying a child it changed somehow. Can't say I believe it…but I at least understand it. It's how they brought order to their lives.

ISHMAEL: It's still strange as hell… Why don't we put all this away…you can get started tomorrow after work…Come to bed.

MARIE: Told you I'm busy… You could stay up with me, though … play some music.

ISHMAEL: …I don't wanna.

MARIE: Oh… so you're gonna be difficult about this?

ISHMAEL: Yep.

[MARIE *pops* ISHMAEL *with a piece of fabric.*]

ISHMAEL [laughing]: Oww!! Domestic violence!!

MARIE [laughing]: You're stupid.

[*They kiss each other.*]

MARIE: I'll be finished soon…I promise. I know it doesn't seem important…but…it is I just gotta do this one last thing for her.

ISHMAEL: Then we can go back to the city?

MARIE: …I didn't say that.

ISHMAEL: I just want things to be like they were.

MARIE: I know.

ISHMAEL: ....Come to Pete's tomorrow night? I'll play song just for you.

MARIE: I'll still be working.

ISHMAEL: ... What about the next night?

MARIE: ...Dinner....with Felix.

ISHMAEL: .....Yeah.

[ISHMAEL *and* MARIE *look at each other for a moment.*]

ISHMAEL: ...Alright....well...goodnight.

MARIE: 'Night.

[ISHMAEL *exits. * MARIE *watches him leave. She removes various spools of thread and places them on the coffee table. She stares at the fabric for a moment. She pulls out a sketchbook and tries to sketch some ideas...she stops and leans back on the couch exasperated.*]

MARIE: How am I supposed to do this, mamma? Where is this supposed to take me?

[*She leans forward and begins to sketch again. Lights fade.*]

ACT 1
SCENE 4

[*Bus stop. Next morning.* ISHMAEL *is sitting on the bench listening to a portable CD player and reading a newspaper.* OLIVER *enters. He walks to the corner and stands next to the sign. He is still unable to cross the street. In frustration he turns to* ISHMAEL.]

OLIVER: Excuse me young man...

[ISHMAEL *does not hear him.* OLIVER *walks up and taps him on the shoulder.*]

ISHMAEL: Yeah?

OLIVER: Sorry to disturb you son. I was wondering…. Would you happen to know any folks around here by the name of Grant?

ISHMAEL: No, can't say I do.

OLIVER: They use to live on this street…some years back.

ISHMAEL: Never heard of them.

OLIVER: What about Tate.....they could be using the name Tate.

ISHMAEL: Can't say I know any Tates either.... Only been in town for a few months. Don't know too many people.

[ISHMAEL *stares at* OLIVER *for a moment.*]

ISHMAEL: ...You look awfully familiar.

OLIVER: Well... thanks anyway. Sorry to disturb you.

ISHMAEL: No problem.

OLIVER: Who you listening to?

ISHMAEL: Cat named Jason Moran

OLIVER: Jason? I know that youngblood. Sat in with him in Berlin, about two years ago. Hell of a talent!

ISHMAEL: No shit! You play?

OLIVER: Little keys, not nearly as good as him… I'm primarily a vocalist. Oliver D.

ISHMAEL: I'll be damned! Pretty boy Tate.

OLIVER: Boy, what you know about Pretty boy Tate?

ISHMAEL: Oh, shit! I can't believe –

OLIVER: You don't look no older than 30, I'm way before your time.

ISHMAEL: Moms and pops had all your albums.

OLIVER: They got good taste

ISHMAEL: You played a gig in Atlanta, at the Jazz Festival I was there!

OLIVER: Well ain't that something

ISHMAEL: You gotta come down to the school!

OLIVER: School?

ISHMAEL: I teach music at the high school. That's where I'm headed now, soon as this damn bus gets here.

OLIVER: Sorry, gotta find my people today.

ISHMAEL: How long you gonna be in town?

OLIVER: Probably for another day or two.

ISHMAEL: Tell you what… A couple of cats get together and jam down at Pete's on weeknights

OLIVER: Old man Pete still got a juke joint?

ISHMAEL: Juke Joint? That place is a national landmark. Anyway, a couple of us get together and jam. I'm talking all-nighters till at least 5 in the A.M.

OLIVER: Don't you gotta teach school tomorrow?

ISHMAEL: Shoot coffee in my veins. Ain't got any choice.

OLIVER: Y'all must be serious about your music.

ISHMAEL: Absolutely….You've gotta stop by and jam with us.

OLIVER: I don't know, son

ISHMAEL: Come by my fiancée's place at around seven this evening. She grew up in this town might be able to help you find your people. We'll have dinner and head to Pete's.

OLIVER: You sure your fiancée won't mind?

ISHMAEL: She'd love it! We rarely have any guest at the house, let alone famous ones. What do ya say?

OLIVER: All right. How do I get there?

ISHMAEL: Just go straight down Cassandra Lane, 7th house on your right. 358.

OLIVER: … 358…

ISHMAEL: Yes sir

OLIVER: 358 Cassandra Lane…Well, I'll be damned I'll. Be. Damned.

[*Lights fade.*]
ACT 1
SCENE 5

[*Bus stop. Early evening. CLAIRE is sitting on the bench sewing. MARIE enters. She is standing beneath a parasol. She sits on the bench next to CLAIRE. CLAIRE turns and looks at her.*]

CLAIRE: Ain't been no sun for a while.

[MARIE *folds the parasol.*]

CLAIRE: Don't know why you walk around with that damn umbrella

MARIE: Parasol

CLAIRE: Hmmm…

MARIE: …It's good to see you.

CLAIRE: …You saw me yesterday, at the funeral.

MARIE: Well…it's good to see you today.

CLAIRE: Really now.

MARIE: Yep…all the way from the school I kept thinking, "I sure hope Ms. Claire is at the bus stop."

CLAIRE: Hmmmm…

MARIE: And here you are.

CLAIRE: Thought about me all the way here, did ya?

MARIE: Sure did.

CLAIRE: Alright… what you want?

MARIE: I wanted to see you.

CLAIRE: Don't play with me child; what you want?

MARIE: Why are you so suspicious?

CLAIRE: Cause I know you.

MARIE: …O.K…There's no rule that says that *I* have to make the burial doll, right?

CLAIRE: Rule?

MARIE: There's no "Costal Girl Handbook" or anything.

CLAIRE: What are you getting at?

MARIE: Mamma always had so much respect for you Ms. Claire.

CLAIRE: Dianne was my heart… bless her soul

MARIE: Exactly, and I'm sure she wouldn't mind it if you

CLAIRE: Stop it right there

MARIE: It's not a big deal.

CLAIRE: I can't believe

MARIE: Pleeeease.

CLAIRE: You are trying to hustle your way out of this.

MARIE: I was up all night

CLAIRE: Good

MARIE: Had to stay after school for parent teacher conferences

CLAIRE: Ain't got no business going to work no way.

MARIE: I've gotta work Ms. Claire.

CLAIRE: You've gotta mourn. Ain't took no time to mourn

MARIE: I'm too tired

CLAIRE: Soon as you lost the baby you were right back in that classroom

MARIE: I gotta stay busy

CLAIRE: You mamma ain't even two days in the ground and you back at work

MARIE: Are you gonna make the doll or not?

CLAIRE: …What's going on with you?

MARIE: Nothing's going on, Ms. Claire.

CLAIRE: ….Let me see what you got.

[MARIE *takes out her sketchpad and pieces of fabric.*]

MARIE: This is it. Spent all night sketching.

CLAIRE: Sketching?

MARIE: Nothing…

CLAIRE: That's cause you wasting time.

MARIE: Thanks for the vote of confidence.

CLAIRE: I don't know why you insist on trying to plan ahead.

MARIE: Got to know where I'm going.

CLAIRE: You've got to know who you are.   That's how we been doing it for generations. That's how Ms. Sarah did it and that's how your mamma did it.

MARIE: I'm neither one of them.

CLAIRE: Then who are you?   We ain't nothin' but the sum total of all the folks that came before us. Now your Nanna, Ms. Sarah, she held an image in her mind...knew ahead of time how that doll would look, the size, shape, and color....she would just pick up that needle and thread and keep right on living. The little house is packed with all these women folk...all the time. Women laughing, gossiping, straightening hair, cooking up some food.   It's our meeting place.   The men got Pete's.   All the women would be up in that little house of yours. Good times. Ms. Sarah counsels some woman about her problems, praying for her and sewing the entire time. Every once and awhile she looks at what she's making and laughs.... a mess of thread and fabric. Always surprises her, what she sees. It's a journey, a place to rest   watching the road unfold as she goes along. Those were the most beautiful dolls I've ever seen.... Your mamma was the same way...You the last one, child. These eyes are getting old... can barely thread a needle, much less finish a whole piece. You've got to be the one to move us forward. I was never any good at making dolls...but you....it's in your blood you've just gotta accept it.

MARIE: ....Where do I begin?

CLAIRE: Just begin.

MARIE: That's easy to say

CLAIRE: Why things always gotta be so complicated for y'all?

MARIE: Life is complicated, Ms. Claire

CLAIRE: Sometimes I think we done raised a whole generation of faithless orphans

MARIE: Oh lord

CLAIRE: Act like you homeless, ain't got no sense of who you are or what you can do.

MARIE: Well, I know I can't make a doll.

CLAIRE: You don't know nothin'. Girl you come from women that could bind the future with the sound of their voices. Those fisherwomen would call out to the sea… loud moans…humming as clear as the dawn. Hmmm…with that kind of power anything is possible….but it takes a light heart….gotta be willing to let go of all the pain and anger…gotta be able to forgive…(beat) She needs a foundation.

MARIE: Who?

CLAIIRE: The doll… a foundation… Start with the legs and feet, child!

MARIE: Huh?

CLAIRE: Start sewing the legs and feet.... keep her rooted....Legs, feet, then the body, arms and hands... save the head for last.

[MARIE *looks at the quilt* CLAIRE *is sewing.*]

MARIE: What are you working on?

CLAIRE: Making a quilt… for you…gonna need something to keep you warm and dry when this weather changes.

MARIE: Excuse me?

CLAIRE: You heard me.

MARIE: What do you see, Ms. Claire?

CLAIRE: Don't worry about what I see you've got eyes of your own? I'm just waiting on you to get some clarity is all?

MARIE : "Clarity"

CLAIRE: I'm serious.

MARIE : My vision is fine

CLAIRE: No it ain't. Carrying too much residue from the past. Gotta plant your feet firmly in the present, girl. Right now. Giving too much energy to the dead, child…. specially the dead that still breathing… folk like Felix Bentecort.

MARIE: We're just friends

CLAIRE: I know y'all just friends…but I'll tell ya…it's a waste …waste of energy

MARIE: Claire!

CLAIRE: I know it sounds harsh…but…. people like that wear you down

MARIE: I've known Felix all my life

CLAIRE: I've known the devil all my life. That don't mean we buddy-buddy… You don't need no running partner. This ain't a relay. This is life…and you won't get nowhere running in the mud. Plant your feet, child.

MARIE: …I hear you.

CLAIRE: Ain't it about time for you to head on home? You know how that boy worries.

MARIE: Yeah… Ishmael's supposed to be having some musician friend over for dinner. You should come.

CLAIRE: Oh no! There'll be enough going on in your house, you won't need me there. Besides, I gotta stay out here a little longer… watch the neighborhood.

MARIE: Who needs the police when we got Ms. Claire?

CLAIRE: Somebody gotta look out for y'all fools.

MARIE: I'll bring you a plate.

[MARIE *kisses* CLAIRE *on the cheek*.]

CLAIRE: All right baby.

[MARIE *starts to leave*.]

CLAIRE: ….Marie.

MARIE: ….Ma'am.

CLAIRE: You know I'm here if you need me.

MARIE: ….Yeah….I know.

ACT 1
SCENE 6

[*Living room.* MARIE *opens the door. She stands at the door for a moment.* ISHMAEL *enters from the kitchen with a bowl and a spoon in his hand.*]

MARIE: Let me guess...fish.

ISHMAEL: And grits.

MARIE: Well.. well ain't you just… precious.

ISHMAEL: What?

MARIE: Trying to fix some Southern cuisine.

ISHMAEL: I'm Southern.

MARIE: You went to college in Atlanta. That don't make you Southern. Now, if you were making some cheese steak sandwiches, we could talk

ISHMAEL: Spent my summers in Virginia, as a child

MARIE: Still don't make you a Southerner

ISHMAEL: And I can make grits

[MARIE *looks into his bowl.*]

MARIE: They better not be lumpy.

[ISHMAEL *lifts the spoon the grits is one big lump.* MARIE *kisses him.*]

MARIE: You still mad at me?

ISHMAEL: Uh…Yeah.

[MARIE *kisses his neck.*]

MARIE: Can we make up?

ISHMAEL: I'll think about it…   How was your day?

MARIE: Long and uneventful…Spent some time with Ms. Claire.

ISHMAEL: Stop by her house?

MARIE: She was at the bus stop.

ISHMAEL: She's always at the bus stop. You'd think she lives there.

MARIE: It's….her studio.

ISHMAEL: Hmmm…

MARIE: I'm worried about her…she was acting really strange today.

ISHMAEL: Stranger than usual?

MARIE: Yeah…I don't know...So, when's company coming?

ISHMAEL: Should be here any moment.

MARIE: You made him sound all mysterious on the phone.

ISHMAEL: I want it to be a surprise.

MARIE: Surprise? … Who is this masked man?

[*The lights come up on the bus stop as* MARIE *and* ISHMAEL *speak.* CLAIRE *sits on the bench sewing.* OLIVER *enters....he stands at the intersection ...still unable to cross the street*.]

ISHMAEL: Someone very important.

MARIE: Famous?

ISHMAEL: Pretty.... well respected.

MARIE: Is his last name ....Marsalis?

ISHMAEL: Bigger than the entire Marsalis clan.

MARIE : Damn...uhmm....Dizzy Gillespie?

ISHMAEL: Sweetheart.... Dizzy is no longer on "our side of the street".

MARIE: Really?

CLAIRE [*to* Oliver]: Go ahead...cross the street, Tate

[OLIVER *looks at* CLAIRE *then takes two reluctant steps past the crossway sign*.]

ISHMAEL: Yeah, It's been couple of years, baby.

[MARIE *starts to gasp for air*.]

MARIE: …Oh… sorry.

ISHMAEL: Are you O.K.?

MARIE: I... –I'm feeling a little nauseous.

ISHMAEL: Could be the fish.

CLAIRE: So, what you waiting on?

[OLIVER *turns to* CLAIRE *and smirks*.]

MARIE: I need to go freshen up.

[MARIE *gets up to leave.*]

CLAIRE: Be gentle with that child, Tate.

ISHMAEL: All right. Yell if you need me.

[MARIE *exits living room.*]

OLIVER: Mind your business, Sister.

[CLAIRE *watches* OLIVER *walk away….Lights fade on bus stop.* OLIVER *is at the front door, which is still open. He looks in then knocks on the doorframe.*]

ISHMAEL: Hey, Mr. Tate. Come on in.

[OLIVER *stands at the doorway for a moment.*]

OLIVER: 358 Cassandra Lane... Ain't this something.

ISHMAEL: Yeah, it's a nice little place.

[OLIVER *stands in front of the large photograph and stares.*]

ISHMAEL: The picture's been in my fiancée's family for about three generations.

OLIVER: Parasols.

ISHMAEL: Yeah, the family heirloom.

OLIVER: Three generations... So, your ...fiancée... a coastal woman?

ISHMAEL: I guess...never heard that term before.

OLIVER: How long you been here?

ISHMAEL: 'Bout four months. Moved down here to help with her mother.

OLIVER: Oh....you still green. You don't know where you are. Travel much?

ISHMAEL: Ain't been but a couple of places.

OLIVER: Traveled a lot when I was your age. Tried to settle down for a moment...you know...play that game. I was never any good at it. Past fifteen years … just been movin' around. Don't think I've slept once in all them years… Music and movement....that's all the fuel you need. One thing I've learned, though you've got to know the lay of the land... got to know its particulars.

ISHMAEL: What do you mean?

OLIVER: Every place has got it's own particulars... The simplest landscapes got they own little undercurrents..... It can pull you right on in the ocean and drown ya if you ain't careful.

ISHMAEL: This little town seems safe enough.

OLIVER: Huh.... spoken like a true Northerner. You ain't in the city no more, boy

ISHMAEL: Don't remind me.

OLIVER: This place...well...let's just say that things around here are a little different... different kind of folk....Generations.. . Not too many men around these parts.

ISHMAEL: Yeah…I've noticed that.

OLIVER: Most of the women folk learned to fend for themselves. Craftspeople. Weaving, making baskets, chairs that sort of thing....some of them learned to fish

ISHMAEL: The fisherwomen....

OLIVER: …Yeah... Don't think too many around here any more... Lived near the ocean. They wear these long flowing dresses...copper bracelets on their wrists...heads shaved. Look like they from another world. Some place ancient. They stand at the shore and cast their lines into the water.... just sit on the beach with their parasols and stare...at the horizon...humming melodies...like they waiting for something....

ISHMAEL: Maybe they're thinking about home.

OLIVER: Maybe. Ain't that what we all thinking about? Home. A place to rest...a place that's safe.... in a world without men…got they own way of communicating. You know how confusing women folks can be

ISHMAEL: Tell me about it

OLIVER: Coastal women even more confusing... and very aware of their power...

[MARIE *enters. She has changed into a flowing summer dress and is putting copper bracelets on her wrist. She is stunning. When she sees* OLIVER, *she stops in her tracks.*]

OLIVER: ....all women got power, boy.

ISHMAEL: Damn, babe...you look...amazing.

OLIVER: Yes. She. Does....

ISHMAEL: Oliver "Prettyboy" Tate, this is

OLIVER: Marie...

[ISHMAEL *looks confused.* OLIVER *walks closer to* MARIE. *She is frozen in place.* OLIVER *starts to hum a melody a sweet yet powerful tune his arms out stretched. He looks as if he's about to cry.* MARIE *stares at him in shock. She pushes past* OLIVER *in a rage and storms out the door.* OLIVER *pauses for a moment then heads for the bar.* ISHMAEL *follows after* MARIE.]

ISHMAEL: Marie.... MARIE!

[ISHMAEL *comes back inside the living room.* OLIVER *is calmly pouring himself a glass of rum.*]

ISHMAEL: What the hell's going on?

[OLIVER *gives* ISHMAEL *a silent toast then drinks…Lights go down on the living room.* MARIE *is sitting at the bus stop next to* CLAIRE *who is stroking her hair.* MARIE *stares blankly into space.*]

CLAIRE: Talk to me sweetie...talk to Claire.

MARIE: Oliver's home...

CLAIRE: I know child...I know.

[MARIE *lays her head on* CLAIRE'S *lap. Lights fade.*]

ACT 2
SCENE 1

[*End of Intermission. As the audience returns to their seats the 4th wall is completely broken.* OLIVER *and* ISHMAEL *are alone on stage, treating the audience as an audience.*]

OLIVER: I ain't played a joint like this in awhile so you gotta excuse me. I'm trying to be as informal as possible. But I need to let y'all know....I ain't taking no request. There will be no Marvin Gaye songs and NO I won't sing that Al Green song you lost your virginity to in the back seat of that mustang. This is strictly some "black classical" shit – so y'all can kiss my ass...[*to* ISHMAEL] You know *"The Road"?

[ISHMAEL plays the opening notes to the song.]

OLIVER [*pleased*]: I'll be damned...see they taught you a lil' something about culture up in Philly.

[*The house lights fade and the focus is on* OLIVER *and* ISHMAEL. *THE ROAD sounds like an old Billy Strayhorn styled jazz standard about the pleasures of life on the road. The two men sing it as a duet.*]

ACT 2
SCENE 2

[*Same evening. Laughter can be heard outside the living room door.* MARIE *enters, followed by* FELIX.]

MARIE: Shhhh

FELIX: Sorry

MARIE: You trying to get me in trouble?

FELIX: Hey Ishmael! What's happening?

[FELIX *walks over to the bar and begins to pour himself a drink.*]

MARIE: Shut up fool. Ishmael....Honey? Ish

FELIX: Maybe he's out with his other bitch

MARIE: There is no other bitch.

FELIX: Well, excuse me

MARIE: Ishmael! Where is he?   Don't you think you've had enough to drink?

FELIX: Yeah.   But y'all got the good shit.

MARIE: He was here before I left.

FELIX: You'd think he'd still be here after all that went down?

MARIE: ...Must be at Pete's.

FELIX: Huh...guess he and old man Tate gotta lot in common

MARIE: They're nothing alike

FELIX: I don't know… whole thing seems rather Freudian

MARIE: Shut up

FELIX: Marie's "looking for daddy"…I would have paid to see the look on your man's face when he found out. I can't believe he didn't know.

MARIE: There was no reason …Oliver Tate is not a part of my life… Ishmael's taking it personally, like I kept something from him

FELIX: You did

MARIE: It has nothing to do with him…nothing to do with us.

FELIX: So, don't fret over it….besides…you're in good hands now.

MARIE: If he heard you say that…you wouldn't have any hands.

FELIX: Well, he ain't here is he?

MARIE: That's cold.

FELIX: It's the truth.

MARIE: ….Shouldn't you be packing?

FELIX: Ooooo... Now that's cold.

MARIE: Wouldn't want you to miss your bus.

FELIX: Don't remind me…two hour bus ride just to get to the freaking airport. This fucking town… If your mom wasn't sick, do you think you would have come back?

MARIE: …I doubt it…but it was mamma – you know…I had to come.

FELIX: And your man was cool with that?

MARIE: He was very supportive.

FELIX: Saint Ishmael.

MARIE: …You're drunk.

FELIX: Yeah…

[FELIX *tries to kiss her* MARIE *steps away and begins to work on her doll.*]

MARIE: and I have work to do.

FELIX : Just reminiscing.

MARIE : Yeah, right.

FELIX : … What's that?

MARIE: What does it look like?

FELIX: I don't know.   Legs...feet. Where's the rest of it?

MARIE: I'm working on it. Legs and feet first...then the body, arms and hands....

FELIX: Put that shit down.

MARIE: No.

FELIX: Sewing.... needle and thread...dolls... it's too goddamn weird.

MARIE: If it's freaking you out   you could always leave.

FELIX: Don't wanna..... Besides...you know…you got a little buzz happening... Ishmael ain't here
MARIE: Please

FELIX: Don't tell me it ain't crossed your mind

MARIE: NO

FELIX: I see you looking at me

[MARIE *starts laughing.*]

FELIX: Girl... I know I 'm fine

MARIE: You're delicious baby...delicious.

FELIX: I see that lust in your eyes....Pure untapped LUST....Girl, you need to embrace your inner freak...

MARIE: My inner FREAK?

FELIX: That sweet sticky chocolate essence that is you...I'm talking bout the real you...not the doll making drunk ass school teacher...The REAL you...the true bitch inside

MARIE: Oh, that's deep

FELIX: STANK and deep.... Like... FUNKADELIC circa 1971

MARIE: Way before my time

FELIX: FREE YOUR MIND! And your ass will follow

MARIE: You know...I left my AfroZodiac poster in storage

FELIX: ...or you could just always...You know....FREE DAT ASS.

MARIE: Same old Felix.

FELIX: You're no fun.

MARIE: I'm working!

FELIX: So....have you talked to Tate?

MARIE: And you were so charming before

FELIX: The man's gotta be in town for a reason. It's been years, right?

MARIE: Yeah…about fifteen….damn….

FELIX: You've been in contact with him?

MARIE: He'd write…a phone call here and there…a birthday or Christmas card. What ever sort of relationship we had was always based on distance….the space between here and there. After mom was diagnosed....I just didn't have anything to say to him. Flying back and forth between here and the city... trying to take care of her. He just didn't seem important anymore. I couldn't stop blaming him for what was happening.

FELIX: She had cancer

MARIE: It was more than just cancer.

FELIX: Does he know the whole story?

MARIE: I don't know. I'm sure no one has told him–[*Beat*]… You know…she didn't ask for anyone else. The whole time. While that cancer was eating away at her...kept asking for Oliver had I heard from her PrettyBoy.

FELIX: You should have told him.

MARIE: Why?

FELIX: He was her husband

MARIE: That's funny. He marries her... has a child....and that makes him her HUSBAND. He's some guy that just...comes along. Strolls in and out of your life. Seasonal

FELIX: Maybe that didn't bother her

MARIE: She had a long winter... and some dark rainy days in between. Oliver Tate is not a safe place to harbor one's soul.

FELIX: Sometimes lying make the living easier.

MARIE: What kind of living is that?

FELIX: I don't think you understand what it's like to live here?

MARIE: Excuse me? You left here long before I did

FELIX: Are you still mad about that?

MARIE: Maybe… it's not important.

FELIX: Say what's on your mind.

MARIE: Felix….we were kids…knew each other our entire lives…I thought you would at least wait…until I was out of high school….   We'd always talked about hopping across the globe together…so yeah I was hurt when you left.

FELIX: ….I'm sorry.

MARIE: But… I got over it….that's what most men do…right? Leave.
I've never been able to understand it.

FELIX: You have no idea what it's like to live in a place like this…no jobs…no future.

MARIE: So you ran

FELIX: I escaped

MARIE: Ran because you were afraid

FELIX: Cause in a place like this I'm worthless… you don't understand… those fisherwomen didn't need men, right.

MARIE: It's not about *needing*…it's about fighting…Fighting to love...and be loved. People run 'cause they're afraid ....afraid to struggle with another person. Oliver Tate spent 15 years running.

FELIX: Ishmael ain't no different.

MARIE: He. STAYS… I'm not the easiest woman to please…Ishmael would never leave me. He won't run away. We've signed a contract ...and we're both too stubborn to break it

FELIX: And you're still not happy.

MARIE: Don't know what happiness is.   Don't think I've ever known.

FELIX: ….I could make you happy…Here...

MARIE: What's this?

FELIX: It's your gift…

MARIE: …Smaller than a breadbox.

FELIX: It's an open ticket…Martinique…*perfect* beaches…whenever you're ready.

MARIE: I can't take this.

FELIX: It's just a ticket…what are you afraid of…O.K… no pressure. [*Beat*] This is supposed to be my send off right?! [FELIX *returns to the bar*] So, let's have a toast!

MARIE: No more rum!!

FELIX: Come on, girl you could always drink me under the table.

MARIE: Alright…one glass… What are we toasting to?

FELIX: …The Ocean.

MARIE: The Ocean.

[*They toast lights fade. An hour later bus stop…*ISHMAEL *and* OLIVER *enter.* ISHMAEL *carries his guitar case.*]

OLIVER: Told ya we had 'em!

ISHMAEL: Amazing. Eating out your hands

OLIVER: You pretty mean on that guitar, boy....

ISHMAEL: I'm still a neophyte...but you...Man, that rendition of *Nature Boy* killed 'em.
OLIVER: I know that's Nat's song, but he ain't never heard me sing it. Seriously though...you've got a lot of talent.

ISHMAEL: I appreciate that, Mr. Tate. It's hard, you know. Pete's is the only place to play around here. After awhile it gets stale...playing with the same cats all the time. Hit a plateau. Stop learning.

OLIVER: Life in a small town.

ISHMAEL: Wish we could have stayed the whole set.

OLIVER: Still got time.

ISHMAEL: ... Gotta check on Marie.

OLIVER: How is she?

ISHMAEL: Don't know. Ain't said much since the other night.

OLIVER: ...Oh....I don't know how y'all tolerate all this damn walking

ISHMAEL: She convinced me to sell my car before I came down.... Said everything was in walking distance

OLIVER: It's hell on an old man's knees.

ISHMAEL: ….I feel like I'm land locked, Mr. Tate. Three blocks away from the ocean, two blocks away from downtown. The only real traveling I do is taking the bus to the high school.

OLIVER: It's a rough place for a city boy. I was born in a small town.....couldn't see myself dying in one. A musician's got to be on the move.

ISHMAEL: Been trying to convince Marie to go back to the city.

OLIVER: Good luck. Spent years trying to convince her momma to leave. Didn't want my child to be raised in some old swamp town. I wanted to go to Chicago
or DC. Someplace that had some culture... folks trying to move beyond the past. She wouldn't do it. Even after the old woman died   wouldn't do it.

ISHMAEL: You and "Nana" didn't get along?

OLIVER: I hated her ass….God bless the dead ….couldn't stand the bitch. One of the most ornery old women you'd ever want to meet

ISHMAEL: Nanna?

OLIVER: From day one we didn't get along. She just straight out told me I was no good. Right in front of my woman. Crazy….use to play that old "Christian" role. Praying to Jesus with the rest of them women in the neighborhood. Praying, eating and making dolls. Them damn dolls

ISHMAEL: Yep

OLIVER: Spookiest shit I've ever seen. Christian my ass…hoodoo plain and simple

ISHMAEL: Hoo doo? …. I dunno about all that
OLIVER: Mark my words boy

ISHMAEL: You sound like them old swamp niggas at Pete's... talking bout how some woman done put the "roots" on them.

OLIVER: Don't you under estimate these country folk.

ISHMAEL: Man, in Philli

OLIVER: Where you think Philli niggas come from….France?

ISHMAEL: You've got a point. …. Why don't you come up to the house? We'll have a drink.

OLIVER: Think we've had enough to drink.

ISHMAEL: Nothing like some rum on a summer evening.

OLIVER: Y'all sure like to get juiced up 'round here.

ISHMAEL: One drink Tate. Besides.… Marie went to dinner with a friend. She'll be a little more social tonight. Maybe the two of you could talk.

OLIVER: Wouldn't want to spoil a pleasant evening.

ISHMAEL: You ain't got much time left. Two days, right.

OLIVER: Yeah…. Tomorrow. Don't got the strength to look into those eyes tonight…I'll stop by tomorrow.

[*Lights fade at the bus stop. Living room. MARIE and FELIX are cracking up. ISHMAEL opens the door. FELIX bolts out of his seat to meet Ishmael at the door.*]

FELIX: Hey Ish; what's up?

ISHMAEL: Thought you'd be gone by now.

FELIX: Just having a little drink …you know …chatting.

[*ISHMAEL and FELIX stare at each other.*]

ISHMAEL: Yeah.

MARIE: Hey, sweetheart.

ISHMAEL: Didn't mean to interrupt your little sewing party

FELIX: Having a lot of fun....you should join us

ISHMAEL: Goodnight, Felix

FELIX: Hitting the sack so soon? Marie, I think your man wants you to tuck him in

ISHMAEL: ...Nigga, I'll

MARIE: Felix....give me a call before you leave tomorrow I'll walk you to the station.

FELIX: Yeah….right….You should come to see me off Ishmael

ISHMAEL: I'll pass.

FELIX: …That's unfortunate...well...y'all have a nice evening.

[FELIX *exits*.]

MARIE: 'Bout as polite as a rattlesnake

ISHMAEL: Told you I don't like that nigga!

MARIE: You need to get over it. And where have you been?

ISHMAEL: I've been out!

[ISHMAEL *goes over to the bar and fixes himself a drink*.]

MARIE: With who? No note, no phone call

ISHMAEL: I'm a grown ass man!

MARIE: Answer my question!

ISHMAEL: Told you I was going to Pete's…..I was hanging with your pops.

MARIE: Oliver.   You were out with Oliver

ISHMAEL: Your father!

MARIE: Are you two fucking?

ISHMAEL: I don't understand what your problem is!

MARIE: You don't know him

ISHMAEL: We're pals.... MUSICIANS....He's a good guy

MARIE: I hate it when you're drunk.

ISHMAEL: I'm not drunk!

MARIE: ….You don't know Oliver Tate. You know absolutely nothing about him

ISHMAEL: Did you plan to tell me anything? You're wearing my ring on your finger. Did you plan to tell me that your father was still alive?

MARIE: He's dead!

ISHMAEL: That your pops is Prettyboy

MARIE: A dead man. I don't care if he's walking around on earth breathing. The man is dead to me.

ISHMAEL: Makes no sense....he may not be perfect but he's still your father. The man is hurting….But you'd rather play with dolls.

MARIE: …Goodnight Ishmael.

ISHMAEL: Yeah….that's right. Send me away like a little kid

MARIE: GOOD. NIGHT.

[ISHMAEL *stares at her in disbelief.*]

ISHMAEL: …Fuck you.

[ISHMAEL *leaves out of the front door.*]

ACT 2
SCENE 3

[*Next afternoon.* MARIE *is sitting in the exact same place as the previous scene. She is maniacally sewing and trying to stay awake. There's a knock at the door. She answers it.*]

MARIE: What do you want?

OLIVER: Can I come in?

MARIE: Ishmael's not here.

OLIVER: I know…he's wasted crashed on my floor at the hotel.

MARIE: Isn't that cozy…Well…hope you didn't come to see me.

OLIVER: As a matter of fact I did....   left my chateau in the South of France...swam the Atlantic just to see you

MARIE: I'm busy, Oliver.

OLIVER: Oliver?

MARIE: I'm in no mood

OLIVER: I just want to spend some time

MARIE: Listen

OLIVER: Please.   Let me come in, just a moment.

[MARIE *turns and leaves him standing at the door. She immediately returns to her sewing.* OLIVER *stands at the doorway for a moment, he doesn't walk in.*]

OLIVER [*from the doorway*]: Watchu working on over there?

MARIE: Close the door... You're letting in mosquitoes.

[OLIVER *steps inside and closes the door. He sits in a chair across from* MARIE. *He stares at her for a moment.*]

OLIVER: Beautiful.   You know, you momma would never admit it but... seems like the older you get the more you resemble my folk. The Tates. Same mouth...them brown eyes always had eyes like mine. Stubborn as hell.... Oh, you ain't got to agree with me. I been talking to your man…the fool had me up all night I know you got an evil streak in you.   Set in your ways; don't want to listen to what nobody got to say. You done figured it out ain't you? Yep…. you know how the world operates it all makes sense to you…. Marie knows more than the rest of us... She's got integrity

MARIE: Well, it's so nice to see you too, Oliver. Glad we could have this little chat. You can leave now

OLIVER: I ain't going nowhere. You done let me in the house now. I'm gonna stay as long as I like.

MARIE: Really.

OLIVER: Damn right.

MARIE: I'm armed.

OLIVER: Good.   A lot of bad people out there. Never know who might come in your house

MARIE: Get out!

OLIVER: Three years! Not a word…stopped answering my calls…returned my letters. Been all over the country looking for you.   Went to your apartment in Atlanta. Your old school. Nowhere   not a trace of Marie Tate.

MARIE: Marie Tate doesn't exist.

OLIVER: What are you talking about?

MARIE: I'm Marie Williams…granddaughter of Sarah Williams…. Marie Tate is a sad little girl waiting for her father to come home.

OLIVER: You can't make me disappear by changing your name.

MARIE: No, you chose to disappear...

OLIVER: I didn't leave you baby

MARIE: I chose my name. You left

OLIVER: I never left you… Left your mother....this house. Why did you come back here?

MARIE: This is my home.

OLIVER: Home? How many times did you beg me to take you away from this place? "Daddy can I come live with you?"

MARIE: I was a child

OLIVER: "Can we go on the road together?"….Your mama wouldn't here of it. Tried to convince her. "Come on Diane let me take the little one on tour with me. She could see the world". No little girl should be stuck in some old swamp town. You were meant to wander the earth, sweetheart.

MARIE: That's your dream.

OLIVER: Our dream…

MARIE: A child's dream.....God.....I put you up in the sky. You were the sun to me. The music....sound of your voice. I was so proud to be your daughter. I was a child....time's a funny thing, though. You grow up and the haze evaporates…No more daddy…no more tears. Can't even cry….my eyes have dried up. But I can see clearly

OLIVER: I'm the same

MARIE: See you for what you really are

OLIVER: The same person you would sing with... every night.

MARIE: What about her, Oliver?

OLIVER: Daddy, just call me

MARIE: You don't deserve that title....What about Mama? What about leaving her and taking her heart with you? How am I supposed to love you after what you did to her....? I wonder if she sees you now. Old. Traveled the world. Ain't as "Pretty" as you used to be. Still uneasy. You look tired, Oliver. Seen the world and still not satisfied. Still hungry. The love of your wife and child just ...wasn't enough

OLIVER: That's not true

MARIE: No, Oliver Tate wants more! More pain, more heartache

OLIVER: I just want to hear our song, baby.   That's all I want.

MARIE: I'm too old for lullabies...shit... I can't even sleep. Nothing on this earth to soothe me. [*She holds up the scraps of fabric.*] Can't even give my mother the one thing she asked for…can't find any peace with my man.

OLIVER: Ishmael's a musician…. You can't expect him to live like this.

MARIE: Why? Because you couldn't.... couldn't stand on a firm foundation. A family. A home. Couldn't struggle with people that loved you.

OLIVER: It ain't got nothing to do with love.

MARIE: Maybe it doesn't.... Maybe I am like you...love just ain't enough. … Months….. Long... endless...months. I watched that woman die… waste away.....Took so long ....a series of gradual steps

OLIVER: ...Baby you should have

MARIE: I took her to the beach…   The weather's just starting to warm up. A breezy warm day. First day of sunshine we've seen in months. I paint her toenails coral. They look like sea shells resting on the sand. The ground is wet ...but firm...impenetrable. We giggle like little girls in our long dresses and straw hats. Momma's parasol twirls in the wind. We tell each other knock knock jokes. She gives me her recipe for peach preserves. "It's all in the jar, honey. Thick glass. It protects the sweetness". Protects the sweetness…. She wants to feel the cool water on her feet.   I watch her walk towards the water…. Her head is as naked as an infant's . She refuses to wear a wig. God ...just look at her… walking towards the ocean ...the sun on her smooth brown head. She looks so new… A different woman. I think about those old fisherwomen along the coast that Nana used to talk about. Casting their lines into the sea. Singing those old songs. Maybe they're heads were clean, brown and new. Ripe persimmons. Protect the sweetness... Mama waves at me. I wave back and laugh. I look up into the parasol. It glows in the sun. … It's funny ...even parasols can't completely block the sun.... I glance back at the shoreline. She's gone….

OLIVER: ...I'm... I don't understand….

MARIE: ...It so quiet. Only waves and seagulls make noise. Seagulls don't sing lullabies. They moan. Long extended moans. Blues singers with white wings.... She always said that she would walk on water.... meet you at the horizon... The boats found her body 15 miles from the shore… Floating in absolute stillness.

OLIVER: ....But...I thought.....she had cancer.

MARIE: …Cancer was killing her….The Ocean set her free…

OLIVER: …My god.

[MARIE *shows* OLIVER *her doll.*]

MARIE: Look… I'm almost done. Everything but the head… I'll save that for last…wait until my mind is clear…when all the memories have been washed away. Legs. Feet. Body. Arms and hands. Where do I put the heart?

[OLIVER *gets up in a daze.   He exits.*]

[*The bus stop. CLAIRE is sitting on her bench sewing. The quilt is large enough to cover her entire lap.* OLIVER *walks towards her.*]

OLIVER: Afternoon sista.

CLAIRE: Mr. Tate…

[OLIVER *sits down next to her.* CLAIRE *notices the anguish on his face.*]

CLAIRE: …Well…looks like Truth done kissed you on the mouth

OLIVER: Didn't even ask me my name

CLAIRE: Brazen hussy, that Truth is… She ain't got no shame. You alright…?

OLIVER: ….Nah…not really…..You got somethin' for me?

CLAIRE: What?

OLIVER: Somethin' for the pain.

CLAIRE: Ain't no cure for pain Tate. What is it you want?

OLIVER: …I just want some peace….peace is all.

CLAIRE: You can't get what you ain't been able to give.

[They look at each other for a moment.]

OLIVER: Ain't got no more lullabies….

CLAIRE: Nope….the air is too thick. It'll rain soon. We'll see what happens after the rain.

ACT 2
SCENE 4

[*Bus stop…early evening. FELIX is sitting at the bus stop with a suitcase. ISHMAEL comes down the street (from the same direction)* OLIVER *usually comes. He looks as if he hasn't slept all night.*]

FELIX: Here comes the music man…

ISHMAEL: Don't say nothing to me, right now, alright?

FELIX: Damn, dawg…think you'd been here long enough to absorb a little southern hospitality

ISHMAEL: Just…not right now, man.

FELIX [*pause*]: …It hurt…don't it?

ISHMAEL: WHAT?

FELIX: No…for real.

[ISHMAEL *begins to walk towards the house.*]

FELIX: I actually feel sorry for you, Ishmael?

ISHMAEL [*turning to face him*]: I don't need your pity.

FELIX: Sympathy… sounds better. Seriously…I understand. I feel your pain.

ISHMAEL: Felix…you don't know who you fuckin with.

FELIX: Yeah…I do. Dawg… you are so …. [*Beat*]… You actually thought you were gonna get her to leave this place.

ISHMAEL: What are you talking about?

FELIX: I mean…It *coulda* happen. Keep a woman away from her element long enough and she just might forget. Just. Might. But you fucked up and let her come back.
See, you and old man Tate…y'all outsiders. And these women… around here …. They always want the outsider. The one that's gonna take them away from all this. The tide, that smell in the air, the ghosts of fisherwomen…but if you look away even for a moment…if you give them a chance to *remember*…it'll pull them right back in. But you ain't know that.

ISHMAEL: But *you* do.

FELIX: Of course….I know these women. I was raised by them.

ISHMAEL: Why did you come back?

FELIX: I never left…not her. I 'm always floating around in the background. Whenever she's daydreaming… looking off in the distance. But you wouldn't have notice that either ….she already got you baited and hooked… fish caught on the line…you know how she does it…(he walks up close to Ishmael) she walks up close to you…maybe this close…and you feel the hairs on your skin start to stand up…Or the smell of her breath soft and sweet like raw honey….or when she drops her voice…just a little bit…and whispers fills up your lungs with clean ocean air…yeah…you feel me…

[ISHMAEL *punches* FELIX *in the face. The two men get into a slugging' match.* ISHMAEL *gets in one good lick to his jaw.*]

FELIX: See… that's what I'm talkin' bout… savagery… don't know how baby girl tolerates it…. but not for long …right?…O yeah… you ain't been home have you…she's probably packing her bags right now…. I gave her a one way ticket to paradise…what you ever give her?

ACT 2
SCENE 5

[*Lights fade...Living room. The entire room is in disarray. There are cushions and pillows on the ground.* ISHMAEL *sits on the chair with a rag on his eye. His shirt is torn and his face is bruised. The doll is torn to pieces and rests on the table as well.* MARIE *storms into the house.*]

MARIE: What's your fucking problem?!

ISHMAEL: He can punch you know

MARIE: Have you lost?

ISHMAEL: Didn't think he had it in him, that bastard's got a mean hook

MARIE: You broke his jaw!

ISHMAEL: He'll be alright. Jaws heal.

[MARIE *notices the torn pieces of fabric on the coffee table. She walks over and picks up the pieces of her doll.*]

MARIE: ...Oh my god.

[ISHMAEL *notices her and laughs.*]

ISHMAEL: Our life is in shambles....and she picks up the dead doll.

[MARIE attacks ISHMAEL.... ISHMAEL *grabs her to keep from being hit. She is kicking and screaming.*]

MARIE: You asshole!

ISHMAEL: When were you gonna tell me... huh? Were you gonna leave a note...explaining the situation or just fly off Martinique...huh? I shoulda been able to put two and two together...

MARIE: We're FREINDS

ISHMAEL: Yeah, RIGHT!

MARIE: I can't believe that you actually think I'd leave with him!

ISHMAEL: What am I supposed to believe....HUH?! ... First, your father pops up from nowhere... now this. ...I don't know what to expect anymore. Everybody in this backwards ass town knows more about my own fiancée' than I do. It's like... I'm some fucking joke.

MARIE: ...I thought you trusted me.

ISHMAEL: Trust...did you trust me enough to tell me about your father...or that you and Felix have a past.

MARIE: What does that have to do with anything?

[ISHMAEL *stares at her.*]

ISHMAEL: You don't get it, do you? I remember sitting on that bandstand…. Cigar smoke thick in the air…. My fingers move up and down the neck of the guitar…. searchin' for a note… a single note. We've been playing for hours …most of the night spent with me hunched on a stool trying to find that note….done sang all the ballads….improvised on every standard ….every chord progression nothing sounds right…I breathe ….then I look up just to rest my eyes… the smoke clears … in the back of the room I see this face in candle light…brown eyes glow…and a small glass of rum resting between her fingers…damn….. my fingers move down the neck… found that note. Everything just fell into place…any woman that could bring that kind of clarity…that kind of simple beauty to my life…well, she's got to be the one… I don't know anymore…but I do know that I can't stay here … You carrying too baggage here…in this place…My arms just ain't big enough …Can't put my arms around you.

[ISHMAEL *heads towards the bedroom.* MARIE *watches him walk away.*]

ACT 2
SCENE 6

[*Living room....later that evening.   There are two suitcases and a box on the sofa.   ISHMAEL'S guitar rests against the side.   ISHMAEL enters from the back with a stack of books.   There's a knock at the door. He places the books in the box, then answers the door.*]

ISHMAEL: Come on in.

OLIVER: Heard you had a little rumble earlier.

ISHMAEL: Good news travels fast

OLIVER: They say you broke the boy jaw...good....I ain't never care for that Bentecort boy.   Whole family sidity as hell.

ISHMAEL: Marie's not here.

OLIVER: Yeah....saw her at the bus stop with that old woman

ISHMAEL: Claire

OLIVER: I suppose.... came the back way....down Nostalgia.

[OLIVER *notices the suitcases.*]

OLIVER: Going on a trip?

ISHMAEL: Yeah..... I am.

OLIVER: .....Oh

ISHMAEL: I'm a musician, Mr. Tate. Gotta get back out there.   Should be able to pick up a little studio work. Who knows, someone might be hitting the road when I get back

OLIVER: The road.

ISHMAEL: Haven't toured in a while....it'd be a nice change of pace.

OLIVER: Spent years out there, boy.   Even after I got married....the road kept calling me. That's one fine bitch....the finest. Ain't never loved any one like I loved her.   Her entire body... asphalt, bus depots, raggedy motels, airports. Heartless woman. She'll use you up.

[OLIVER *stares at the picture on the wall.*]

OLIVER: You walk around with no blood in your veins. Heart pumping on music and desire. Nothing else.

ISHMAEL: This is your last night, right?

OLIVER: ...Yeah.....I guess it is...hmmm....   Don't think I got any reason to stay.

ISHMAEL: ...Sorry.

OLIVER: Ain't your fault. That's how it be sometimes.

[OLIVER *walks over to the bar*.]

ISHMAEL: Mr. Tate...why....I… I don't understand how a man could leave his family like that. No disrespect. It's just ...It doesn't make any sense to me.

OLIVER: ....She every sing for you, boy?

ISHMAEL: Who? Marie?

OLIVER: Yeah....my baby girl....Met her momma at an old blues joint down in Sarasota. Prettiest little red gal I'd ever seen. Right out of college...all educated with a bunch of fancy talk. Sanity little thing. Peculiar too. Walks around all the time with a parasol. Regardless of the weather... sun shining, gray skies, even at night. Always got that parasol. Makes me laugh. Have to hide that damn thing the first time we make love.... Now, that was something else... early morning ...look into her eyes...I melt....feel her all around me. Nothin' but an ocean of sweat...our flesh...our tears... Ain't never been no religious man... but it is the closest thing to prayer I've ever experienced...breath and sound... one unending circle. Sound. ....Comes out of nowhere. I see her lips moving but the sound comes from some other place. Her pores. Strands of hair. The room itself. Ain't never heard nothing like this before. ..I feel ...this...warmth... slowly rise up my spine. The room swims in light. The sun. Sound. Her voice wakes up the sun. When she's pregnant with Marie she sings all the time. I rest my head on her belly...her voice and the rhythm of my little girl's heart....It's no wonder Marie comes out singing. At night I rock my baby girl in my arms.... tiny little thing....she sings me to sleep...hmm…don't think I've slept since. Walking the earth in a daze... blinded by memory...

[*At the bus stop.* MARIE *has her arm around* CLAIRE. *They both sit under the parasol.* MARIE *watches as* CLAIRE *explains a stitch for the doll she's working on.* MARIE *lets the parasol down.*]

OLIVER: ...Parasols? They protect you from yourself. Sometimes the light is too bright... least it was for me. What can a man do for a woman who calls up the sun?

[OLIVER *walks towards the door*.]

OLIVER: You can't leave her boy. You the only person she got left to sing to.

ISHMAEL: She's never sung for me.

OLIVER: She's got to feel safe. Got to know she can rest… in your arms. Got to know that you won't leave her.

ISHMAEL: Like you left her mother…

OLIVER: Some of us run. Some of us stay. That fool curled on the floor. Drunk out of his mind. Crying like a baby…he ain't going nowhere. You stronger than I am boy. Why chase the road – you found your music.

[OLIVER *leaves. Lights up on* CLAIRE *and* MARIE *at the bus stop.*]

CLAIRE: No since whining over it. What's done is done.

MARIE: So close. Legs, feet, body, arms, hands

CLAIRE: Can't go back and change it. Gotta start from scratch.

MARIE: Not enough time.

CLAIRE: Always enough time.

MARIE: Don't know how to begin.

CLAIRE: Well don't look at me...you've figured it out for yourself Trust your hands and heart. Let that needle and thread map the way for you.

MARIE: I can't …it's just too much…Ishmael's leaving…I…

[ISHMAEL *walks over to the bus stop.*]

CLAIRE: It's alright, baby…let go.

MARIE: It's just…too much…

CLAIRE: Let go of the pain sweetheart…

MARIE: It's…no

CLAIRE: Mourn for you baby…for your mother…for all that you've lost…go ahead…it's alright.

[MARIE *rests her head on* CLAIRE'S *shoulder.* CLAIRE *covers her with the quilt.   The sound of thunder is heard.* MARIE *begins to cry.*]

CLAIRE [*to* ISHMAEL]: He's gone…isn't he?

ISHMAEL: …Yeah.

MARIE: I miss my daddy, Claire

CLAIRE: I know sweetheart…I know.

ISHMAEL: Come inside, baby…it's gonna rain

CLAIRE: You go on inside, boy…I'll stay out here with her. Been waiting for this rain a long time. Can't run away from it now.

[*Light fades.   The sound of pouring rain.*]

ACT 2
SCENE 7

[*Living Room. Next morning. It's still raining outside. OLIVER sits at the bus stop under an umbrella a suitcase is next to him…ISHMAEL is sitting in a chair in the shadow of the windowpane. He plays a more complex variation on *MARIE'S THEME. MARIE is lying on the couch asleep, covered in the quilt that CLAIRE made. She holds the completed doll in her arms. Excess fabric and thread are on the coffee table. She slowly awakens…stretches and looks around the room as if for the first time. She caries the doll in her arms and enters the shadow of the windowpane with ISHMAEL. MARIE stares out where the window would be and begins to swing/twist from side to side like a little girl, to ISHMAEL'S music. MARIE starts to hum the melody that OLIVER hummed earlier, the same melody that ISHMAEL is playing. She begins to sing the lyrics to the song her voice is crystal clear. The rain begins to subside. OLIVER lets down his umbrella and looks in the direction of the house…soft lavender and orange light begins to fill the open sky that surrounds the room causing the shadow of the window pane to vanish. OLIVER smiles and walks away. ISHMAEL plays until the song is over. He looks at her and smiles.*]

ISHMAEL: 'Mornin.

[*She proudly hands him the doll. ISHMAEL puts down the guitar and stands, gently holding the doll in his hands.*]

ISHMAEL: ….It's beautiful. I'm sure it's just what she wanted.

MARIE: Hope so.

[*MARIE looks out toward the window.*]

MARIE: You think he's safe?

ISHMAEL: Tate? Yeah…he's safe.

[*There's a moment of silence. MARIE looks at ISHMAEL.*]

MARIE: …What happens now?

ISHMAEL [*jokingly*]:.Breakfast?

[ISHMAEL'S *attempt at humor has failed.*]

MARIE: …I'm talking about *us*.

ISHMAEL: …I don't know…we'll have to play it by ear.

[MARIE, *not satisfied with* ISHMAEL'S *response, turns back towards the sunlight.* ISHMAEL *walks up behind her slowly. He wraps his arms around her waist. She slowly relaxes in his arms.*]

ISHMAEL: I wish I could …it's just… so much has happened…it's gonna take some time.

MARIE: Hmmm…*time.*

[*Long pause. They both ponder the sadness of the present and the insecurities of the future.* ISHMAEL *looks towards the window.*]

ISHMAEL: ...Looks like we finally got some sun.

MARIE: For a little while.

ISHMAEL: ...Yeah... For a little while.

[*Lights fade.*]

The Divine Order of Becoming

By Carla Stillwell

World Premier 2003

The Divine Order of Becoming
Director's Notes

The Divine Order of Becoming, like many plays, examines a rite of passage. There are many things that make this examination unique: the usage memory, the employment of poetry, and most importantly the truthful depiction of life, language and circumstances that define this Black mother and daughter and their relationship. As a director, I viewed the main character, Erica, as a woman standing at a gate that would transform her life. The play takes place inside the moment of her mother's death, which propels her through that gate. The story is a set of images in which Erica is seen blossoming out of her past, yet the audience can still see her poised in the frame of that transitional gateway. Erica can be seen moving rapidly from the posturing of a bratty child to the silhouette of a capable, loving young woman. With careful distillation, the story uses sharply defined moments to etch its repeating stacking images that move towards maturation through a frightening, heartbreaking journey.

We live in a time when most Americans will be touched by cancer in some way. This theme makes *The Divine Order of Becoming* relevant to a wide audience. It is rare to meet someone who doesn't know a survivor or who hasn't lost someone they love to this disease. In my own experience, cancer has introduced loss and fear and sorrow but mercifully and painfully, in most cases, cancer has been slow at its work. And so, in many ways, it also gives us an opportunity to experience a kind of poetry in living. When death is approaching, or standing just visible in the distance, we are invited to contemplate issues such as love, living and the afterlife. Erica Victor is devastated by her loss, but also has some gracious chances. She gets to give her mother the attentive care that she received growing up, and she also gets to prove that she's prepared to take care of herself and the wild eventualities of adulthood. Most importantly, Erica has a chance to say good-bye. It is here that *The Divine Order of Becoming* is so gorgeous; it has rich, curving contrasting places where love, agony, beauty and waste alternate back and forth and beg that they be contemplated as they truly exist side by side.

Directors must respect all of the fun and mismatched patterns of this play. The greatest challenges come in staging the poetry and defining the space. First, the poetry is placed in a script that uses down-to-Earth language. It stands out and is meant to do so. As the poetry provides the emotional pulse of the play, it must be presented carefully, respectfully, and with balance. It should be treated like a heart. When making decisions about the space, it is sometimes hard to remember that the story begins in a hospital. Because it is a memory play, the action unfolds in a lot of different places: the kitchen, the car, the hospital and the living room by the window. It is important to find those textures and items that stand out in memory and give a moment its outline.

Lastly, this one point must be made: Elder and Erica are written as Black Americans in a way that is rarely seen on the American stage. So frequently, non-white characters in plays spend a lot of time talking about or struggling against the injustices of America' white supremacist systems. *The Divine Order of Becoming* not only skips talk of racism, economic inequity, and general deconstruction of skirting Mr. Charlie, but portrays characters that are distinctly Black. For instance, one of the things that Erica recalls is the first time she relaxed her mother's hair. Later, when Elder is hospitalized, one of her daughter's many duties is to make sure that her mother's hair looks good. As a teenager, I remember the first time my mother asked me to do her hair and how it was a moment of pride for me. A mother asking her daughter to fix her hair is a powerful way of displaying trust and of recognizing the daughter's beauty. Scene after scene, the depiction is crystalline. *These* characters are Black, two Black women in a play having a universal experience. With no desire to explain, apologize or whitewash their blackness, these two characters could not be cast as white.

The Divine Order of Becoming is a love song. The syrupy parts must be sung with honesty, and the torchy parts attacked bravely and gracefully so that their heights of scale are well achieved. Erica is the Lover and her Mother, Elder, is the Beloved as Erica reviews their time together. The tempo changes over and over, as does the key. But well orchestrated, the impact is deep and almost physical for its witnesses. It touches in the very empty Mother spot where we always feel and fear loss.

The Divine Order of Becoming
Playwright's Statement

About the Play...
This story takes place in the moment when life takes a sharp, distinct turn. With poetry, prose and the conjuring of memory's past, we watch a young woman struggle to let go of the relationship that she and her mother developed during her 20's. We mourn with her as she applies the lessons passed to her through lecture, argument, and out right silliness to rise above the pain of loss.

...Carla Stillwell

The Divine Order of Becoming
Original Cast and Staff

Original CAST

Daryl Charisse ....Elder
Demetria Thomas...Erica

Production Staff

Director .... Kim Crutcher
Production Stage Manager ....Evelyn Danner
Set Design... Danjuma Gaskin
Lighting Design... Shepsu Aakhu
Costume Design...Carla Stillwell
Dramaturgy...Mignon McPherson Nance
Technical Director ....Sean R. Neron
Sound Design... Larry Nance
Music Direction...Red Clay
Musical Performance... Red Clay
Producer...Reginald Lawrence

CHARACTERS

Elder/Eve Victor, African-American woman, mid 60's
Thirty/Erica Victor, African-American woman, 30's

Staging

[*Chicago, '90-'00. The story sits in a single moment, the moment of application. We find* THIRTY *in the moment of* ELDER'S *death.*]

ACT 1

[*In black, the sound of beeping electronic devises that you hear in hospitals is intermingled with the pounding of percussion instruments. The sounds fuse and crescendo until there is silence. Lights up on the stage. The space is a black box. There are 3 cubes placed on the stage. There are shelves on the walls with different trinkets, and coat hooks on the walls with various colored costume pieces hanging from them. 2 colored doors open onto the set. The stage is divided into three areas of light: the empty place, the shadow of the window and then. The silence is followed by the faint whispering of wind that blends with the sound of a flute. A woman in her 30's is hovering in the shadows. Lights up to full. A woman in her 60's enters the stage and begins rearranging the cubes. She sits two cubes facing one another, and grabs a bowl. The older woman mimes snapping beans. The 30 year old woman, gets her own bowl and crosses into the scene.*]

ELDER: There are never enough beans. No matter how many beans I buy, they cook down to little or nothing and there are never enough.

THIRTY: I'm sick of this…

ELDER: Well then don't eat.

THIRTY: This is too many beans! If this isn't enough beans, then all of you people are addicts and need a program…12 steps, 6 steps, beans anonymous, something…

ELDER: You people?

THIRTY: Yes, you people: y'all, mama an 'em, the fruit of your womb and your husband in there, and you, old woman!

ELDER: I told you about calling me old…

THIRTY: This isn't even what I want! I'm sitting here, snappin' beans, and I want a pie! A smooth and creamy, delicious sweet potato pie. I got to beg you to make me a pie, but you will make me snap a million beans for your other children, it's not fair.

ELDER: Your sisters.

THIRTY: Your other children, I don't like them.

ELDER [*amused*]: You love them.

THIRTY: But I don't like them, never have. Make them snap a bean!

ELDER: They don't know how.

THIRTY: Yes they do.

ELDER: I want you to do it.

THIRTY: I want you to make me a pie.

ELDER: Make your own pie.

THIRTY: If I could make my own pie, I wouldn't be asking you.

ELDER: I'll teach you.

THIRTY: No you won't! You're just saying that to get me to finish snapping beans.

ELDER: I'll teach you.

THIRTY: When?

ELDER: When we're done with this. Somebody's got to learn. Might as well be a rotten little baby girl.

THIRTY: I told you about calling me a baby.

[*Silence*]

THIRTY: Can I write it down?

ELDER: What?

THIRTY: The pie recipe, can I write it down.

ELDER: Yes, but if you tell anybody, I have to kill you.

[*Beat*]

THIRTY: I want to learn how to make a cake from scratch too…

ELDER: It's easy…I'll teach you. [*beat*] You gonna write that down too?

THIRTY: Yep.

ELDER [*smiling*]: Then you won't need me.

THIRTY [*smiling*]: Nope. I think I'll use my new culinary skills to find a rich husband. We'll move to the Bahamas and have 2.5 kids and a dog.

ELDER: Just gonna leave me huh?

[*Beat*]

THIRTY: Nope. You can go. But your husband and your other children can't visit.

[*Lights fade out on* ELDER *she exits. One stool becomes illuminated with a single white light. This is the empty place.* THIRTY *crosses to the stool. She speaks to an unseen presence.*]

THIRTY:

> I stand in this moment
> Trying to hold
> Together the
> The memories
> That are fragmenting
> In my mind

[*The shadow of the window is illuminated.* THIRTY *gravitates to it.*]

Then I notice the
Window
I'm facing the window
Looking backwards
Over my shoulder
Wondering why I can't feel
The sun on my face
Well shit
I'm
Looking backwards over
My shoulder
That's why I can't
Feel the sun
On my face
So I turn
Around
To the window
But the sun
is really bright
and hurts my eyes
so I
look backwards
over my shoulder
again
I
do this
long enough
and I
get a crick
in my neck

[*A wave of sadness creeps up as* ELDER *enters the space and pulls a cube into the shadow of the window. She is carrying a mirror and a pair of tweezers.* ELDER *holds the mirror up and looks at her face. She examines herself for a moment then begins to pull chin hairs.* ELDER *watches her before entering the scene.*]

THIRTY: What are you doing?

ELDER: Trying not to grow a full beard!

THIRTY: Well, why can't you do that in the bathroom like normal people? Anybody walking down the street can see you picking chin hairs.

ELDER: I can see better here.

THIRTY: I don't how you can see anything with the glare from the sun on that mirror. It 's too bright.

ELDER: That's the point. No chin hair can hide in the sunlight. Not much can. Like all that dust on that damn table. If you had of dusted in the daytime, like normal people, then you would have seen it. Little vampire.

THIRTY: Whatever Mama.

[*The empty space and window start to morph into a single light. Both lights blink and the window fades.*

The empty space remains. THIRTY *stands still for a moment.*]

THIRTY:

then I

can't feel

I can't

feel

a thing

I'm…

[ELDER rises and stands by THIRTY]

ELDER: Numb. [*beat*] Numbness isn't bad. People always talk about being numb like it's bad. When you're numb you can't feel anything. When you can't feel you don't hurt and when you don't hurt you can deal with it. Whatever it is at the moment, and trust me it is always there. There will never be a point where there is not an "it". And sometimes it is so strong and bleak and razor sharp that if there were no numbness you would kill yourself because the pain is too much. You should thank God for numbness.

THIRTY: But I should feel…something, anything.

I sit in this

Chair in my mind

Try and force

Myself to

Feel/see

the sun

All I feel is the why, but

There is no answer, no reason for this…

ELDER: There is always both an answer and a reason. You don't always want to hear it, because sometimes the answer and the reason are: that *it* is.

[*Lights transition.* THIRTY *begins to clear the stage of everything except two of the cubes and a pressing comb.*]

ELDER: How far back you gonna go?

[THIRTY *stands agitated and confused. She holds the comb for a while and places it on one of the cubes. Lights transition as* THIRTY *grabs* ELDER *who is shaking, holds her for a moment, then enters the scene.* ELDER *picks up the pressing comb. She sits and begins the motion of pressing her hair.* THIRTY *watches for a second, then snaps abruptly into the scene.*]

THIRTY: Mama…Let me perm your hair.

ELDER: Why?

THIRTY: Because you just look hot sittin' there over the smoldering stove with that hot, greasy hot comb. Let me perm it.

ELDER: I let your sister perm my hair once, and I was bald for months…

THIRTY: But Mama, that was 100 years ago and the perms are different now. They don't have lye anymore, so it won't break your hair out. I perm my hair. My hair is growing…

ELDER: Your hair is growing…

THIRTY: Please let me?

ELDER: I can just keep pressing it…

[ELDER *raises the comb to her head*, THIRTY *lunges forward and grads her wrist.*]

THIRTY: Mama please…don't do it!

ELDER: [*snatching her hand back*]: Have you lost your mind? You could have burned me!

THIRTY: I'm sorry Mama, but I can't let you keep going on like this…it has to stop…put the hot comb down, it is not your friend.

ELDER: Is everything a movie of the week with you…

THIRTY: Please Mama, just hear me out…It would knock 20 minutes off you getting ready for work. Let me do it…We can do it now, you don't have anyplace to be until later, I'm not going out until later and I have an emergency perm kit in my room.

ELDER: An emergency perm kit?

THIRTY: The perm kit I use in an emergency…when the naps just creep up on me and I got to straighten 'em out right then…

ELDER: Oh…I see

THIRTY: Please…you will feel soooo much better when you can just get up and leave the house without having Dante's inferno blazing on your face before you get dressed…Just think of it Mama, your tresses would be soft and supple…the wind could blow and your hair would actually move…flow in the breeze… for once you could smell like something other than hair grease…Mama you would embark on a whole new life…a hair grease free life…would you please just trust me on this…

[*Beat*]

ELDER: Ok, come on…do it now before I loose my nerve…and when I'm bald as a goose, what am I gonna do then…

THIRTY: Trust me Mama…

[*Lights soften to the empty light as* THIRTY *combs* ELDER'S *hair.*]

THIRTY:

> like a blanket
> the feeling
> like a wool
> sweater
> the moment
> will be
> with you
> forever
> even when
> the seasons
> change
> moments

twinkle like
stars

[*Lights come up on* ELDER *sitting on the stool with* THIRTY *standing behind her combing her hair.* THIRTY *snaps into the moment with* ELDER.]

ELDER: Curl it off of my face…

THIRTY: Why? I thought you liked your bangs in the front…

ELDER: I'm too old to have all that hair around my face. When you get past a certain age, you shouldn't have hair hanging in your face. Just calls attention to the wrinkles.

THIRTY: But then you can see all the gray…You want to put some color in it? Maybe an auburn…that's kinda the natural color of your hair…

ELDER: Maybe…just a little color…

THIRTY: I'll do it so it doesn't cover the gray, just makes it look like highlights…

ELDER: That'll be nice…you can do it Saturday.

THIRTY: Awright.

[*Lights soften to the empty light on* ELDER.]

THIRTY:

They glisten
like fresh
snow
under the street light
outside at night
moments

[ELDER *becomes illuminated.*]

ELDER: I am quiet beautiful.

THIRTY: Your beauty knows no bounds. Next time I'm gonna clip your ends.

ELDER: I don't want it short…you got it to grow to a very nice length…

THIRTY: It won't be short. Just clipping not cutting…I'm done…More hair.

ELDER: [*surprised by* THIRTY'S *choice of words*] What did you just say?

THIRTY: More hair.

ELDER: [*amused*] 'More hair', and you act like you don't listen! What do you know about 'more hair'?

THIRTY: That's what you used to say to me when you finished my hair…'more hair'

ELDER: Do you know why I said it?

THIRTY: No, not really…

ELDER: The old folks used to wish you more hair so that your hair would always grow…like wishing somebody good luck.

THIRTY: [*smiling*] Well then, More Hair.

ELDER: [*smiling*] More Hair.

[*Lights transition to empty place.* THIRTY *becomes agitated and confused.* ELDER *crosses to* THIRTY *to comfort her.*]

ELDER:

> even moments
> that don't seem
> bright sometimes
> glisten
> they sparkle
> with truth

THIRTY:

> but truth
> like the sun
> in the window
> burns too brightly

[THIRTY *begins frantically lining up the cubes.* ELDER *grabs* THIRTY *to stop her but she breaks free and continues.*]

ELDER: You can't stop this…No matter how far back you go, you can't stop what has happened…

THIRTY: [*to* ELDER]

> I scoop the
> Pieces of memory
> Up in my hand
> And lay them out
> Like ants at a picnic
> Looking backwards
> Over my shoulder
> There is a moment
> That exists
> That makes
> me
> Forget about
> The sun
> Or the crick
> In my neck
> And I
> Need to find it

[*Once the cubes are arranged,* THIRTY *stops abruptly and stares at them, she grabs a blanket, she is shaking.*]

THIRTY:

> These things that
> We cried about
> did not require
> tears
> and things
> that we found
> amusing
> did not require
> teeth or lips
> we lend
> so much
> energy to
> circumstances
> of happenstance
> that seem so
> mundane
> in this moment
> but the idea of the mundane
> only comes in
> retrospect

[*Lights transition. THIRTY crosses to the cubes, lay across them and covers herself with the blanket. She is sobbing uncontrollably. ELDER sits on the edge of the cubes next to her.*]

THIRTY: Mama what am I going to do…

ELDER: There's nothing you can do except wait until next semester and go back.

THIRTY: I can't sit out a whole semester!

ELDER: Why not?

THIRTY: Because I can't. I have to finish.

ELDER: Sitting out won't stop you from finishing. It might take a little longer, but so what …

THIRTY: But it's not fair. I did everything I was supposed to do. I did all my paperwork, and got it in on time, got it in early, and everything, and my money isn't there because this woman didn't do her job and now I can't go to school, and it's not fair.

[*Beat*]

ELDER: No it's not fair…so what? This is not the first injustice you will suffer. So what are you going to do? Lay on the couch and cry and whine for 3 months? Don't nobody care about your tears. You aren't doing anything other than making yourself sick. You have a problem and you have dealt with it the best way you know how. Now you have to move on. You have a job that you haven't been to in 3 days. Do you want to loose your job?

THIRTY [*calming*]: No.

ELDER: Then you need to go to it. Get up tomorrow, and go to work. Tell your boss what's going on and tell him you want more hours because you won't be in school this semester. Then save the extra money. You'll have this semester and all summer to save money. If this happens again, you can at least have enough money to pay for one semester until things get straightened out. I'll help you if you need it…but you won't. [*grabbing* THIRTY *and holding her tight*) I never had to whip you twice for the same thing.

THIRTY: What?

ELDER: I never had to whip you twice for the same thing. If I beat your ass about something, I only had to do it once. If you ever did that thing again, you didn't let me know about it. You've always been quick about things like that. I don't think you will ever be without money for school, or anything else again.

THIRTY[*laughing/sobbing*]: Nope.

ELDER: Shit happens, such is life.   Always gotta have a plan B. The next time somebody messes with my baby like this she'll be ready.

THIRTY: I'm not a baby…

ELDER: No, not to the rest of the world, you're a big girl to them, so you have to start acting like one. You have to handle your business. Even when your sad and hurt and things are broke, keep your composure and handle your business. Don't you ever spend 3 days on the couch crying again. You hear me?

THIRTY: Yes…

ELDER: Don't even spend 1 day crying. When it goes down, start planning. Handle it. You hear me?

THIRTY: Ummhmm

ELDER: This is nothing to cry about. You're stronger than this. Stronger than any of it.

[ELDER *hugs* THIRTY *one last time, lays her back down and tucks her in. The lights transition the shadow of the window.* ELDER *crosses and stands in the shadow of the window staring at* THIRTY.]

ELDER:

You felt

feel

deeply

and

see shapes of pain

but you

are just now

seeing

the natural

shade of

pain

you know

pain has

a distinct color

and scent

and you have neither

seen nor smelled

it until today

and

I want

To take it all

From you now
But I can't

[ELDER *crosses to* THIRTY, *takes her hand*.]

ELDER: …if I could make you understand now, I would… I can't protect you from it.

THIRTY: Yes you can, you...

ELDER: This is not my decision. Do you think I would ever hurt my baby, if I had the choice.

THIRTY [*incoherent*]: I need to sweep up The pieces…

ELDER [*holding* THIRTY]: I know. I'm sorry I told you to stop…you can stay and do this for a little while longer...sweep up the pieces. But I will have to go. You will have to let me go…

THIRTY [*pulling away*]: No I don't! It's just me and you here and if you stop this, nobody will know!

ELDER [*grabbing her again*]: It does not work that way…Listen. Do you hear that sound?

THIRTY [*shaking and confused*]: No! What sound? There is no sound!

ELDER: There is noise in this absence…the sound of transition, and everybody knows it. You know it, and we can't go back because it's already been done. You can stay and lay out these pieces of memory for a bit, but it can't be undone…

THIRTY:

I keep looking
backwards over
my shoulder trying
to keep the hands
of the clock from
moving

[ELDER *turns to* THIRTY]

ELDER: But they keep moving anyway don't they?

THIRTY: Yep.

ELDER: Baby…[*beat*] Come on now, if you're going to sweep up, you've got to make sure you get everything, and don't sweep it into a pile and leave it in the middle of the floor. Sweep to clean.

[*Lights transition as* ELDER *rises and begins to circle* THIRTY. THIRTY *rises as the lights become harsh. She begins to counter* ELDER. *They size each other up.* ELDER *stops abruptly in front of* THIRTY *they are nose to nose*].

ELDER [*screaming*]: You are acting like a child! I don't believe that I am having this conversation with you! Why is this even a conversation!

THIRTY [*standing her ground*]: I'm not a child! I am an adult, you are an adult, and grown people talk to, not at each other…you never just stop talking…

ELDER: Trust me little girl, my silence is not what you want.

THIRTY: How in the hell do you know what I want? You don't know me! Neither of you know me! You look at me and see a child, you have never taken the time to know me, who I am, what I want, and where I stand! How will I ever be grown to anybody else if I can't be grown in my own damn house?

ELDER: Well that's the first problem, this is not your house. This is our house, we allow you to live here.

THIRTY: I pay rent here!

ELDER: You give me $200 dollars a month. You can't rent a room at the goddamn Y for $200 a month. Hell, that don't even cover your phone bill. I would like to see you live anywhere else for $200 a month…

THIRTY: My phone bill? You don't use the phone…

ELDER: You are missing the point…It's my phone, it's my house and my responsibility for you ran out when you turned 18. If you don't want to be treated like a child, don't act like one. Grown people don't stand in the middle of their parent's kitchen and whine about taking care of the house that they live in, being grown doesn't give you a license to be nasty…

THIRTY: Well, didn't you just say it was *your* house?!

ELDER: But you live here with other people and as long as you wish to live in this house, hell as long as you live anywhere on the face of this earth you have to clean the toilet and wash the damn dishes and pick up your funky clothes from off every available surface. Any place you live you have a responsibility to keep it livable. You cannot continue to stay here if you can't respect this house…

THIRTY: Are you kicking me out?

ELDER: No. I'm giving you your options. See you grown, and grown people get to choose where they live. You can stay here as long as you like, but this is my house and if you stay here you will act accordingly. If you can't do that, then you need to find somewhere else to live.

THIRTY: Oh, so because I won't bow down and kiss your ass and let you treat me like a child, I have to move? I can't be grown in your house. Can't nobody be grown here but you huh? I am too damn old for you to "make" me clean my room Mama!

ELDER: Why do you keep telling me you're grown? I know when you where born…I know how old you are…why you telling me? Who you trying convince? Let me give you a hint sugar, grown people don't have to keep saying it. The day you get grown is the day that you get your ass up in the morning, see the dirty dishes in the sink and wash them without somebody telling you…The day you contribute to this house without a schedule then we can talk about how grown you are…Until then take your ass in there and pick up some of that shit up off the floor or get the hell out on my house.

[THIRTY *stands silent. She and* ELDER *stare at one another for a moment and* THIRTY *finally sits on one of the cubes.* ELDER *exits as lights transition to the empty place.* THIRTY *speaks to an unseen presence.*]

THIRTY:

> There was a hand
> on my cheek
> gently turning my
> head forward
> toward the
> open window

[*The window becomes illuminated.*]

toward the
sun
I remember that
and everything is
tinted

[*Confused for a moment*]

The tint, what color was it? I don't remember.

[*Silence.* THIRTY *begins to move frantically through the place clearing it of the blankets and rearranging the cubes. She stops abruptly.*]

Green.
Green is our favorite color
Me and you we
Share green
It's your color so
I began to see
in shades of
green
I decided to
color my
memories
green
Make them
the color of
grass
and
healing
and
peace
They were
Neither
In that
moment
but that is
the color they
would become
I didn't know
where else to
go
to find the
green
So I sat
and allowed
memory to
shade its self
with green
couldn't go
to
sisters

or
friend
only
found comfort
in green
called
on green
to wrap its self
about my
shoulders
hair
eyes
heart
Green holds
the fragile pieces
of my mind together
Memory
green
comes in many shades
The pieces
of memory
lay
on the
kitchen
floor
and
counter
and
sink
Hospital
Floor
The pieces now
shrouded in
green
and it was the color of my uniform when I was little
and you came to pick me up from school

[*choking back tears*] I remember now.

[ELDER *enters from the shadows*.]

ELDER: Now what?

THIRTY [*sobbing uncontrollably*]: I don't understand…

ELDER [*moving to her side*]: You keep calling them, and they keep coming, but what are you going to do with them? Because if you don't see the truth in these moments you keep lining up, I can't do what I need to do, because I don't want to leave you like this…

THIRTY: …and you have to leave?

ELDER: Yes. If you're going to keep calling, listen. I'll wait as long as I can…

[ELDER *retreats to the shadows*. THIRTY *begins to break down again, but she catches herself.*]

THIRTY [*calm*]: keep going now…moments all in a row.

[THIRTY *runs frantically and retrieves coat, glove, hat and backpack from one of the hooks and begin to pace.* ELDER *has entered the scene and is sitting on a cube with a coffee cup in hand. Lights transition.*]

THIRTY: Mama, I am buying a car!   I swear fo God if it's the last thing on earth I do, I am buying a car!

ELDER [trying not to giggle]: What happened to my baby?

THIRTY: Ok, so first the cab didn't come this morning right?

ELDER: UmmHumm…

THIRTY: It was what 5:30 in the morning and it's what, like 2 degrees outside this morning?

ELDER: Yes…that's what they said on the news with the wind chill…

THIRTY: So I just say to hell with it, I'll take the bus…I'll be 45 minutes late for my damn job but, whatever. So, I walk the 6 blocks to Jeffery and I'm standing there and standing there and standing there and ain't no bus coming. So I go and read the sign and it says that the bus don't start running until 6:00 am…

ELDER: The #14 doesn't start running until 6?

THIRTY: Now I'm gonna be an hour and a half late for work, so by the time the bus gets there I am good and pissed right…

ELDER [fully amused]: UmmHmm

THIRTY: I get a seat and sit down and as soon as the bus got on the Drive this raggedy, man starts preaching!!

ELDER: Preaching?

THIRTY: Yes! He goes into full fricking praise and worship service on the #14 and I listened to it as long as I could Mama…

ELDER: Oh Lord…

THIRTY: I tried to just be quiet and put on my headphones and drown him out, but I swear Mama, he got louder… as soon as I put on my headphones he got louder, just to spite me…

ELDER: Just to spite you?

THIRTY: I swear fo God…

ELDER: What did you do?

THIRTY: I just couldn't take it anymore and I screamed, "Would you just shut up, shut up, shut up!" And some other stuff I said, but I'm not gonna repeat it because, even though I say a few bad words in front of you, you are still my Mama and I can't repeat all the bad words I said on the bus.

ELDER: Well thank you…

THIRTY: Your welcome.

ELDER: One of these days you're gonna get yourself killed with that mouth…

THIRTY: Then it got real quiet and everybody was just staring at me, so I just put my headphones back on, then after a couple of minutes he goes "Lord, the devil is on the bus this morning trying to hold my tongue Jesus…"

[ELDER *erupts with laughter.* THIRTY *observes her for a moment and begins to laugh collapsing on a cube across from her.*]

THIRTY: Mama, that is not funny! He called me the devil…

ELDER: Well when you show somebody your little pointy horns and you make a mean face at them and tell them to shut up, what do you expect them to call you?

THIRTY: I just got off the bus at the next stop and walked the rest of the way. I was almost two hours late for work.

ELDER: Did you tell them what happened?

THIRTY: Yeah, but they thought I was lying…

ELDER: 'Cause that kinda mess doesn't happen to most people…

THIRTY: …and it's not gonna happen again, because I'm never taking the bus again…ever! I am buying a car! Tomorrow is Saturday, and I'm gonna get up early and go to a dealership and find a car!

ELDER: A car?

THIRTY: Yep. I have to be at work too damn early to depend on our fair city's transit system.

ELDER: A car is a lot of work…

THIRTY: I know, but Mama come on, two hours just to get to work…besides that, I would actually be able have a life, go out and kick it. I would be able to run errands around here too…

ELDER: It would be nice to have a car around…

THIRTY: Yes it would…

ELDER: It would be real handy to get groceries in and pick up other little stuff…

THIRTY: UhhHun…and if your ride doesn't go to work on a particular day, I could take you…I get off early enough.

ELDER: That's true…

THIRTY: Well then it's settled, us is getten a au-to-mo-beel to morrie!

[THIRTY *rises to leave.*]

ELDER: I'll go with you…

THIRTY: I'll be fine Mama. I think I can pick a car without my Mommy.

ELDER: I'm sure you can, but I thought that maybe I could help you a little bit…but if you're too grown for your Mama's help…

THIRTY [*raising an eyebrow*]: What kind of help…

ELDER: Do you have money for a down payment?

THIRTY [*turning to ELDER slowly*]: I have a couple of dollars put away…why?

ELDER: Well, I have a couple of dollars I may be able to give you. Help you a bit.

THIRTY: Mama you don't have to do that…

ELDER: If you're going to use it to help me, I think I should help you out a bit…

THIRTY [*smiling*]: Oh yeah…

ELDER: Yeah…

THIRTY [*smiling bigger*]: …tomorrow about 10:00?

ELDER: Sounds good…

[*Beat*]

THIRTY: Thanks

[*Lights transition as* THIRTY *exchanges her winter coat for a spring jacket. She moves her cubes to face* ELDER *and takes the coffee table position.*]

THIRTY [*rising to leave*]: Alright Mama, I'm gone.

ELDER: What time will you be home?

THIRTY: I don't know. I might stop and hang for minute after work. Why, you need something?

ELDER: Karin needs to get to the train around six.

THIRTY [*instantly angry*]: Then Karin needs to get her fat ass on the bus around 4:30.

ELDER: Well, I already told her you would…

THIRTY: I don't know why you did that, 'cause I'm not taking her nowhere!

ELDER: Why can't you ever just do what I ask you to do? I ask you to do one thing and it's always a big problem.

THIRTY: No, Mama…When you ask me to do something for *you,* it's never a problem. But I will not allow you to rearrange my schedule for your children. I ain't got no kids, and I am tired of bending over backwards for yours.

ELDER: They are your family too. If your sisters need some help, then you should give it. You will drive anyone of your friends from here to hell and back, but you won't take your own sister to the train…

THIRTY: Here we go…

ELDER: All I ever wanted was for my girls to be close and help each other…

THIRTY: And who do they help! They don't help you! And they sure as hell ain't never did shit for me!

ELDER: Do not curse at me!

THIRTY: They are leeches Mama! The other two don't call until it's time to buy their kids something for the holidays, or they need a place to keep their bags when they roll into town, while they go play with their faux middle class Negro friends. And Karin…if you don't have anything to give her ass, you can't find her! You can't ask her to walk to the store for you, and did I mention that none of them have ever done anything to help me. Their entire existence is an inconvenience to both of us, so why do you keep asking me to help your ungrateful children, and more importantly, why do you keep giving and giving to people who clearly don't care about anybody but themselves?

[*Beat*]

ELDER: Because they didn't have what you had.

THIRTY [*crossing to leave*]: Not this again…

ELDER: …it was too much shit around when they were small. Your father was always drunk. There was never any money. We lived with my Mother, so when it was time to discipline somebody, there Mother was the whole time in the way, and I was no older than you are now. Are you ready to be somebody's mother? It was just always something and I didn't get to teach them properly.

THIRTY: Well, Mama, that has nothing to do with me…*(stops to calm herself)* I will do whatever you ask me to do for you and Daddy. But I can't help you with your children. You keep telling me that I have to be grown, and be responsible, and I've been doing that. But you don't expect that from them.

ELDER: Because I didn't get the chance to teach them…

THIRTY: So what! Ever since I got that car…hell, ever since I've been old enough to do anything, you've been singing the same damn song…help Karin with this, pick Janis' kids up from there, it's Joan's birthday, help me bake her a fucking cake! Not once I have I ever heard you ask them to do anything for me!

ELDER: Because you don't need their help, you have me. They didn't.

THIRTY [calming]: Mama, I will take you, pick you up, do whatever you ask, because I appreciate your help…

ELDER: You don't understand…

THIRTY: No, I don't. They're users. You know that, so no, I don't understand…

ELDER: They are emotionally arrested. Those girls saw and experienced things that no child should ever witness…

THIRTY: That was 20 some years ago. Daddy was a drunk and Granny was evil, so damn what! They aren't the only people in the world to have some drama growing up. They have been out of this house almost as long as I've been alive! When will you stop being responsible for them, and hold them accountable for their shit. If I have to take responsibility for my shit, why don 't you expect them to do the same thing?

ELDER [*rising*]: Because I was able to sit down and have a conversation with you, and say, in no uncertain terms, "Take responsibility for your shit". I have never said that to either one of the others, so how would I expect them to know? You are speaking on issues that you know nothing about. All you remember is the sober father, the grown mother, and the senile grandmother that was too crazy to stick her nose in how I raised you. The police weren't breaking up fights, and the ambulance wasn't coming to take your mother to the hospital because her drunken husband had bashed her head against the sink. They need help now, because I didn't help them when I was supposed to.

[*Beat*]

THIRTY: I have to go to work now Mama.

ELDER: Will you do this for me today?

[*Silence*]

THIRTY: Yeah, I can do it today.

[ELDER *exits as the lights transition into a single spot on* THIRTY. *She speaks to an unseen presence.*]

THIRTY:

The funny thing
about looking
backwards
is that if
you look back
long enough
all the objects
in
space
life
time
start to
come closer
to the
here
and
now

[THIRTY *begins to explore the object on stage, as lights transition to the empty place. She picks up a glass figure reflectively.*]

When you
back track
through
space
life
time
looking through the distortion
of the past

there are
moments
when the change
comes and it
seems abrupt
at the time
but the transition
was planned
by whom
I am not sure
but it was
seamless
less effort than
the view
when I'm not
looking
backwards over my
shoulder
or
when I refuse
to look out
of the window
and face the
sun
in those
moments when
I let my
eyes rest
on the
clothes I'm
wearing at
the time
or the
objects
in the room
and…
that is the
moment
of feeling
and confusion
I can feel
and I can't
concentrate
because
I see the past
closing in on
me and
I am very conscious
of the clothes
that I'm wearing
at the time
and I
hurt
In this moment

I can see
Beyond it
Fragility in
One that
Is not
In this moment
I see
it confuses me
Is this what it is?…divine order at work.

[*Lights begin to fade as* THIRTY *sits on a stool with her head in her hands.* ELDER *is watching from the shadows.*]

ACT 2

[*In black there is the sound of a phone ringing in the distance. Lights up on* THIRTY *rushing into the place wearing a jacket and a carrying workbag. She comes to an abrupt halt center stage.*]

THIRTY: Hello-Hey Mama…yeah, I just got in…what's up? Oh, well yeah…I'll be there in about, umm, 15/20mins? No, don't come down stairs…I'll call when I get there…ok
Bye

[THIRTY *stands in the place dazed for a moment. She speaks angrily to the unseen presence.*]

THIRTY:

I have recently
become fascinated with
clouds
they move
with speed
and
agility
like
lions and crocodiles
they
come out of
nowhere
they're just
there
sometimes
especially when
you're up
high in
a plane
they appear
to be soft
and fluffy
and safe
even when
they're dark
and full of
weather
there's something
not so bad
about them
until
one of them
comes and
snatches the
roof off
your fucking
house
but
what fascinates
me is that
clouds
like

lions

or

crocodiles

have flawless

camouflage

and

they stalk us

like we're

gazelles or wildebeest

feeding

in packs

or drinking from

the watering hole

and before

we see/smell/sense

the danger

the clouds have

ripped the roof

right off

the top

of the fucking

house

[ELDER *drifts into the place and begins to slowly and methodically sit two cubes side by side.* THIRTY *begins shaking her head violently and starts to leave the space.*]

ELDER [*stopping* THIRTY *with her voice*]: You can't run now. You keep calling them…why? What are you calling them for? If you're gonna…

THIRTY: I know this shit! I don't need this shit again!

ELDER [*uncompromising*]: This is exactly what you need. This is the important part.

THIRTY [*angry*]: I will not look into the face of this evil again! This is what put us here! In this fucked up lie! You just want to leave!

ELDER [*her tone even stronger*]: No, I have to leave…you want to hide. And what's more important is that you know you can't. I won't let you hide. [*Beat*] Come on.

[THIRTY *reluctantly moves closer to* ELDER. *Lights transition as the two women sit.*]

ELDER [*visibly shake*]: I was so embarrassed…

THIRTY: What happened?

ELDER: I don't know. I was sitting at my desk and had to pee. When I stood up to go to the washroom I felt this be whoosh of blood just flowing out of me. I just barely got to the washroom. There was blood everywhere. Thank God Audrey came in behind me to see if I needed something. I had left these pants in my locker months ago. So I was able to clean up enough to get home…

[*Silence*]

THIRTY: Well, what do you want to do?

ELDER: Do when baby?

THIRTY: Now. You hungry? You want me to stop somewhere and get you a little something…need something from the drugstore before we go home…
ELDER [*managing a smirk*]: No baby, I just want to go home and lay down.

THIRTY: Well…do you feel alright now?

ELDER [*hesitant*]: I feel a little light-headed, that's all…

THIRTY: If you lost that kind of blood…you still bleeding?

ELDER: Yeah…

THIRTY: Mama, that doesn't sound good to me…

ELDER: No, I don't think it is…

THIRTY: You think you ought to go home? Maybe we should go to the emergency room…

ELDER: I don't think I need to go to the hospital…

THIRTY: Mama, anytime you just start bleeding like that for no reason…well, that's just not normal…

ELDER: I know.

THIRTY: I think you need to go see about it…

[*Silence*]

THIRTY: Let me know now if you want to go through emergency…the exit is coming up…

ELDER: I don't feel like sitting in there all night…

THIRTY: Mama…

ELDER: I don't want to stay there by myself…

THIRTY: I'm going with you…

ELDER: But it'll probably be real late when we get out and you have to go to work early tomorrow…

THIRTY: Mama, I ain't worried about that damn job! What, they gonna fire me because I had to take my Mama to the emergency room?

[*Silence*]

ELDER: Where are you going?

THIRTY: To emergency.

ELDER: I didn't say I wanted to go to the emergency room…

THIRTY [*soft*]: Mama, I think you have too.

[*Lights transition as* THIRTY *rises, begins to pace*]

THIRTY: So, what are they saying?

ELDER: It looks like, from the x-rays, that I have, what did he call them, fibroids.
THIRTY: Plural?

ELDER: Yeah, he said it's about 3 from what he can see, but he's making an appointment for me to go through the o.b./gyn clinic tomorrow morning at 9. He says they would want to remove them as soon as possible or I'll keep having this problem.

THIRTY: Well, yeah I would think they need to be removed. When we get home, I'll leave a message at work that I won't be in tomorrow.

ELDER: I can get a cab…

THIRTY: Whatever Mama…Can you leave now?

ELDER: Don't say whatever to me!

THIRTY [*excited*]: Mama, I can't talk to you if you ain't makin' sense…How you gonna take a cab anywhere and you can't get from point A to point B without blood running down your leg…

[*Silence*]

ELDER [*embarrassed*]: Lower your voice…

THIRTY [*softening*]: I ain't worried about that job…*(beat)* what are we still waiting for?

ELDER: The nurse has to come back with my appointment information and release papers and things… where's my coat?

THIRTY: I took it out to the car, I had to take a walk, too many sick people…I'll bring the car around front for you…

[THIRTY *begins to exit*]

ELDER: I wish she would come on. We gotta do this all over again tomorrow…

THIRTY: Same Bat Time, Same Bat Place

ELDER [*smirking*]: You said it Robin…

[*Beat*]

THIRTY: Why do you always get to be Batman?

ELDER: Because I'm sick and the sick person always gets to be Batman.

THIRTY: You are a lying monkey…

ELDER [*mock outrage*]: You calling me a liar?

THIRTY: When I was little, you said you had to be Batman because I was too little, now it's because you sick …you are full of lies, Mama lies. I am an adult and I would like to be Batman for a change!

ELDER [*amused*]: You can be Batman when I die…

THIRTY: Now how is that right…

ELDER: I don't have to be right, I'm the Mama.

THIRTY: One day soon, you gonna let me be Batman.

ELDER: There will be enough years in your life when you get to be the superhero. For now enjoy being my sidekick…is that how y'all say, "cool".

THIRTY [*amused*]: Yes ma'am.

[*Lights transition to the empty place. THIRTY grabs a cube and takes it center stage, speaking to the unseen presence.*]

THIRTY:

The pieces
of my
Mind
Split
In half
And I have
Both sides
Of the conversation
I'm me and them
Them and me
Some would say
That's
Crazy
I feel
crazy

[ELDER *emerges and speaks from the shadows*].

ELDER: Some call it coping.

THIRTY [*smiling*]: Coping? Sounds better than crazy.

ELDER [*smiling back*]: When you get a little older, you won't mind being called crazy.

THIRTY: Will I mind feeling crazy?

ELDER: You'll come to accept that it's par for the course. You'll own it, and appreciate that at least you're feeling. Isn't that what you wanted?

[TIRTY *pauses for a moment to ponder the question, then begins to shake with sadness.*]

THIRTY [*breaking down*]: I thought so, but this…this feels so bad. *(beat)* Mama, I want to stop now…

ELDER [*crossing closer to THIRTY with deliberate steps and words*]: This is neither bad nor good. This is. These feelings, these memories, you can't keep using them as a buffer from the truth of now. You can't un-scramble the Order to suite you. When you walked in and saw the light, you asked to feel. You called everything you thought would make you feel good. But the Divine, the only concerns it has is that you feel, experience the truth.

[ELDER *exits. Lights transition.* THIRTY *agitated, paces frantically through place then slows her speed. She stops abruptly and stands facing the audience.*]

THIRTY: Yes…Hi, I'm her daughter Erica…(*nervous, sits*) Oh, yes, ok…There were 4 tumors…Ewww… what is that? That's a tumor? Ewww…Ok…can I go back to see her? Thank you.

[THIRTY *rises, shaky. Lights transition to the empty place. She speaks to the unseen presence.*]

THIRTY:

Scared.
In this moment
I see
Beyond it
Fragility in
One that
Is not
In this moment
I see
my eyes don't
burn
so I shouldn't
be scared of
I just want to
stay in these
clothes
then there is a point…

[THIRTY *inhales. She is washed in the light from the window. It dims and fades out as she is speaking.*]

…a point in your
Becoming when
you start to
notice that
the sun isn't
always painfully bright
you notice that
it dims a bit
from time to
time
but you're not sure
as to why
it takes a while
to notice the clouds
you start to
realize that
you're being
followed
stalked
it takes
a few years

before the
clouds become
suspect

[*The stage lights begin to flicker.* THIRTY *grabs a purse and two bags. She opens one of the doors and stands by it. Lights transition as* ELDER *enters. Her movements are labored.*]

THIRTY: We is home!

ELDER: Thank God!

[ELDER *crosses to a seat.* TIRTY *begins to fuss around her. Propping up her feet, giving her blankets, etc.*]

ELDER: Girl, those steps are gonna be death of me…Thank you baby.

THIRTY: You want some tea? I bought some ginger tea when I went to the store yesterday.

ELDER: Yes, I believe I would like a cup.

[*Beat*]

THIRTY: Well…they showed me your womb…

ELDER: What?

THIRTY [*amused*]: The doctor came out and showed me this picture of your uterus. I know way more about you than I ever needed to.

ELDER: Now he knows he had a lot of nerve! Why would they show you my uterus? Why are they taking pictures of my insides anyway? They didn't ask my permission…My uterus is my personal business!

THIRTY: They do that now. To put in your file for future reference…

ELDER: In the future they need to reference me before they go around showing people my insides.

THIRTY: He was explaining your procedure to me.

ELDER: I'm glad they told somebody, 'cause they damn sure didn't tell me what happened. Just told me that they got all the tumors and that's it.

THIRTY: Well, that was pretty much it. That they were all gone. One of 'em was a big sucker too. Nasty…but he said he got 'em all. Nothing else to worry about.

ELDER: Good to hear that…

THIRTY: Oh, and you have a follow-up appointment. They want to see you in 6 weeks.

ELDER: I wonder if they plan on taking more photographs of my privates…

THIRTY: Mama…

ELDER: Maybe I ought to shave real good for the pictures…

THIRTY [*shocked*]: Mama please!

ELDER: Put a little lipstick on it…

THIRTY [*stifling a giggle*]: Oh now Mama, that's just tacky!…

ELDER: I heard on one of them news shows that the young girls are piercing them now a days…

THIRTY: What you gonna get a stud or a hoop?

ELDER: Think I want me a hoop…

THIRTY: Then you'll be setting off the metal detector at work…

ELDER: Stop doing all that nasty talk around me, I'm your mother…

THIRTY: You started it!

ELDER: Do you have any respect…

THIRTY: I'm going to make tea!

ELDER: You don't want to talk to your sweet old mother anymore?

THIRTY: Naw, cause you got problems. You want a sandwich or something, nasty mouth old woman?

ELDER: I would like a toasted turkey sandwich please. I would also like for you to bring me my tea and sandwich and sit here and talk to me.

THIRTY: I don't know if I can talk to you anymore. I might not be tall enough to ride this ride.

ELDER: I think you are.

THIRTY: Mama, you're a mess…a hot salty mess!

[*The sound of the phone ringing is heard. The women freeze. Lights transition to the empty place. Silence. The phone keeps ringing.*]

ELDER: Aren't you gonna get it?

THIRTY: No.

ELDER: You are prolonging the inevitable. Whether you answer or not, the moment still exist because it has happened and cannot be undone. The days between things being ok and things not being ok still passed. You didn't go back to stop it, because that's not possible. [*beat…the phone is still ringing*] Now go on…

[ELDER *retreats to the shadows. The lights flicker and transition as* THIRTY *walks and stand down stage.*]

THIRTY: Hello. Who's calling? Oh, um…just a moment…Mama, phone

ELDER [*calling from off stage*]: Who is it?

THIRTY: It's a Dr. Werner from the hospital…

[*The lights flicker again, and she becomes very angry.*]

THIRTY:

I

caught a cloud

following

me

it was all quite

surreal

when you

notice nature

is turning on

you

in that

moment

the cloud

creeped up

on me

without warning

BOOM

The roof…

is that a leak?

Didn't know the clouds had it in for us.

[*Lights transition. ELDER enters the space and sits, her breathing is heavy and erratic.*]

THIRTY: What's wrong? What was that all about?

ELDER [*trying to catch her breath*]: He, he said they found some abnormal tissue and wants me to come in tomorrow afternoon.

[*Silence*]

THIRTY: What time?

ELDER: 1:30.

THIRTY: I'll leave work about 12:30 then. That should give me enough time to get home and get you to your appointment.

ELDER: OK.

[*Silence*]

THIRTY: They just said abnormal, nothing else?

ELDER: No.

[*Silence*]

THIRTY: We'll see tomorrow.

ELDER: UmmHmm

[THIRTY *and* ELDER *are isolated in the empty place.*]

ELDER:

> My eyes
> turned inward
> and I saw my
> own soul
> tremble
> shadows passed
> across my mind
> my body shook
> from the inside
> internal tremors
> stronger than a
> thousand volcanoes
> erupting all at once
> but outwardly
> I'm not sure
> if I moved at all

THIRTY:

> I reached out
> and I touched
> your hand
> it trembled

ELDER: It did tremble?

THIRTY: Because you were…

ELDER/THIRTY: Scared.

THIRTY [*jumping to her feet, screaming*]: And your fear made me angry! I am angry! I look/looked at you and I get/got mad at everything and everybody. I'm mad at the window and the sun and the crick in my neck that I get from looking over my shoulder trying to get an answer and I get mad at the clothes that I'm wearing right now and I hate the clouds…loath and despise the clouds! I am angry!

[*Beat*]

ELDER: Anger and hurt are the same emotion from different perspectives.

THIRTY [*defeated*]: You walk around thinking you're safe from the weather. There is no raincoat or umbrella or roof that can keep you dry…I don't want to be angry, hurt, scared, but the alternative is…

ELDER: Numbness.

[ELDER *looks at* THIRTY *for a long moment.* THIRTY *begins to pace. The window is illuminated. The sounds of birds and percussion are heard.* ELDER *hands* THIRTY *her coat and purse.* ELDER *then puts on her own coat, gets a purse while they speak.*]

THIRTY/ELDER:

Nature is not
my friend this morning
the sound of
the birds
seem to
be too loud
and the sun
is coming into
the window
too brightly
I usually enjoy
morning dew
on the windshield
this morning
it's just annoying
To have your
senses bombarded
by nature
I never thought
that waking up
would be
oppressive

[THIRTY *moves slowly through the space. She reluctantly sets up a waiting room.* ELDER *hands her coat to* THIRTY *and exits. Lights transition to then with the window still illuminated.* THIRTY *grabs a magazine and sits on a cube. She flips pages as time meanders and several shadows pass across window.* ELDER *enters and stands dazed. She notices* ELDER *and rises.*]

THIRTY: What did he say?

ELDER: Where's my coat?

THIRTY: Right here…

ELDER: Hand it here so we can go…

THIRTY: Mama? What's wrong…what did he say? Mama…

ELDER: It's bad.

THIRTY: What is it!

ELDER [*sitting*]: He said that there is a, a cancer…

THIRTY [*sitting*]: Oh.

ELDER [*mouth dry and unable to swallow*]: In my uterus…He wants to do surgery…

THIRTY: What kind of surgery?

ELDER: A, um…hysterectomy. He, he said that should remove the cancer. That's the only way to get all the cancer. That's what he said.
[*Silence*]

THIRTY: You gonna have the surgery?

ELDER: Do I have a choice?

[*Beat*]

THIRTY: When?

[ELDER has drifted to a far away place.]

THIRTY [*grabbing her Elder's hand*]: Mama…the surgery? When are you supposed to have it?

ELDER [*snapping back to the moment*]: Next Friday…He said they can do it next Friday.

[THIRTY *reaches into her bag and pulls out a date book.*]

THIRTY: The 20th?

ELDER: Yeah, I think that's the date he said.

THIRTY: How long you got to be in the hospital?

ELDER: He said 5 days I think…I don't remember that now.

THIRTY: Let's go…

[THIRTY *begins to gather the coats/purses.* ELDER *remains seated.*]

THIRTY [*softly*]: Mama…come on.

[ELDER *pulls herself up slowly.* THIRTY *helps* ELDER *into her coat.* ELDER *exits.* THIRTY *crosses down stage center.*]

THIRTY: I'm gonna need to be off on the 20th. My mama is having surgery…Well what do you want me to do? No, there is no one else to take her…My father is sick himself, two of my sisters don't live in the city, and the other one don't drive, it's just me. Look, I don't understand what there is to talk about, I have to take my mother to the hospital, why is this a conversation…What, do you think I'm making things up? My mother has cancer…Yeah, then they found out hat she has cancer!…I could give a good goddamn what it "looks" like to you or her…I'm a grown ass woman, I don't have to lie to you or…You know what, fuck it…I said fuck it, fuck the job and fuck you!

[*A wash of light comes up over the stage and* ELDER *is sitting on a stool with her feet propped up and a blanket across her knees.* ELDER *snaps into the scene with* ELDER.]

THIRTY: Hey you! How you feeling?

ELDER [*smiling*]: I'm feeling ok. What took you so long to get here?

THIRTY: Every Negro on the south side was all trying to get home all at once. I brought you a present…

ELDER: Is it chicken?

THIRTY: Fried and greasy…

ELDER: Thank God…I'm starvin' to death! Four days of hospital food…

THIRTY: I can't even imagine…So, any word on blowing this joint?

ELDER: He said tomorrow I should be able to go home.

THIRTY: Good. [Beat] Janis called you, and so did Joan…

ELDER [anxious]: You didn't tell them anything did you?

THIRTY: No…They both called at times when you would have been at work…

ELDER: Good.

[Beat]

THIRTY: Mama, you really should tell them…

ELDER: Look, I have enough to deal with, those girls will turn this into a big thing and I just can't deal with that now.

THIRTY: I'm just saying, you're their Mama, I don't like 'em but…

ELDER: Do not tell them anything! You and your father are the only two people who need to know. Besides, now it's nothing to tell. He said that they checked and there are no more signs of cancer since the surgery …so there, it's done. I'll be home tomorrow and that's it.

[Beat]

THIRTY: Very well…

ELDER: Did you bring my tweezers? I can feel the chin hairs poppin' out as we speak.

THIRTY: Yes ma'am. I brought a comb and curling iron too, because your head looks like a whisk broom.

ELDER: Oh my God! You mean I been sittin' in here looking like a pick-a-ninny and you didn't tell me!

THIRTY: You just had surgery, I didn't think you cared. But now that you're feeling better…

ELDER: Please come over here and do something about my head. Lord why didn't you tell me?

THIRTY [amused]: Why are you concerned about your hair Mama? Got your eye on some man.

ELDER: Girl, don't play with me…come over here and do what I said now…

THIRTY [singing]: Mama looks like a broom, Mama looks like a broom…

ELDER: I am sick and you are upsetting me!

[THIRTY digs in her bag and pulls out comb and curling iron.]

THIRTY: So, the surgery took care of everything?

ELDER [hesitant]: Well, they recommended that I also do some chemotherapy…

THIRTY: And…

ELDER: I don't see the point in it. If they got all the cancer, why take the drugs.

THIRTY: What did Daddy say?

ELDER: Pretty much what I was thinking. [*Beat*] What do you think?

[*Silence*]

THIRTY: Well…I think…that stuff is very hard on you. I remember how sick Daddy was from it. I…I guess I agree with you.

ELDER: You think I shouldn't?

THIRTY: Mama, I think you should do whatever you think is best. If you don't think it's best to do, and if Daddy doesn't think it's best, then I don't think you should do it.

[*Lights fade out on ELDER. THIRTY is left in the empty place.*]

THIRTY:

I find myself
frequently
speaking the
language of the
poets
speaking in
verse
and
metaphor
and
rhyme
when
I begin to
slip into
this language
I feel grown up
and silly
I never wanted
never considered
being one of
the thinkers
then I
vacillate between
the language of
poets and
the common
vernacular
because I'm not
quite sure
which language is
best to connect
with myself/she
or articulate

the question
the ugly questions
seem
so much prettier
through clever turns
of phrases
when spoken
through the common
vernacular
ugly is just
ugly
so I hide
in the language
of a poet
Maybe if I layer
this hateful existence
with enough
pretty language
I can make all
this ugly
disappear

[ELDER *steps into her light*]

ELDER: You use to just cover your ears and hum.

THIRTY: The more time that goes by, the louder the ugly gets.

ELDER: Ugly can cause quite a racket.

THIRTY [*crying*]: The pretty words aren't working either.

ELDER: None of it is meant to stop the ugly. Ugly exist. It is. You can't cover your ears. You can't dress it up, and this moment that we're stuck in now…sweetie you have to let it end. We both have more work to do beyond this moment. You have a job here, and I got duties…

THIRTY [*shaking her head violently*]: Don't say it!!!!!!!!!

ELDER: You're procrastinating.

[*Lights flicker and the stage goes black for a second. Lights come on abruptly.*]

THIRTY: You ready?

ELDER: Did you put that baby's gift in the car?

THIRTY: For the twentieth, eleventh, millionth time Mama, yes! Everything that should be in the car is in the car except you! Now come on…say goodbye to Daddy and come on!

ELDER: I said goodbye to that man. Do you have the directions?

THIRTY: Mama, don't ask me another question about this trip…

ELDER: You have never driven this far before, and you damn sure have never done it with me in the car, so

I want to make sure you don't get me lost somewhere.

THIRTY: Look you, I can follow directions and I drive better then ¾ of the population, so get in the car and don't stress me woman.

ELDER: You drive like a man. Too aggressive, just makes me nervous…please don't get out there on the highway with all that horn honking and cursing…

THIRTY: Mama, I know how to drive.

ELDER: This is 12 hours. Did you get to bed at a decent hour last night. What if you fall asleep?

THIRTY: Ok…I'm going to get in the car. When you're done talking, feel free to join me downstairs, at which point we will embark on a nice road trip to see your hateful children and their off-spring and listen to Aretha and Stevie and Anita while we enjoy the countryside.

ELDER: I don't like when you dismiss me…

[THIRTY *covers her ears and hums*.]

ELDER: I am your mother! You shouldn't want to be so ugly to your own mother.

[ELDER *exits*. THIRTY *stand silently for a long moment in the empty place*. THIRTY *slowly and methodically clears the stage of everything except the two cubes*. *Lights transition as* ELDER *enters, walks in then exits through another door*. THIRTY *does not join the scene this time*. *Her tone is distant and sad*.]

THIRTY [*near tears*]: You wrong Mama. I told you I had to go and you raced me to the bathroom and that's just wrong. Who drove the whole trip? Me, that's who!…and the driver should get to go first!

ELDER [*from off stage*]: You're young, you can hold it.

THIRTY [*still distant*]: Wrong, wrong, wrong…

[ELDER *enters*. THIRTY *stands and adjust her mood trying to go back to the moment the way it actually existed*. ELDER *walks slowly to a stool and sits*. THIRTY *notices her mothers face*. *She pauses briefly*. *Then continues to speak*.]

THIRTY [*faux enthusiasm*]: Janis got all mad yesterday, because when we were at the mall, everybody kept telling me that Ryan was so cute and that she looked just like me. It's not my fault my little snuggle bunny looks more like her TeeTee Evie than her evil mother…

[*Silence*. THIRTY *lets the façade fall completely*. *Again, her tone is distant and sad*.]

THIRTY: You ok Mama?

ELDER: I saw blood.

THIRTY: When?

ELDER: Just now.

THIRTY: Coming from where?

[ELDER *looks at* THIRTY *then away*. *Lights transition as* THIRTY *and* ELDER *both move their cubes to face the audience.*]

ELDER: What does that mean?

THIRTY: What are saying?

ELDER: How long…

THIRTY: 12 to 18 months… [*exploding*] What the hell is your problem! How dare you sit here and tell my mother when she's gonna die…you are not God! Admittedly, all you fucking doctors have a God complex, but it's just a complex…you have no idea what the fuck you're talking about.

[THIRTY *paces frantically then sits.*]

ELDER: He says that there are some treatments I…we can try…

[*Silence*]

ELDER: …chemo.

[*Silence*]

ELDER: I would need you to help me get back and forth for chemo and doctors appointments…

THIRTY: That's not an issue Mama.

ELDER: What do think?

THIRTY: What do you want to do?

ELDER: I want to live.

THIRTY: Then you will.

[*The empty place and the shadow of the window become illuminated, but the light in the window is dim. ELDER moves a cube into the shadow of the window and grabs her mirror and tweezers. She tries to pick chin hairs but her hands are shaking badly. ELDER looks worn, tired. ELDER looks on from the distance. ELDER frustrated slams down the mirror and looks over her shoulder.*]

ELDER: You leavin'?

[*Again, THIRTY tries to enter the scene as it actually happened, but the waves of sadness are evident.*]

THIRTY: Yeah…see ya later.

[*Silence*]

THIRTY [*crossing to ELDER*]: You need anything from the store?

ELDER [*smirking*]: Let's see…I would like my taste buds back, my hands to stop shaking, my vision to clear up, and a ginger ale for my stomach.

THIRTY [*smiling back*]: I think I can do 1 out of 4.

[She bends to kiss ELDER. ELDER grabs THIRTY'S face in both hands and stares at her for a long moment. When she releases her, THIRTY begins to straighten up. ELDER grads her hand and pulls her down next to her.]

ELDER: You know what I was thinking about just now?

THIRTY: What?

ELDER: I think you must have been 18 months old or so. Your father came home from god knows where, drunk, and screaming about needing money for some rum. He had just give me this money earlier in the evening so I hadn't had time to go to the store and get grocery's yet. I still had the money and he knew it. It was always bad when he was drunk and knew I had money. He was screaming and hollering, "Bitch that's my fucking money! You better get up off my fucking money right now!" Right up on me screaming. Now, you were sitting on my lap the whole time, and I'm telling him that I ain't givin' him shit. At some point I realized that I wasn't holding you any more. I was hiding behind you, because I knew he wouldn't get drunk enough to hit you. And in what was to date the lowest, most cowardly moment in my life…me using my baby as a shield from getting my ass beat, you stood up on your little fat legs and swung your fist at him and screamed "weave her a wone!". *[Beat]* You didn't cry. You didn't whine. At 18 months old your first instinct was to fight. Any crying and whining you do now, you learned that from me. *[breaking down at her next thought]* I looked at you just now and you know what I thought? I been hiding behind you for the past few months…

THIRTY: Mama don't say that…

ELDER *[breaking down]*: You've been fighting, because I can't. I can't take this! I am in pain…constant pain…

THIRTY *[desperate]*: Mama, this is temporary! We will get through this. If I have to hook myself up to an IV and take the damn chemo for you, we will get through this. It's almost over. The doctor said there is some shrinking of the tumor, and…

ELDER *[smiling sadly]*: But that's not fair for you. Little girls shouldn't have to fight so hard.

THIRTY *[holding ELDER]*: That's my way, you just said that. Let me fight, you get better.

[The lights dim, then transition to the empty place as ELDER moves the cubes to the hospital position with blanket over ELDER'S knees. Her stool is lit. ELDER is listless. THIRTY paces, agitated.]

THIRTY:

> …and the clouds
> covered up the
> sun completely
> there was darkness
> everywhere

ELDER: Come here. Sit down.

THIRTY *[shaking]*: No. They moved to fast. They were closing in on me, I knew that Mama, but I never expected them to cover up the sun. I can't sit there. That light scares me.

ELDER: It's not like the light in the window. You can't turn away from it. You have to see it. One day, you'll know it, like I know it. But for now, you just have to see it.

[Stage lights flicker again and black out for a second. Lights come up.]

THIRTY [*forced enthusiasm*]: So what's the good word for the day.

ELDER [*listless*]: They say that from my test it looks like a reduction on the lymph nodes by 17% since last time.

THIRTY: That's good!

ELDER: Did you bring me some ginger ale.

THIRTY: Yeah, here…

[*She hands* ELDER *the ginger ale. ELDER sips slowly in silence.*]

ELDER: I don't know if I can keep doing this.

THIRTY: Werner said you only have 2 more treatments to go…

ELDER: I don't know if I'm gonna make it. I'm so tired. Tired of being sick. Tired of being tired.

[*Silence*]

ELDER: Baby…am I gonna live?

[*Thirty freeze.*]

[*Beat*]

THIRTY [*choking back tears*]: Of course…you have to be there when Michael Clark Duncan and I say our vows…

ELDER [laughing]: Come over here and do something about my head. I know I just look a mess.

[THIRTY *gets out a comb and stands over her mother. She hesitates before she speaks.*]

THIRTY: Mama, your hair is breaking really bad.

ELDER: I know.

[*Silence*]

THIRTY: I was thinking…maybe we should cut it before it falls out. Maybe if we just cut it real low, then it won't break as bad. You won't go completely bald.

ELDER [*choking back tears*]: You're probably right. When you gonna cut it.

[THIRTY *bends down and grabs scissors*]

THIRTY: Let's do it now…get it over with.

ELDER [*crying*]: Ok.

THIRTY [*still choking back tears*]: Ok.

[THIRTY begins to cut ELDER'S hair. ELDERsobs silently. Lights fade out. Lights come up. THIRTY has given ELDER a mirror.]

ELDER [*sniffing*]: It's not too bad…you can see all the gray…

THIRTY [*sniffing*]: That's ok…your gray is silvery and nice. It's kinda of cute. Maybe I'll cut my hair real short.

ELDER: You wouldn't be as pretty as me…

THIRTY: Well of course I wouldn't…

[*Beat*]

THIRTY: More hair.

ELDER: More hair.

[*Beat*]

THIRTY: I'm going home old woman, I have had enough of you today.

ELDER: You know, I asked the nurse and she said that if you stayed with me they would bring a cot in the room for you to sleep on.

THIRTY: You want me to stay?

ELDER: It's just that, I have a hard time getting around to the bathroom and stuff with the I.V. and the nurses take so long when you call…

THIRTY: Well, let me run home and get some clothes, you can tell them I'll be staying tonight. You're coming home tomorrow, right?

ELDER: That's what they say…

THIRTY: One day in the hospital…I think I can manage that for my Mama…I'll be right back.

[THIRTY bends down to kiss her mother. ELDER grabs her arm.]

ELDER: You're a good girl, do you know that?

THIRTY [*taken aback*]: You're not half bad yourself.

ELDER: Thank you baby…I love my baby girl…

THIRTY [*choking up*]: Don't be nice to me until you get through with this stupid chemo for good. This is cutting into my dating. I'll be back.

[*Lights transition*. ELDER *exits*. THIRTY *stands facing the audience, enraged*.]

THIRTY: I don't understand what happened. Yesterday she was fine. You said she could come home today. What the hell is septicemic? …a blood infection? How did she get that? How does your blood get infected?…Look, stop speaking in tongues…what are you telling me? You're telling me that you people talked her into taking the goddamn chemo, and now that's what's fucking killing her? This is a fucking joke! So, you poisoned my mother! How do you plan on fixing it!!!!!!!!

[*Silence*]

What? Now, today? My mother is dying? At this very moment she's not gonna live no matter what? Is that what you're telling me? You are a lying sack of shit! GO TO HELL!

[*Lights transition as* THIRTY *paces in a frantic circle.* THIRTY *stops abruptly and faces the audience. She is physically broken.*]

THIRTY: They can't get the infection under control.   [*crying/defeated*] It's been over 36 hours and at this point…Janis, will you call the other two. Yeah, Daddy is here, he's with her now. I think you should probably come soon. Good, see you tomorrow.   [*chuckle*] Yeah, I think you might have to buy me a couple of drinks…Yeah, love you too. Be careful coming ok. Ok. Bye.

[THIRTY *falls to the floor.*]

THIRTY [*crying*]:

My coping
Gets all jumbled up
And confused
I don't know
Which parts
I said
Or what was
Said to me
I don't know
If it was
Really said at all
Or if I heard the
Conversation in some
Secret space
In time where
Words escape
Us
Have I left the room
Or am I
Watching

[ELDER *enters and sits on a stool illuminated with the blanket on her knees.* THIRTY *falls at* ELDER'S *feet in the light, defeated, still sobbing*].

THIRTY: I don't understand Mama…Why? Why me? Why am I here? Why did I have to snap beans and clean puke and sleep in the hospital and cut your hair and …why me?

ELDER: Why not? You're the only one I got to raise. You're my baby, but you needed to be a big girl, and everybody grows up differently. This is the way your steps were ordered. Now you can move on. Do the rest you your work. Take care of yourself

THIRTY: No, I can't. I'm the baby. I need you.

ELDER [*laughing*]: Yes you can. You've been taking care of yourself, and me, and your father for the past year now. You don't need to see me any more.
You have me. You are me. I was able to give you the best parts of me.

THIRTY: Please…stay.

ELDER: I'm out of time here. My work is somewhere else now. Let me go. It's divine. It 's already been done.

THIRTY: I love you Mama.

ELDER: I love you baby…

[ELDER *bends down and kisses* THIRTY *on the cheek.* ELDER *exits.* THIRTY *collapses into the empty spot, and screams.*]

THIRTY: It's not fair…not fair, not fair! COME BACK!

[THIRTY *screams incoherently for a long moment. Then grows silent. She rises abruptly. Shaking she begins speaking as if rattling of a to do list.*]

THIRTY: First, stop crying. Nobody cares about my tears.

[THIRTY *wipes her eyes.*]

…can't lay on the floor and cry. We have to get her body to a funeral home and call everybody, the girls and Daddy…

[*She becomes very still*]

THIRTY: I want to cry…Later. Fight. Gotta cope…that sounds better for now…better than crazy, Be a superhero, with a prettier cape. A green cape…

[*She begins to cry again.*]

THIRTY: I can do this…I can do this…I'm a big girl…I'm a fighter…I can do this.

[*She crosses to* ELDER'S *light and sits in it*]

THIRTY: You have to help me…

[*She wraps herself in* ELDER'S *blanket.* ELDER *appears from the shadows and watches.*]

[*Lights fade*]

[*End play*]

Thank you
by Shepsu Aakhu

Yesterday, I had a very interesting experience: I actually wanted to be in two places at the same time. This is vastly different from the *NEEDING* to be in two places at the same time, which happens to most of us on a daily basis.

A show that I wrote and directed, *Kiwi Black*, is running at North Park University. It is full of young hungry artists and youthful exuberance, And, of course, Andre Teamer, an actor who makes me want to write just to hear the words come out of his mouth.

A few miles down the street, my latest play, *Softly Blue,* is in its world premiere run. It is a show that I wrote and designed. It is a dark and powerful little play that intrigues me, and in the most pleasant of ways continues to surprise me.

In the car ride between these two temples of my familiar, I had a moment to reflect upon my privilege. I am privileged. One can't work in this business and believe otherwise. Things that once existed only in my mind are brought to life by a legion of artists. Ideas are made flesh and set free to dance, cry, and be. For a few brief days or weeks, a lifetime of work (albeit a short one) is once again validated.

But that is not the privilege that I have spent the last 24 hours or so overwhelmed by; that privilege is to have known all of you. I entered this field with absolutely no training. Everything that I am and everything that I do was facilitated by many who have given of their time, patience, and their passion. They are my teachers, formal and otherwise, and I am forever in their debt.

Aum Mu Ra, George Blaise, Danjuma Gaskin and Shawn Wallace: Thank you for letting me play before I could keep time, for holding my hand and hitting me in the back of the head when I needed it, and for allowing me to learn without shame or ridicule.

William S. Carroll: Thank you for telling me to tell my stories instead of waiting for someone else to do it for me.

Mignon McPherson (Nance), Charles S. Hall, Kim Crutcher, Terry Cullers, Tiffany Trent, and Arie Thompson: Thank you for opening my eyes to the possibilities of my work, for challenging me to be better, and for helping me to see theatre as a process as much as a product.

Sean R. Neron, Mark Franklin, Maggie Fullilove Nugent, Regina Walton-Ciss, Jessica Kuehnau, Kanika Sago, Evelyn Danner, Sharlet Webb, Juarez Hawkins, Daryl Charrise, Betty Sibon, Razor Wintercastle, Tom Birch, and Dirk DeLaCour: Thank you for showing me worlds both large and small created from near nothing. From you I have learned to dirty my hands to make the things that I value. I have seen you paint the sky with light, shape and layer fabrics into delights and toil on sets until deep in the night.

 I have stolen everything I know about design from all of you, and I plan to keep on doing that.

Efé McWorter, Shirley Carney, Hiwoté Tamrat, Chad Eric Bergman, Larry Nance, Kevin Douglas, Carla Stillwell, Rodney Stapleton, Chuck Smith, Stacey Ballis, Robin Robinson, Tsehaye Herbert, René Townsend, Adrian Capehart, Arnold April, Cynthia Weiss, Jackie Terrassa, Jackie Samuel, Tiffany Trent, Hilal Tamrat, my students, and my own children: You have taught me to be an educator, and in doing so helped me to better understand my own art. You are the people who helped me to understand the importance of "what you want to teach", and "how you need to teach it". You have taught me patience and perseverance, to set high standards, and to expect them to be accomplished. But most importantly, I have learned to be more compassionate for those in whose lives I play some small part. I have learned how to build worlds from you as well.

To those actors who have given so freely of their time, too often paid at a rate far below what your talent demands, I thank you. To Andre Teamer, Demetria Thomas, Kevin Douglas, Elisabeth Isabue, Morocco Omari, Carla Stillwell, Mark Morgan, Gina Taliaferro, Robert Hines, Al Bozwell, Charles Michael Moore, Tina Marie Wright, Angela Walsh, Leonard House, Kate McCandless, Carl Barnett, Joe Giovanetti, Tanya Renee Lane, Alana Calco, Rebecca Thompson, Honey Beverly Crawford, Quinton Wilks, Rell Burks Smith, Darius Jones, Antione P. Brunson, James T. Alfred, Yvonne Huff, Jason Delane (Lee), Sati Word, Heather Ireland, Cynthia J. Maddox, Mark D. Hayes, Warren Jackson, Simeon Henderson, Derrick Jones, Eddie Brown, Nihara Nichelle, Lydia Diamond, Jesse AJheydei Standford, Brittany Davis, Chris Lambreth, LaNisa Frederick, Joslyn Jones, Tory O. Davis, Earl Fox, Alana Arenas, Tabitha Cross (Mathews), Lisa Biggs, Sharif Atkins, Darwin Harris, Christopher McMorris, Terry Cullers, Mashari L. Bain, Jameelah McMillian, Freeman Coffey, Rodrick Jean-Charles, Lydia Fasse, Julia Oh, Marie Francois, Seirra Cleveland, LaFern Watkins, Kenneth Johnson, Edwin Holmes, Felicia Bradley, Aaron Carter, Karen Stephens, Latrice Bailey, and others too numerous to mention (but certainly not forgotten): From the bottom of my heart I thank you. I have learned from you as well, and you have given me so much in our short time together. You are appreciated.

To Lydia, Nambi, Addae, Mom, William S. Carroll, Lisa Biggs, Larry Nance, Carla Stillwell, Deidre Searcy, Mignon, Kevin Douglas, J. David, Ena Isis, Godfrey Donchima, Aaron Carter, Inda Craig-Galvan, Nicole McIntosh, Tina Jordan, Camille Banks, Terry Fitzpatrick, and Rene M. Butler: You are my writing teachers. It is as much through your work as my own, that I can call myself a writer. Through every keystroke and glide of the pen I have learned from your efforts as well as my own. You are amazingly talented writers and I am honored to learn in your company.

For the choreographers who remind me what I could have been (probably not) had I continued to dance: Thank you Sabrina Tyus, Roxi Fuqua, Imani Foster, Jennifer Savarirayan - Stidellie, Tabitha Russell-K., the Andrea's (Wukitch and Vinson), Aum Mu Ra, and Boogie. I don't dare dream worlds as beautiful as the ones you have created.

I am in awe of your talents.

Every time I watch a Biography/ Inside the Actors Studio/ True Hollywood Story or other such nonsense, I am amazed by the answer to this question: "Who were your major influences?" They say something like "Stevie Wonder, Richard Pryor, or Sidney Poitier." As much I respect these artists for their contributions and their sacrifices, they have never lifted a hammer to build a set for me, never patiently studied my lines to figure out how to make them alive, never corrected my form, edited a script, sewn a costume, bathed a set in lights, washed it in meticulously arranged sound, or spoken a word of encouragement when I was low. Stevie Wonder reminded me of how beautiful Black people are, but it is through this community of artists that I witnessed and participated in such beauty.

In response to the question, the celebrity never says, "My major influences were the people that I work with everyday". Well, I'm saying it. You are my deepest most powerful influences. I am nothing without you. You gave birth to me. I have been nurtured by you. I am forever in your debt. You are appreciated.

With deep affection
Shepsu Aakhu

298

About the playwrights

SHEPSU AAKHU

Presently, Shepsu teaches and directs theatre at North Park University. He is also a founding member and playwright in residence with MPAACT, where he has developed several critically acclaimed works including: *Softly Blue*, *Relevant Hearsay*, *SOST, Kiwi Black*, *Kosi Dasa, Fascia, The Glow of Reflected Light, The Abesha Conspiracy, Beneath A Dark Sky, Piece-Meal Clan,* and *Otherworld Lovers*.

In 2004, Shepsu Aakhu was awarded the prestigious Artistic Fellowship in Scriptworks by the Illinois Arts Council. He is the recipient of the 16th annual Theodore Ward Prize for Playwrighting (*Kiwi Black).* He is a five time nominee for best Original Stage Play (Aldridge Award) by the BTAA of Chicago. Shepsu received the Ira Aldridge Award in 1999 for *The Abesha Conspiracy.* He has also received a nomination for best new work by the Joseph Jefferson Awards Committee *(Kiwi Black).*   Other projects currently in development include the stage plays: *Ten Square, Port Chicago, Atwood, A Thousand Negative Confessions* and *STEEL,* a commissioned musical for the Westside Theater Guild of Gary, IN.

Screenplays include: *Mel-Bay*, *The Preacher's Game,* co-written with J. David Shanks, the film adaptation of his stage play *Beneath A Dark Sky,* and *The Ballad of Sadie Hawkins,* a commissioned work for the Westside Theater Guild. Monologue selections from several of Shepsu's plays may be found in *The Alibi Transcripts* (Sakhu Press 2001.) *Kiwi Black* is available in the anthology *Seven Black Play*s, edited by Chuck Smith (Northwestern University Press 2004).

NAMBI E. KELLEY

Ms. Kelley is an award-winning, published, and produced playwright, including projects for the Steppenwolf Theatre in Chicago and Lincoln Center in New York. Honors include: TCG Candidate for Playwriting, Goodman Theatre, Chicago, 2004-05, Eugene O'Neill Playwrights Conference nomination, 2004, The Chesterfield Writer's Film Project, Paramount Studios, finalist, 2004; 3 children's plays commissions for Unibooks, Seoul, Korea, 2004; ACT Theatre/Seattle Repertory Nomination for Women's Playwright Festival, 2003, Ovation Awards Nominated Production, Los Angeles (HOW KINTU BECAME A MAN) 2003,Williams College Playwright-in-Residence, 2003 Stalwart Originality, Williamstown, Massachusetts, Peace Maker of the Year Award, The Peace Museum and Ben & Jerry's Ice cream (Health Works Theatre commissioned violence prevention play),Prop Thtr New Plays Festival (HE, SHE & MY WHITE MAMA and BUS BOYZ),Best Original Writing Nomination (HOOCHIE MAMA), Black Theatre Alliance. Professional affiliations include, The Alliance of Los Angeles Playwrights, The Playwright's Center Minneapolis, The Dramatists Guild, and playwright-in-residence with Chicago Dramatists and MPAACT.

AADAE MOON

Addae Moon is a Southern based playwright, director and bluesman. He is a graduate of the Playwriting program at Ohio University (M.F.A.). His other works include *Bottletree, Kissing Piranahs, Mood Indigo, Strange Fruit* and *Moon Women Eat Pecan Pie.* He is currently working on *Terminus* and *Ballad for Lila.*

CARLA STILLWELL

Carla made her introduction as a playwright in Chicago with the one woman piece *Carla...In Search of My Silky Underthings* in the spring of 2000. Her first full length piece, *Defending Myself,* ran at the Victory Gardens Theatre in 2002. Both works were produced by Ma'at Production Association of Afrikan Centered Theatre (MPAACT). Excerpts from *Carla...In Search of My Silky Underthings* appear in the *Alibi Transcripts,* a book of African-American monologues for stage. She has also toured with MPAACT throughout the U.S. as an actor, and holds the positions Director of Artistic Development/ Production Coordinator and Playwright-in-Residence for the company.

Carla's acting career and training began with a touring children's theatre company at the age of 10, and she has been performing in and around the greater Chicagoland area for 23 years. Most recently, Ms. Stillwell's play *The Divine Order of Becoming,* a work which celebrates the bond of a mother and her child, closed after a successful run in Chicago in March 2005. *The Divine Order of Becoming* was also nominated for a Jeff Award and Black Theatre Alliance Award. She has also entered into her first comedic collaboration with Chicago's renowned comedy team *kevINda.* She dedicates her career to the loving memory of her parents, Charlene and Raymond Stillwell, and her very first drama teacher, Zaheerah Muhammad.

Plays for Production

The Abesha Conspiracy
Playwright: Shepsu Aakhu
World Premiere: 1999 , Originally produced by MPAACT, Chicago Illinois.
Setting: America (Chicago/Mississippi) & Addis Abba, Ethiopia,   Various settings minimally suggested:
Airport terminal, house, garden, bedroom.
Time: 1980-1999
A full length drama (2 acts)
3M/3F   Some roles are doubled
Production has choreographic elements
Two languages are utilized English(90%) & Amharic (10%)
Production contains media elements (Sound, video and/or slide)
Slide elements available
Sound media available
Language tapes available
$12/script
$75/performance

Synopsis
The Abesha Conspiracy follows the story of Joseph and his Ethiopian wife Sosena as they journey to
her homeland. It is a journey of the soul that connects a husband to a wife, parent to their child, and an
individual to their culture. Based on the playwright's perceptual experiences on a post nuptial pilgrimage
to Ethiopia. The Abesha Conspiracy is a layered exploration of the emotional and cultural conflicts that
exist between continental Africans and the Diaspora. It is an invasive, sometimes satirical, exploration of a
collective unconscious, it is a fearless examination of self, the vaunted "African Mythos", and the realities
of contemporary African and African American society.

Beneath A Dark Sky
Playwright: Shepsu Aakhu
World Premiere: 1998 , Originally produced by MPAACT, Chicago Illinois.
Place: Rural southeast Texas. Two settings minimally suggested: Front porch and yard, fishing pond.
Time: 1970-1998
A full length drama (1 act / 90minutes)
2M/2 F   A roles may be divided, expanding cast size to 2M/2F
$12/script
$75/performance
Synopsis
Beneath a Dark Sky is a touching memory play of African-American life in rural southeast Texas.
Willamena has an enduring relationship with an otherwise ostracized grandfather, all the while struggling
to come of age with a transient father of her own. Not so much a play in the traditional sense, "Beneath
A Dark Sky" is storytelling in it's most ancient and powerful form. We are invited into the world of
Willamena Levy, where we share the events which shape her world and perceptions.

Blaxploitation: The Remix
Written by Kevin Douglas, Inda Craig-Galvan, and Carla Stillwell
World Premiere: 2006 MPAACT Chicago Illinois
Place: Various Minimally suggested.
Time: present day America
Sketch Comedy 90 Minutes
2M/3 F Roles may be divided, expanding cast size to 4M/4F
$12/script
$75/performance
Synopsis
BLAXPLOITATION: THE REMIX is a collection of original sketch performances that are unabashedly

courageous and provocative in their take on race, class, and American politics.

Bus Boyz
Written by Nambi E. Kelley
World Premiere: 2005, Originally produced by MPAACT and Prop Thtr, Chicago Illinois.
Place: Chicago Illinois: Various location minimally suggested
Time: present
A full length drama (2 acts)
4M/1 F Some roles are doubled.
 Production has choreographic elements
$12/script
$75/performance

Synopsis
"Men are like buses" are the words of Mary who is looking, but not desperate to find Mr. Right. And, so come the many men who transport themselves in and out of her life. There is "Ford the Fleabag", Rob the flip", and "Dussell the Love Muscle" just to name a few. But Mary is interested in finding true love, not just a constant parade of new and newer buses. What happens when a chance meeting with a bus named Vernon goes sour forcing Mary to face her relationship with her absentee father? BUS BOYZ is a comedy tracing the dating life of Mary in her hot pursuit of the "L" word: love takes place in the moment when life takes a sharp, distinct turn.

Carla... in Search of My Silky Underthings
Playwright: Carla Stillwell
World Premiere: 2000 (Exoskeletal Blues) - Originally produced by MPAACT, Chicago Illinois
Place: Chicago IL . One settings minimally suggested: Nightclub
Time: 1975-2000
One Act drama (40minutes)
1F
$12/script
$35/performance

Carla... in Search of My Silky Underthings is based on the true life experiences of Carla Stillwell. Performed as an intimate dialogue between the artist and the audience. The work displays a bold honesty. With liberal doses of respect and irreverence the play tackles sex, dating, parenting, chronic illness, and the need for creative expression.

Chris T.
Playwright: Nambi E. Kelley
World Premiere: 2000 - Originally produced by MPAACT, Chicago Illinois.
Place: America at the turn of the millennia. Various settings minimally suggested:
Time: The coming of the millennia
A full length drama (2 acts)
4M/2 F   Some roles are doubled, some are not gender specific.
Production has choreographic elements
$12/script
$75/performance

Synopsis
Chris T. asks intriguing questions about our belief systems, from politics to faith. What happens when the Prezo-dent of the world gets on T.V. and proclaims that Jesus Christ never existed? The world is cast into a series of devastating events. Chris T. is the story of every man, embodied in the characters Mama Pajama, Sassafras, Jethro, Charles, Max and the title character, as they take a journey of faith and spirit which begs the question: Can love exist where chaos is king?

Defending Myself
Playwright: Carla Stillwell
World Premiere: 2002, Originally produced by MPAACT, Chicago Illinois
Place: Chicago IL . One settings minimally suggested: Apartment
Time: 2002
A full length drama (1 act / 1hour 45minutes)
1 M/1 F
Production has choreographic elements
Dramaturgical materials available
$12/script
$75/performance

Synopsis
Defending Myself is a physical exploration of the power dynamics in love. We witness Richard and Aza from the anticipations of first date flirtation and intense heat to the familiarities of daily routine and the "little things" that make all the difference in loving/sharing /giving/receiving/ possessing self or a lover. Writer Carla Stillwell says of her impulse for the piece: "There are few words and no labels that articulate what happens in private between two people. We just don't know that unless we are in it." Therefore, through movement, dance, and layers of sound, she explores what happens when words run out.

The Divine Order Of Becoming
Written by Carla Stillwell
World Premiere: 2005, Originally produced by MPAACT, Chicago Illinois
Place: Chicago IL. Multiple settings minimally suggested: Apartment, car, hospice
Time: Present
A full length drama (1 act / 1hour 30minutes)
2 F
Production has choreographic elements
Dramaturgical materials available
$12/script
$75/performance

Synopsis
This story takes place in the moment when life takes a sharp, distinct turn. With poetry, prose and the conjuring of memory's past, we watch a young women struggle to let go of the relationship that she and her mother developed during her 20's We mourn with her as she applies the lessons passed to her through lecture, argument, and out right silliness to rise above the pain of loss.

Fascia
Playwright: Shepsu Aakhu
World Premiere: 2001 , Originally produced by MPAACT, Chicago Illinois.
Place: Chicago, Illinois & the Yazoo City Mississippi. Various settings minimally suggested:
Time: 1940-2001
A full length drama (2 acts)
12 roles 6M/6 F   If roles are doubled, 4M/4F.
Production has choreographic elements
Two languages are utilized English(99%) & Yoruba (1%)
Dramaturgical materials available
Language tapes available
$12/script
$75/performance

Synopsis
Fascia is a blend of Yoruba belief systems grafted onto a contemporary African-American family.   Fascia is the struggle to understand a singular moment in the life of an entire family. The baggage that makes the

seemingly simple ....so damn complicated. We follow the story of cousins who though once inseparable, now find themselves distant and detached. The concept of time is folded in upon itself allowing four generations of the family to interact, and influence each other. In the end we a are left with a concept of family which stretches far beyond the western nuclear family to accommodate those whose once lived, and those who are yet to come.

Gabriel's Threshold
Playwright: Shepsu Aakhu
World Premiere: 1997 (Afrosynthesis) - Originally produced by MPAACT, Chicago Illinois
Place: Small town, Midwest. One setting minimally suggested: Front porch.
Time: The late 1980's.
One Act drama (30 minutes)
3M/1F
$12/script
$35/performance

Synopsis
Gabriel's Threshold allows the audience to stand witness as victims of random violence turn the tables on their assailant. In a world were violence is glamorized, Gabriel's Threshold exposes the physical and emotional devastation caused by these acts, with none of the glitz to numb the pain.

Girl To Be Named Later
Playwright: Nambi E. Kelley
World Premiere: 1996 - Originally produced by MPAACT, Chicago Illinois.
Place: Chicago, Illinois. Various setting minimally suggested:
Time: The late 1980's-1990's
A full length drama
7 characters/ 5 when doubled.   Gender flexibility in 4 roles
$12/script
$75/performance

Synopsis
Girl To Be Named Later reflects the tension and turmoil of its main character who teeters on the edge of sanity. Wanting desperately to escape a life filled with pain, but afraid to venture out of her mother's shadow, Ohh Child -Peach retreats into a world of fantasy. Unfortunately the world she creates is one filled with disturbing fragments from the world she is trying to flee.

The Glow of Reflected Light
Playwright: Shepsu Aakhu
World Premiere: 2000
Originally produced by MPAACT, Chicago Illinois.
Place: Ontario Canada (cabin), Various other settings minimally suggested:
Time: 1832
A full length drama
6M/2F
Production has choreographic elements
$12/script
$75/performance

Synopsis
The Glow of Reflected Light is loosely based upon the Canadian communities founded by William King, Hiram Wilson, and Josiah Henson. It is an exploration of the historical context which ushered such communities into being, and the myriad paths which brought about their inevitable decline. *The Glow of Reflected Light* provides some rare and enormously valuable glimpses into the interior lives of American slaves, freemen and women, fugitives, freedom fighters, and nation builders. This provocative drama has

been exhaustively researched, sampling a wide variety of manuscripts and archival materials in the United States and Canada. The result is a story which resonates with the authentic voices of ordinary people in extraordinary circumstances.   At it's core *The Glow of Reflected Light* is an examination of the self, community, history, and progress.

Hoochie Mama

Playwright: Nambi E. Kelley
World Premiere: 1997 (Afrosynthesis) - Originally produced by MPAACT, Chicago, Illinois.
Place: Anywhere America. One setting minimally suggested: The Glad-as-Night and the Pips E-stablish-ment.
 Time: The mid 1990's
One Act romantic drama (30 minutes)
3M/3F
$12/script
$35/performance

Synopsis

Hoochie Mama magnifies and further distorts every stereotype ever concocted about Black life: dread locked Jamaicans, steppin' fetchit characters, homeboys, buppies, pimps, hustlers, mammies, coons, and bucks. Set in the fictitious Glad-as-Night and the Pips E-stablish-ment, *Hoochie Mama* centers on a confused main character trying desperately to smother his "Blackness" as a result of such stereotypes. Displaying the hallmarks of a Nambi E. Kelley production *Hoochie Mama* utilizes rhythmic dialogue and extravagantly drawn characters to elevate it's language into poetry.   The result is a play which begs the questions: Who do we think we are, and who are we trying please?

The Inside

Playwright: Lydia Diamond
World Premiere: 1998 - Originally produced by MPAACT, Chicago Illinois.
Place: Chicago, Illinois. One setting minimally suggested: An apartment party,
Time: The late 1990's
A full length drama
3 F   Many roles are doubled for dramatic effect.
$12/script
$75/performance

Synopsis

The Inside presents us with a piercing take on race, academia, art, and sexuality, all viewed through the prism of this highly original character. By turns amusingly ironic and heartbreakingly vulnerable, Emma serves up her interior life with astonishing honesty. "It was your typical, painfully liberal, pre-professional anti-establishment artistic event". So recalls Emma, a Black college student who comes to crisis at a party given by, and populated with her white peers. Challenging the distinctions separating performance art and traditional narrative, *The Inside* utilizes a unique format that blends monologue and ensemble work. Emma speaks directly to the audience, aided by a chorus of actors who serve alternately as an extension of herself, or as voices from her past, her present, and her fantasies.

Kiwi Black

Playwright: Shepsu Aakhu
World Premiere: 2003, Originally produced by MPAACT, Chicago Illinois.
Time: 2002
A play in two acts
6M/1 F   (Various none speaking roles)
$12/script
$75/performance

Synopsis

Kiwi Black is a piercing take on class, the American work ethic, and the non-traditional family, as experienced by two complex and conflicted characters. With gritty realism, abstract humor, and blurred boundaries Joe and Lennox (father and son) serve up the challenges of their evolving relationship, and the tumult of their interior lives. Lennox as described by his father is "...trying to turn the corner on being a man". Joe as described by his son is "...willing to do anything to survive". Aspirations of a college education come into conflict with the realities of collection agencies and the daily hustle to make ends meet, leaving Joe and Lennox to navigate their relationship through uncharted territory .

Kiwi Black blends monologue, ensemble work, live music, and surrealist staging to explore the many faces of love and devotion that exist between a father and his son.

Kosi Dasa

Playwright: Shepsu Aakhu
World Premiere: 2002, Originally produced by MPAACT, Chicago Illinois.
Place: Mythical Afrikan Village
Time: mythical
A full length drama (2 acts)
4M/3 F (Principals) 1M/1F (Ensemble minimal) Expandable to suit production vision
Production has choreographic elements
Two languages are utilized English(97%) & Elombian (3%)
Dramaturgical materials available
Language CD available
$12/script
$75/performance

Synopsis

A magical landscape of myth, ritual, and folklore await in Shepsu Aakhu's *Kosi Dasa*. "Stories are passed from mouth to mouth, with the supple caress of secret words wrapped inside a full kiss". No Eyes and Diata are a young couple, flirting with love as they await their passage into adulthood. Their lives are changed forever as each must accept sacrifice in the name of community, family, and spiritual beliefs. Told using elements of traditional African storytelling, African and Indian Dance, Brazillian and Asian combat styles, and live musical accompaniment, Dasa examines the beliefs which bind one spirit to another, individuals to community, and community to it's divine aspects.

MiLK

Playwright: Nambi E. Kelley
World Premiere: 1998 - Originally produced by MPAACT, Chicago Illinois.
Place: Chicago, Illinois. Various setting minimally suggested:
Time: The late 1980's-1990's
A full length drama
3 F/3M
$12/script
$75/performance

Synopsis

MiLK traces the story of three adolescent girls living in the shadow of a Chicago housing project. We follow "Baby" and her spirit force "Womaclown" as they tackle the difficult issues of coming of age in such a difficult environment. The playwright skillful utilizes rhythmic dialogue to elevate the character's street language into poetry, thus bringing out the mystical elements hidden in the everyday world. *MiLK* takes an audience through a painful yet beautiful life journey that is as rich and nourishing in it's poetry as it's unifying image of milk.

The Missing Peace
Adapted from the short story by Edwidge Danticat

Playwright: Mignon McPherson
World Premiere: 1998 (Exoskeletal Blues) - Originally produced by MPAACT, Chicago Illinois
Place: Ville Rose, Haiti. Various setting minimally suggested:
Time: October 1991
One Act drama (adaptation) (25 minutes)
Additional consent required from author: Edwidge Danticat
3 F/2M
Two languages are utilized English(90%) & Kreyol (10%)
$12/script
$35/performance

Synopsis
The Missing Peace picks up one month following the coup which overthrew the people elected president, Aristide. The whole country is tense. The poor are still mourning the lost of their president, and the continuing murders by the military of their brethren. *The Missing Peace* follows the story of LaMort, an illiterate, sheltered, Haitian adolescent who attempts to aid a Haitian-American journalist find her missing mother amid this backdrop of political unrest. Together the two women search to find redemption, and personal peace in a world where all that is conventional is at war.

Moon Women Eat Pecan Pie
Playwright: Addae Moon
World Premiere: 1997 (Afrosynthesis) - Originally produced by MPAACT, Chicago, Illinois.
Place: Atlanta, Georgia. One setting minimally suggested: Southern diner
Time: The mid 1990's
One Act romantic drama (30 minutes)
3M/3F
$12/script
$35/performance

Synopsis
Moon Women Eat Pecan Pie is a charmingly warm and slightly melancholy play which illuminates the divisions and connections in contemporary African-American society. Pitting snide college girls against "country" local men *Moon Women Eat Pecan Pie* folds back the layers that separate the classes and exposes the very real attractions that remain.

Notes from the Bottletree
Written by Addae Moon
World Premiere 2004 Originally produced by MPAACT, Chicago Illinois
Place: Atlanta, Georgia. Various setting minimally suggested: Gallery exhibition, Apartment, Darkroom
Time: 2004
One Act drama (80 minutes)
2M/1F
$12/script
$75/performance

Synopsis
Danger, art, beauty and a haunted past drive this provocative new play set in "intown" Atlanta. This modern lyrical tale exposes a passionate young photographer, Jules, as she searches for clarity in both her life and work. Her father has recently passed away, and Red, her estranged brother, is on his way to Atlanta from his

most recent prison stay for an unwelcome visit. The brother and sister must face their shared memories and determine what is to be done with the family home. In the midst of this struggle, Jules, with the help of her painter/sculptor boyfriend Che, is putting the finishing touches on a photography exhibit and art installation that could be her big break. Jules is a woman trying to reconcile her past, present and future while coming to terms with her relationships with the three important men in her life.

Otherworld Lovers
Playwright: Shepsu Aakhu
World Premiere: 1996 - Originally produced by MPAACT, Chicago Illinois.
Place: Cote d'Ivoire, West Africa. Three settings minimally suggested: An apartment, a village dwelling, and a outdoor bench.
Time: Early 1990's
A full length romantic drama
3M/4 F   Roles may be doubled reducing cast size to 3M/3F
Production has choreographic elements
Three languages are utilized: English (80%), French(18%), & Twi (2%)
Language tapes available
$12/script
$75/performance
Synopsis
Otherworld Lovers takes us to the cultural landscape of the Cote d'Ivoire to trace the story of a newlywed couple plagued by a gentle, yet jealous spirit. The wife returns to the village of her ancestral roots in order to unlock the mystery of her infertility and the increasing visitations she has from an Otherworld Lover. *Otherworld Lovers*, a romantic drama, explores the themes of gender roles, traditional values, and religion in modern day west Africa.

Piece-Meal Clan
Playwright: Shepsu Aakhu
World Premiere: 1997 - Originally produced by MPAACT, Chicago Illinois.
Place: Champaign Illinois.
Time: Early 1990's
A full length drama
4M/5 F
$12/script
$75/performance
Synopsis
Piece-Meal Clan centers around Desmond and the family of mostly unrelated individuals which has been pieced together for him, or by him to provide stability. Tensions arise when Desmond's long absent father attempts to claim a place for himself inside the clan. We have an opportunity to view the internal dynamics of the clan, and the relationships that maintain it both as a social institution in African-American life, and as a volatile backdrop for a boy coming of age.

Relevant Hearsay: Stories From 57...
Adapted from the Short Stories of Shirley Carney

Written by Shepsu Aakhu and Mignon McPherson Nance
World Premiere 2004 Originally produced by MPAACT, Chicago Illinois.
Place: Rural Southeastern Texas and Houston Texas, Rural Mississippi.
Time: 1950-2004
A full length drama
2M/4 F (Can be reduced to 1M/3F)
$12/script

$75/performance
Synopsis

At fifty years of age Shirley Carney began to write short stories. Her stories reflect the journey of a black woman nearing a half century of living. Ms. Carney's voice is distinctive and her characters capture the complexity of her varied experiences. She was born in rural Mississippi, transplanted to Chicago by her teens, served in the Navy during the Vietnam era, and became an unwed mother, all before her 21st birthday. Now living in Texas she continues to straddle the fence between urban sensibilities and rural practicality. She says of her stories; Some are true. Some mostly true. Some "Dragnet". The names have been changed to protect the innocent.

Relevant Hearsay... Stories from 57 is an adaptation culled from Ms. Carney's as yet unpublished body work. It is not so much a staging as it is a sharing of that which should be spoken, and that which needs to be heard. Episodic in nature *Relevant Hearsay...* is true to the tradition of storytelling; each of the stories presented is crafted as an examination of language and community.

SOST

Written by Shepsu Aakhu
World Premiere 2003 Originally produced by MPAACT, Chicago Illinois.
Place: Chicago Illinois & Addis Ababa Ethiopia
Various settings minimally suggested: Various apartments/homes, yard.
Time: 1980-present
A full length drama (2 acts)
3 languages
English 95%
Amharic 5%
Oromo sparingly
Dramaturgical materials available
Language CD available
$12/script
$75/performance

Synopsis

SOST is an Ethiopian story that concerns itself with the African mind and it's struggles with the mythology and reality of America. *SOST* reflects the playwrights many years among Ethiopians immigrants. This play reflects the incredible subtlety between the spoken and unspoken. So much of what is communicated exists in what is "not" said, "not" acknowledged, and "not" shared. It is a culture that is both foreign and familiar... grounded in family, tradition, and an often unnerving preoccupation with being polite.

SOST concerns itself with three sisters who have found themselves in America for a variety of reasons. Each must forge new relationships in America and each other while reconciling with the reasons why they each have left their distant home.

SOFTLY BLUE

Playwright: Shepsu Aakhu
World Premiere: 2006
Originally produced by MPAACT, Chicago Illinois.
Place: 2 Apartments in Chicago, various other settings minimally suggested:
Time: 2002
A full length drama
1M/1F
$12/script

$75/performance

Synopsis

How do two people ever find each other in twenty first century America? And when they do find each other how do they ever get to know each other? Our society is full of illusion, isolation, and overt deception. Can you trust the people that you invite into your life? Can you trust your own judgment when it comes to finding companionship? These are the questions that haunt Dakota and Sloan. Two characters desperate for companionship, and equally desperate to guard their own dark secrets. In Softly Blue we witness the delicate truce that exists in managing that which we want know, and that which we prefer to be illusion.

Third Day

Playwright: Larry Nance
World Premiere: 2000 (Exoskeletal Blues) - Originally produced by MPAACT, Chicago Illinois
Place: Chicago, Illinois.
Time: Late 1990's
One act drama (25 minutes)
2M
$12/script
$35/performance

Synopsis

Third Day delicately maneuvers around a relationship between a minister and Robert his gay son. Full of self-righteousness the Rev. Archer refuses to accept his son's sexual identity. When the Rev. Archer dies Robert is plunged into a world of self-doubt and self-examination as he struggles with whether he will attend his own father's funeral.

Vital Signs

Playwright: William S. Carroll
World Premiere: 1994 - Originally produced by MPAACT, Chicago Illinois.
Place: Solitary confinement in a Federal correctional facility. One setting minimally suggested:
Time: 1970-1994
A full length drama
1M
$12/script
$75/performance

Synopsis

Vital Signs follows the life of a nameless inmate, who finding himself locked in solitary confinement, makes a ritual of the continual retelling of his life story. His story is a not so gentle reminder that there are those who took up the call for freedom and justice, and as a result are living out their lives in prison. African-American political prisoners who helped change the nation, only to be forgotten, and abandoned by those whom they sought to protect. Vital Signs is a reflection upon the forgotten "living" such as Assata Shakkur, Geronimo Gi Gaga Pratt, and Dharuba bin Wahad. Casualties of an undeclared war on American injustice... Causalities of the short memories and even shorter attention spans that now form our collective consciousness

Within the Dream

Playwright: Deidre Searcy
World Premiere: 1999 - Originally produced by MPAACT, Chicago Illinois.
Place: Chicago, Illinois. Various settings minimally suggested: An apartment, classroom, etc.
Time: 1960's-1990's
A full length drama
3M/3 F
Production has choreographic elements

Production has Video elements
Video Media available
$12/script
$75/performance

Synopsis

Within The Dream examines the technological and historical legacy passed on to "Gen Xer's". In a bizarre happenstance, media technology has been wed to the history of the generations before. What generation has ever inherited their parents and grandparents history, not in faded newspapers, novels, history books, and paintings, but rather in media footage, movies, and soundscapes, frozen yet faded, all magnetized, digitized, and pre-package for your consumption?

What does it mean to inherit such bounty, such responsibility? What relevance, if any, do these "artifacts" from the last half of the twentieth century have on a new generation Within the Dream examines the difficulties of two siblings struggling to answer these very questions?